PENGI
BEYOND

Yoginder Sikand studied econoat the Jawaharlal Nehru Universiy, ... ,
in history at Royal Holloway, University of London. He works with
the Centre for the Study of Social Exclusion at the National Law
School, Bangalore. He is the author of more than a dozen books,
including *The Origins and Development of the Tablighi Jama'at
(1920-2000): A Cross-Country Comparative Study*; *Sacred Spaces:
Exploring Traditions of Shared Faith in India*; *Muslims in India
Since 1947: Islamic Perspectives on Inter-Faith Relations*; *Bastions of
the Believers: Madrasas and Islamic Education in India*; *Religion,
Peace and Dialogue in Jammu and Kashmir*; *Voices Against Terror:
Indian Ulema on Islam, Jihad and Communal Harmony* and *Jihad,
Peace and Inter-Community Relations in Islam*. He freelances for
several newspapers and magazines, having written mainly on religious
conflict and communalism, but now, being tired of the subject, is
searching for something more meaningful to explore. He thinks the
Buddha makes sense, and wants to work in that direction.

BEYOND THE BORDER

BORDER

An Indian in Pakistan

Yoginder Sikand

PENGUIN BOOKS

PENGUIN BOOKS
Published by the Penguin Group
Penguin Books India Pvt. Ltd, 11 Community Centre, Panchsheel Park,
New Delhi 110 017, India
Penguin Group (USA) Inc., 375 Hudson Street, New York, New York 10014, USA
Penguin Group (Canada), 90 Eglinton Avenue East, Suite 700, Toronto,
Ontario, M4P 2Y3, Canada (a division of Pearson Penguin Canada Inc.)
Penguin Books Ltd, 80 Strand, London WC2R 0RL, England
Penguin Ireland, 25 St Stephen's Green, Dublin 2, Ireland
(a division of Penguin Books Ltd)
Penguin Group (Australia), 250 Camberwell Road, Camberwell,
Victoria 3124, Australia (a division of Pearson Australia Group Pty Ltd)
Penguin Group (NZ), 67 Apollo Drive, Rosedale, Auckland 0632,
New Zealand (a division of Pearson New Zealand Ltd)
Penguin Group (South Africa) (Pty) Ltd, 24 Sturdee Avenue, Rosebank,
Johannesburg 2196, South Africa

Penguin Books Ltd, Registered Offices: 80 Strand, London WC2R 0RL, England

First published by Penguin Books India 2011

Copyright © Yoginder Sikand 2011
Illustration copyright © Kallol Majumder 2011

All rights reserved

10 9 8 7 6 5 4 3 2 1

The views and opinions expressed in this book are the author's own and the facts are as
reported by him which have been verified to the extent possible, and the publishers are
not in any way liable for the same.

ISBN 9780143104247

Typeset in Adobe Garamond by SÜRYA, New Delhi
Printed at Replika Press Pvt. Ltd, Sonepat

Go forth, o bhikkhus, for the good of the many, for the happiness of the many, out of compassion for the world, for the welfare, the good and the happiness of gods and humans . . .

—The Buddha

contents

preface and acknowledgements

Although many Indians and Pakistanis share much in common—to the extent that they could be called a single people—it is remarkable how little has been written by Indians about Pakistan, and vice versa, other than in a fiercely polemical mode. Almost everything that Indians write, read or hear about Pakistan is invariably about some negative development or the other there—the sinister machinations of its duplicitous politicians, the firebrand rhetoric of its rabble-rousing mullahs and radical Islamists, the continuing sectarian and ethnic violence that threatens to tear apart the country, and so on. Few Indians know about what life is like for 'ordinary' Pakistanis—which is precisely what this book is about. It is based on two journeys that I undertook to Pakistan, one, in 2006, which lasted for a month, and the other, briefly to Islamabad, the country's capital, in 2008.

I owe a heavy debt of gratitude to scores of people, in both Pakistan and India, who made my journeys to Pakistan and this book possible. Most of them, central characters of the book, are mentioned herein, but I have had to change the names of some in order to protect their identities. To all the many Pakistanis who fed, housed, guided and cared for me, a very hearty *shukriya*. May your tribe increase! *Zindabad*! I can never forget your love.

To Kamini Mahadevan and Ravi Singh, I owe a heavy debt

of gratitude for giving me the opportunity of doing a third Penguin book. Many thanks to Paloma Dutta for being such a careful editor.

Without the love and concern of my mother Mira, and my sisters Nigar, Percy, Surya, Sona, Puppy, Jiggly and Sizzy this book would certainly not have been possible.

A big thank you to all of them.

Bangalore   YOGINDER SIKAND

one

the land of my ancestors

I guess I first heard the word 'Pakistan' at the same time as I heard the word 'India', and that, too, in the same sentence. 'India and Pakistan are at war!' my father exclaimed one afternoon, on rushing back home early from office. That was in December 1971, when I was four years old and we were living in Calcutta. Was this an occasion to rejoice or to mourn, I wondered. I could not make out, because the excitement my father exuded could have been interpreted either way. All the same it was clear that 'Pakistan' was something that I was meant to hate and fear, though, of course, I had not the faintest idea where or what that dreaded monster was.

In the following years, what I heard and read about the two countries—at school, on television and over the radio, in the newspapers and from relatives and friends—only seemed to reinforce negative images of Pakistan, as a country inhabited by a people I necessarily had to dread and even to define myself against. Pakistan and Muslims were equated as one, while India and the Hindus were treated as synonymous. The two countries, as well as the two communities, were said to be absolutely irreconcilable. To be Indian necessarily meant, it seemed, to be uncompromisingly anti-Pakistani. To question this assumption,

1

to entertain any thought other than the standard line about Pakistan and its people, was tantamount to treason.

But I was, I suppose, a heretic from early on. As in many other things, I refused to toe the generally accepted line on Indian patriotism. I read up as much as I could about Pakistan (and other 'exotic' lands, such as Tibet and Africa). I even made a Pakistani penfriend, a Baluch boy from Quetta. We corresponded for half a year or so, but then the letters became infrequent and finally stopped. The mail service between India and Pakistan was becoming increasingly unreliable, possibly because the authorities on both sides wanted to reduce communication between their peoples to the minimum.

My father's family was from East Punjab, so there was little that I could learn about Pakistan from them. On the other hand, my mother's parents hailed from what is now Pakistan, and from them I heard much about the land of their birth. Every other year, we would visit them in Ooty, up in the Nilgiris in Tamil Nadu, then a placid hill station, unafflicted by swarms of tourists. Nana, my maternal grandfather, had been the head of the Epigraphic Department. He knew over a dozen languages, or so Nani, my mother's mother, claimed. He was born in Abbotabad, a town in Pakistan's North-West Frontier Province. Nani's family came from Sargodha, near Lahore, but had later shifted to Gujranwala, today one of the largest cities in Pakistani Punjab.

On our visits to Ooty, Nana and Nani would regale me with tales about life in pre-Partition Punjab, so fondly did they recall those days and so eagerly did I listen to them. True, they were bigoted about Muslims and thought that Pakistan and India could never live together in peace. But still, they had an emotional attachment to the land that now lay beyond a border that they could never cross. That was the land where they had been born, where the ashes of their ancestors had been scattered for millennia.

'If you've been to Pakistan,' I would ask them, 'why can't I also go? You had your homes there, so, isn't it possible for me to go and live there?'

Nani's face would change at once. She would twist her eyes into a knot and loudly hiss, 'Those Musalmans drove us out from our land, and they will never allow us back.'

Nana, who was generally reticent, would nod his head in agreement. He rarely spoke, being entirely dominated by Nani. Naturally, then, it was she who would relate Nana's story, while he sat like a serene Buddha in his rocking chair, nodding his head every time she turned to him to seek his confirmation about certain facts of his life.

'Your Nana came from a family of rich dry-fruit merchants,' she would start. 'They lived near the Afghan border, in an area inhabited by fanatic Pathan Muslims. There were only a few Hindu families in that area, all of whom were traders and moneylenders. Because they had money, they were protected by the Pathans, who adopted them as honorary members of their respective tribes.'

So far so good, I would think.

But inevitably, this would be followed by a torrent of abuses against the Pathans who had hosted the Hindu migrants to the area, including Nana's family—merchants who had left their homes in Punjab, centuries ago attracted by the handsome profits to be made by importing goods from Afghanistan and lending money to the thriftless Pathan tribesmen.

'The Pathans are very dirty and bloodthirsty people. They hardly wash. And worse, they even eat the mother cow!' Nani would go on. 'Like our own family, Nana's family and all the other Hindus in Abbotabad never ate food cooked by Pathans or any other Muslims. Even to drink a drop of water from a glass touched by a Muslim was considered to be a sin.' The Hindus lent money to the Pathans and sold things to them, but, she stressed, they never allowed them into their homes.

'*Hai na, ji?*' she would turn to Nana to ask, but without waiting for him to reply, she would continue, 'In our childhood, so strict was the law of caste purity that if a Hindu and a Muslim were crossing a bridge at the same time from opposite sides, the Muslim would get off to let the Hindu through first.' And in the railway stations, she would add, there were separate drinking fountains for Hindus and Muslims.

'But why, Nani?' I would interrupt her.

'Because they were Muslims and our Hindu *dharam* teaches us not to eat with impure people or even to consume anything touched by them,' Nani would snap back.

At such times Nani would resemble, I thought, a venomous serpent stirred from its sleep by an unwelcome intruder.

As for Nani's own story, I do not know how much of it was true and how much wishful thinking.

'My family came from Sargodha, from the village of Giroth. They belonged to the Batra clan, and owned most of the land in the village, along with thousands of acres in the surrounding areas,' she would claim.

Because they were Arora moneylenders, Nani's clansmen must, I assume, have stealthily obtained much of the land that they owned from the local, largely Muslim, peasants who, as elsewhere in western Punjab and Sindh, were heavily indebted to Hindu merchants, into whose hands their lands passed because of their inability to repay their loans. Nani's father looked like a typical village moneylending *sahukar* in the one picture that she had of him. He was short and rotund, and wore a giant onion-shaped turban on his head that ended in a tail like a cock's comb. He sat like a petty potentate on a carved throne-like chair. The slim walking stick that he held in his hand, and that reached almost up to his chin, was made of pure ivory, or so Nani boasted.

'*Nahin, nahin.* Of course not! He was not a moneylending Bania,' Nani would angrily retort when I would ask her if that was what his profession was. 'Rai Bahadur Udai Bhan Batra,' she would proudly announce, 'was the leading medical specialist of his times. He did his MBBS from Lahore University, decades before the Partition, at a time when it was extremely rare for Indians to do so. He was appointed as civil surgeon in Sargodha and then in Gujranwala, and was decorated by the British for his services.'

A beam of great pride would flash across her face.

'Decorated?' I would ask. 'You mean he was given flowers to decorate himself? Or was he dressed up in some sort of special costume?' I could not understand why any British official might have wanted to do that to Udai Bhan Batra. After all, as his picture clearly indicated, he had not been physically attractive by any means.

'Didn't your mother teach you what that means?' Nani would retort unpleasantly. 'It means he was given an honorific title, that of Rai Bahadur, by the British themselves! Imagine!'

'Oh! But why, Nani?' I would pester her.

'Because he served the British well. He was a good doctor, too. And he stopped the deadly bubonic plague from spreading just as it was entering Gujranwala.'

For Nani, her father's association with the British was a source of great pride. 'English officials would often come to our house for dinner. Few other Indians in Gujranwala enjoyed the same privilege. We had a separate kitchen that was used for cooking meat and chicken when they were invited, and a special cook for this, too. And, my father would be regularly invited to parties held in the Cantonment by British officials. There'd be ballroom dancing and drinking and that sort of thing. Of course he didn't do all that, but he would mix with the British officers and some of them were his close friends,' she would go on, her chest puffing out with evident pride.

Nani's pet subject were the bloody riots of 1947, which she

had escaped as she was already married by then and had shifted with Nana to Ooty, some three thousand kilometres south of Gujranwala, where the rest of her family lived. 'The merciless Muslims butchered so many Hindus. They kidnapped and raped our women. They looted our homes, envious of us for our wealth and prosperity,' she would shudder as she spoke.

I could see tears welling in Nana's eyes as he gently rocked himself in his chair.

'Luckily,' Nani would go on, her voice choked with emotion, 'our family managed to flee. They hired a big truck and, one week after Pakistan came into being, they got into it, leaving their wealth, their many buildings and their vast estates behind, and fled across the border to Amritsar.'

One of her cousins, Nani once mentioned, decided to stay behind in Pakistan, and converted to Islam, and so was able to save his life and lands. All that Nani could recall about him was his name: Ram Nath Batra. She had had no news of him after the Partition and, for all she knew, she said, he could well be dead by now.

That thought greatly saddened Nani, but it certainly excited me. The fact that I might have relatives in Pakistan—Nani's cousin, his children and their grandchildren, who would probably be my age—made me even more curious to know more about that country. It certainly confirmed my suspicion that Pakistan could not be as bad as the stories I had heard. After all, I thought, I had relatives living there.

If Nani and Nana were to be believed, the holocaust of 1947 in Punjab was an entirely one-sided affair, involving Muslim mobs slaying hapless Hindus wherever they could find them. Like so many other Hindu refugees from West Pakistan, as also most other Indians, they had been reared on that myth which brooked no questioning whatsoever. I never heard about the other side of the horror-filled story till I got to Pakistan many years later where, for the first time, I learnt about Muslims being done to death by Hindus and Sikhs in as ghastly a manner and on as enormous a scale.

'What about the local Muslims? Did you have good relations with them?' I would ask Nani.

'*Arey* nahin!' Nani would reply, quaking with disgust. 'We kept a long, safe distance from them. We had some Muslim servants—the peasants in our fields, our camel-herders, the potter, the sweeper, the men who took care of my father's stables and so on. But no Muslims—not even those few in the area who were educated and rich nor even those who worked for us—could ever enter our house.'

Like Nana's family, Nani's, too, had been sticklers for absurd Hindu rules about 'purity'. They regarded Muslims, in addition to Untouchables, as ritually polluting. They abhorred the very thought of social interaction with their Muslim neighbours, although they lived as a small minority in a Muslim-dominated district and were heavily dependent on Muslims for their thriving businesses.

We are, all of us, creatures of our times and our social and political contexts. It would be uncharitable to blame Nani and Nana entirely for their anti-Muslim feelings or their visceral hatred for Pakistan, for such sentiments were, and still remain, widespread and deeply rooted in Indian society. That there was obviously some truth in what Nani had told me about the violence that accompanied the Partition I had no doubt. But I also knew that there was another side to the story that she perhaps did not know, or, to put it less charitably, that she had chosen not to believe. I wanted to find out the real story about Pakistan for myself. I could not take what my grandmother had told me for granted.

As the years rolled by, I, like many other Indian children, grew up constantly bombarded with horror stories about Pakistan. I heard much of this in history class at school, where we learnt that Pakistan came into being as a result of a demand on the part of the Indian Muslims for a separate country of their own. We were led to believe that this demand had the backing of almost all the Muslims of India. It was only later that I learnt about the role of Right-wing Hindu forces in the creation of Pakistan as well as the staunch opposition to the demand for Pakistan on the part of many Muslims. The subliminal message that our history books sought to send out was that Muslims were 'anti-national', that they were not to be trusted and that they could never live in peace with people of other faiths.

We had only a few Muslims in our class, and they were regularly taunted by a group of toughies for being 'crypto-Pakistanis', their pathetic insistence on the contrary notwithstanding. Cricket matches between India and Pakistan took the form of mini-wars. If India won, there would be a party at school and a minor celebration at home as well. If Pakistan won, a sort of mourning period was observed, and my father turned sullen and grumpy, although I, of course, could not care less since I abhorred cricket. I cannot say that I did not imbibe any of the negativity about Pakistan that I witnessed all around me, but I certainly did not obsess about it passionately. I had my prejudices, of course, based on ignorance, but hatred for Pakistan was never an article of faith for me as it was for many of my relatives and peers at school, even at a young age.

One summer, sometime in the late 1970s, my father paid a short visit to Pakistan on business. When he returned, he told us about his colleague in Karachi who worked in the same shipping company as him, a certain Mr Akram, with whom he had stayed. He had refused to let my father stay in a hotel. Those three days appeared to have had a miraculous impact on my father, who could not stop chattering about how wonderful a host Mr Akram had been; how, to his pleasant surprise, Mrs Akram had short hair and did not wear a *burqa* ('very emancipated', he must have said, or so I imagine); and how their two daughters went to an English-medium school (and not, contrary to what he must have expected, to a *madrasa*). 'They are just like Indians, no difference at all,' he told us, and that made me even more eager to visit Pakistan.

So, the day my father returned from Karachi, I began poring over an atlas, and in a few days' time had charted a journey to Pakistan that I wanted him to arrange for me through Mr Akram. I would travel from Amritsar to Lahore, and then go all the way up to the Himalayas and the Afghan borderlands, ending my trip down south in Karachi. En route, I would stop at places with exotic-sounding names that I spotted on the map: Jhang, Mianwali, Rawalpindi, Peshawar, Bannu, Waziristan, Swat, Malakand, Quetta, Gwadar, Sadhu Bela and Thatta. I would also go to Sargodha, where I hoped to visit Giroth, Nani's ancestral village, and to Abbotabad, where Nana was born. I might also, in the course of the journey, I mused, finally locate Ram Nath Batra, Nani's long-lost relative in Lahore.

I excitedly told my father about my plans. He probably knew that nothing would come of them, but he suggested that I write to Mr Akram. Two weeks later, I received Mr Akram's reply. Excited, I tore open the envelope, sure that Mr Akram had written to inform me that he had arranged my visit. Neatly typed, the letter, which I still have in my possession, read as follows:

Dear Yogi beta,
    Thanks for your letter.
    I have heard a lot of good things about you from your dear father, who visited us in Karachi some weeks ago.

Much though I wish you could come to Pakistan on my invitation, I fear it will not be possible. You are a young boy, hardly ten years old, and I do not think you will be able to travel on your own to the places that you have mentioned in your letter. Perhaps you should think of undertaking such a journey when you are older, when you can manage things on your own and when, also, you will be able to remember all the places that you visit.

Do accept my apologies.

Regards,
Uncle Waris Akram

That, then, was the story of my first abortive attempt to visit Pakistan.

Another occasion arose, around a decade later, when I was a student at St. Stephen's College in Delhi. I did not learn much in class (most of our teachers were dreadful bores and I was forced, against my will, to major in Economics, so I found the classes doubly tiresome), but the one source of considerable enlightenment for me in college was the Informal Discussion Group, the IDG for short. The IDG's mandate was to invite people of note—activists, journalists, politicians and so on—to the college to address the students every Friday after dinner, which would be followed by a question–answer session.

One Friday, in the last semester of my third year in college, shortly before I was to graduate, the IDG invited the Pakistan High Commissioner in New Delhi for a lecture. I cannot recall what his presentation was about—he must have repeated the same tired platitudes about the need for good neighbourliness between India and Pakistan, I suppose—but at the end of the lecture he announced that General Zia ul-Haq, then President of Pakistan, would be delighted if a group of students from the college could visit Pakistan, because Zia himself had studied at St. Stephen's College in the years immediately before the Partition.

Most of the students present at the meeting probably did not take this offer seriously, but I and, unknown to me, three others, did. The next day, I shot off a letter to the President mentioning what the High Commissioner had said and asking him if I could take up his offer. I addressed the letter simply to 'General Zia ul-Haq, President of Pakistan, Islamabad, Pakistan', not quite sure if the letter would reach its destination.

Months passed, and I forgot all about the letter. Then, one day, in August 1988, by which time I had enrolled at the Tata Institute of Social Sciences in Bombay for a course in Social Work, I received a frantic call from my mother.

'Rush to Delhi at once. Your Pakistani visa has come through. I just got a call from the High Commission telling me that. I've also received a letter to that effect, signed by General Zia himself,' she excitedly said.

'But Mumma, my passport is with you in Calcutta. Suppose I fly down there, pick it up, and fly all the way to Delhi and if I don't get the visa, wouldn't it be an awful waste of money?' I wailed. Those were the days before the advent of courier companies, STD booths and e-mail.

'It's worth the risk, beta,' Mumma insisted.

'No, Mumma! I've just joined the course here and I don't want to miss any classes,' I answered.

I could really kick myself, even now, thirty years later! The three other boys who had responded to Zia's invitation got their visas and travelled to Pakistan at the expense of the Government of Pakistan, and were regaled like state guests. They even had a private audience with the President and were taken by special helicopter to a number of historical sites across the country. And for all my concern that going on the trip would have meant missing classes at the institute I had just joined, three months after taking admission there I quit, finding the whole approach to social work too tame and charity-oriented, and geared to promoting corporate greed.

I made a third abortive attempt to visit Pakistan in the early 1990s, when I was a student of sociology at the Jawaharlal Nehru University in New Delhi. At a conference on Dalit rights organized by a local NGO, I met two Pakistanis from Lahore, a middle-aged man and a woman slightly older than him. They spoke eloquently and with passion about the plight of the Dalits in Pakistan. Since no one in the audience, including me, even knew of the existence of the almost three million Pakistani Dalits, their presentation generated considerable discussion.

I chatted with the couple after the conference got over. Khurshid Kaim Khani, the man, was a Leftist activist from Sindh, and worked mainly with landless Dalit labourers or *hari*s, who were heavily exploited by the local landlords. His family hailed from Ganganagar in Rajasthan but had shifted to Pakistan in the wake of the Partition. The woman, Khurshid's friend, was Khadijah Gauhar, a noted writer and social activist. Born in Gujarat and raised in Karachi, she had graduated from the London School of Economics, after which she shifted to South Africa, where she took an active part in the struggle against apartheid. She now lived in Lahore and managed a free clinic up in the mountains in the former princely state of Gilgit, in Pakistan-administered Kashmir. The two frequently visited India—as often as they were able to secure visas.

Since she lived in Lahore and appeared to know just about every Lahori whose name I took, I asked Khadijah if she might know Ram Nath Batra, Nani's cousin who had chosen to stay behind after the Partition. Nani had said that she suspected he still lived in Lahore, where their family had had considerable ancestral property.

'Batra? Hmm . . . I've heard of one Mr Batra, but his name isn't Ram Nath. He's called, if I remember correctly, Rab Nawaz,' answered Khadijah.

That must be Ram Nath himself, the thought struck me. On

converting to Islam he must have retained his surname and adopted two Muslim-sounding forenames with the same initial letters as his previous names.

I suggested this possibility to Khadijah. 'Yes, that's quite likely,' she replied. 'I've heard that Mr Batra was once a Hindu and that he might have turned Muslim, perhaps to save his property. I'll check on that when I get back,' she promised.

Three weeks later, I got a call from Khadijah who, by then, had returned to Lahore. Yes, she said, it was the same Mr Batra, originally from Giroth in Sargodha, Nani's cousin. He now lived in a bungalow in Gulberg, the swankiest part of Lahore, with his wife Mohini, who was also a Hindu convert.

Khadijah had spoken to Mohini Batra on the phone.

'She was shocked out of her wits when she came to know that I had met you, a distant relative. Of course she did not even know that you existed,' Khadijah related. 'She wanted to know more, about your Nani and her brothers and sisters, but since I know nothing about them I've given her your address, and you both can correspond and you can tell her all that she wants to know'.

And so, eighty-year old Mohini Batra and I became pen-friends. We would write to each other unfailingly once a month, exchanging news of ourselves and our families. Most of her family, Aunty Mohini wrote, had settled in India. She and her husband were now among the few 'upper' caste Hindus who had remained behind in Lahore, a city that, prior to the Partition, had had a Hindu majority. They had formally converted to Islam, although she never disclosed why and I did not have the heart to ask. Religion and nationalism were two topics about which she was loath to mention anything at all. 'Let's not talk about them. There are so many other things to discuss and share,' she mentioned in one of her earlier letters. Instead, we wrote about less sensitive subjects—the monuments and markets of Delhi and Lahore, the prices of vegetables and house rents, news about our families, and so on.

One summer morning, a year or so after we had started corresponding, I heard a voice call out from below my room in Nani's house in Delhi. 'Arey Yogi *puttar*! Yogi beta!' an old woman's high-pitched voice wafted up to my window.

I peered down to see a wrinkled, white-haired woman sitting in the front seat of a Maruti car. As she saw me, she broke into a toothless smile, quaking with joy. 'Puttar, it's me. Your pen-friend, Aunty Mohini from Lahore!'

I scampered down the stairs and out of the entrance gate. Aunty Mohini was struggling to get out of the car, but I firmly seated her back and bowed down to touch her feet. That was the first time in my life I had ever done that to anyone.

'*Jeetey raho, mere puttar*! Have a long life, my son!' said Aunty Mohini, choking with emotion, the words barely able to escape her lips. A stream of tears trickled down her cheeks and smudged her crumpled *dupatta*. Then she took me into her arms and held me in a tight, warm embrace. I did not want to withdraw myself from her.

'Imagine, puttar!' she choked on her words. 'I'm here to see your Nani after fifty years! *Hai Rabba*! This divide, this conflict, this hatred in the name of religion and nationalism! How cruel our fates have been!'

By this time Aunty Mohini was so overcome with grief that I feared she might collapse. 'Where's your Nani, my sister Sheila? Call her, beta. My eyes thirst to see her,' she spluttered as she struggled to wipe her tears.

'Nani!' I called out as I raced inside the house. Nani was in the kitchen, scolding Sita, her Nepali home-help. 'Nani!' I ran up to her. 'Guess who's here? Mohini, the wife of your long-lost relative, Ram Nath Batra, from Pakistan!'

Nani stood dazed for a while, trying to digest what had just hit her like a bombshell. I expected her to hobble out of the house as fast as she could with her walking stick, and then there would be, I thought, a tearful meeting of long-separated relatives who had not met for half a century. Nothing of the sort happened, however. Instead, Nani turned menacingly to me, twisting her face and looking half-crazed. 'She's become a *Musalmani*. I don't want to meet her. She isn't welcome in my house. You can tell her that. Ask her to go,' she growled and went back to scolding the hapless Sita.

I cannot forget Aunty Mohini's terror-struck face when I told her, in as gentle a manner as possible, that Nani did not want to meet her. Nor can I forget how I broke down uncontrollably and said how disgusting I found Nani's behaviour.

Aunty Mohini took my hand in hers. 'Beta, if that's how she wants it, what can we do?' she whispered, gently planting her cheek on my forehead. Then she called for the driver and the car sped away.

Aunty Mohini and I stopped corresponding after that. And since it was all because of Nani's deplorable behaviour, my relations with Nani turned increasingly bitter. Shortly after, I decided to leave her house and shifted to a room in the university hostel.

Two years later, I received an invitation card from Aunty Mohini. One of her sons, a top Pakistani civil servant, was getting married, and she wanted me to attend the function. It was good to hear from her again. It had put to rest the lurking fear that she might think that I had in some way been complicit in Nani's despicable treatment of her. Armed with the letter, I approached the blue-domed pseudo-Mughal-style complex of the High Commission of Pakistan in New Delhi. I filled in the visa forms and handed them, along with my passport and the invitation card, at the visa section. There, I was told that investigations would be made regarding the invitation and that I should contact the High Commission within a fortnight for news about the visa.

Two weeks later, I was back in the serpentine queue outside the High Commission, confident that the investigations had revealed the veracity of the invitation and that, therefore, I should have my visa in hand that very day. After waiting for more than half a day, I finally got my turn to stand in front of the prison-like bars of the diminutive window of the room that housed the visa section. A dark, cantankerous middle-aged man with a wisp of a beard sat before me. He spoke Urdu, but with such a heavy Punjabi accent that he was almost incomprehensible. I gave him my passport details. He turned around and, shuffling through a pile of passports all waiting to be stamped, drew mine out.

He rudely tossed my passport over the counter to me. 'Visa application rejected,' he growled.

But why, I asked him. Surely, I feebly protested, my papers were all in order. I hoped that I might be able to make him reconsider his decision.

'Our investigation reveals that this invitation is not genuine,' he barked.

I knew at once that the man was lying, that it was not the invitation but, rather, the 'investigation' that was not genuine. Perhaps no investigation had been carried out at all. I said so to the man, unable to conceal my irritation. My response so angered him that he tore my passport from my hand, and, plucking out a pen from his pocket, he drew a large 'R' on the passport's last leaf. That stood, he said with unconcealed sadistic glee, for 'Rejected'. And that meant, he went on, that I could not visit Pakistan as long as my current passport remained valid—a period of more than four years.

And so the years rolled by, and although I was able to travel to more than two dozen countries in Asia, Africa, Europe and North America, the possibility of ever being able to visit Pakistan seemed as remote as ever. Meanwhile, I had developed an interest in Islam and Muslim societies, doing a PhD from London on a global Islamic missionary movement, then a post-doctoral project from the Netherlands on Islam and inter-faith relations, and penned half a dozen books on various aspects of Islam and South Asian Muslim history. I also started writing regularly on Islamic and Muslim issues for a host of newspapers, magazines and websites. One of these was a leading Pakistani journal based in Lahore.

One day, in December 2006, by which time I had taken up a research project at an institute in New Delhi, I was chatting with the editor of this journal on the Internet, and he asked me if, given my interest in Muslim issues, I had ever visited Pakistan. Surprised to learn that I never had, he offered to arrange a Pakistani visa for me if I so wanted. I pounced on the offer at once, though half disbelieving him. A week later, I received an e-mail message from him informing me that all was clear, that he had spoken about me to people in the 'right places' in Islamabad's officialdom, and that all I needed to do now was approach the Pakistan High Commission in New Delhi, hand over my passport, get the necessary visa, and take the next flight to Lahore. It was as easy as that, he said.

The next morning I bundled myself into an autorickshaw and sped down the posh Chanakyapuri, where most of the foreign embassies in Delhi are located, and arrived at the graceless complex that houses the Pakistan High Commission.

Outside the forbidding walls of the High Commission, sitting on little stools with makeshift foldable tables in front of them, a dozen men were selling visa application forms and clicking away at ancient, noisy typewriters. Pakistani visa forms had to be typed out, rather than filled in by hand, and that too in quadruplicate. This bizarre rule translated into thriving business for these men. Many of the people who crowded around them were unable to read and write. After they had typed in their details, the men grabbed their thumbs, pressed them on to ink-pads and then again on to the visa forms.

Pakistan High Commission

I stood by a booth and waited for my turn, which came up an hour and seven customers later. I purchased a set of four visa application forms for twenty rupees and handed them to the typist.

'Are you a Muslim?' he looked up at me and inquired as a stream of red *paan* liquid trickled out of his mouth, down his chin and on to his badly stained shirt.

'Hmm, I don't know,' I answered, wondering why he had asked me this question.

'What do you mean?' he angrily shot back. 'You either are Muslim or you are not. From your name you are evidently not Muslim,' he concluded for me, and took out a separate set of forms, meant specifically for non-Muslims, from a drawer of his table to fill in.

I wanted to see as many places in Pakistan as possible, but there was a limit of six places that Indian citizens could visit in Pakistan on each trip, details of which they had to enter in their visa application forms. I applied to visit Lahore, Gujranwala, Hyderabad and the ruins of the ancient city of Moenjo Daro. In the first three of these cities, I had friends with whom I planned to stay. They were located in the Punjab and the Sindh provinces, and were sufficiently far apart from each other to give me the chance of possibly seeing some smaller places *en route* as well. I was tempted to apply to travel to two more places, in the North-Western Frontier Province and Baluchistan, so that I could see all of Pakistan's four provinces. I had no friends in those provinces, however, and the typist warned me that since those were troubled areas, the High Commission authorities might get unnecessarily suspicious and might then even decline to give me a visa at all.

The forms filled in, I entered the embassy compound, climbed up a flight of stairs and walked into the portals of an imposing building. Men dressed in starched shalwar-kameez and woollen waistcoats strode in and out of rooms, bearing files tucked under their arms and looking busy. I hesitantly knocked on the door of the chamber of the officer I had been instructed to meet by my friend, the editor of the Lahore-based journal.

'Come in,' I heard a loud grunt in Urdu from behind the door. I slowly pushed the door open and found myself in a commodious, well-appointed room. A large Persian carpet covered almost its entire floor. A leather-covered couch occupied one corner of the room, next to which were carved wooden racks neatly stacked with books and a few curios. Above these, was a framed portrait of Muhammad Ali Jinnah, the founder of Pakistan. Grim, stern and unsmiling, he was dressed in a *sherwani* that was buttoned up to the neck, and *churidar*s that bunched up at his ankles. On his head he wore an oval-shaped *karakul* fur cap. This was the costume that he had adopted quite late in his life, after he had doffed his Western attire when he decided he needed to look more 'Islamic' in order to gain Muslim support for his Pakistan scheme.

I looked to the far end of the room and spotted a corpulent, middle-aged man sitting behind a massive mahogany desk. He looked sloppy even in his well-pressed suit. He had a nose shaped like a button mushroom, and his eyes were small, shifty and distinctly unfriendly.

'Oh, come in, sit down,' said the man without looking up, and guided me to a seat in front of him with a wave of his hand. He finished signing a bundle of papers that his peon had handed to him and then turned towards me. 'So, you want to visit Pakistan, I am told,' he said.

'Are you a journalist?' he asked, raising his eyebrows and looking now like an angry beetle.

Before I could answer, he went on, 'I read a book review you had written some days ago in *Kashmir Times* about Dalits in

Pakistan. What you wrote is absolute rubbish, Mr Sikand. There are no Dalits in our country.'

'But that was just a summary of what the book said, sir,' I replied hesitatingly, pretending to be polite. 'I did not add anything of my own.'

'No, no,' he snorted. 'This book has been written with the carefully calculated purpose of defaming Pakistan before the international community. Who is the author of the book?'

'He's a Pakistani, who works for a leading local NGO,' I answered uncomfortably. I mentioned the author's name, from which it was evident that he was a Hindu from Sindh. That revelation, I feared, was bound to make matters much worse for me.

'These NGOs get money from abroad to give their country a bad name. Some of them are even liberally supplied with booze and women to carry out their plots against the country,' he charged. 'In any case,' he added, 'I've never heard of the word "Dalit". As I said, there are no Dalits in Pakistan.'

He turned to his peon and asked him if he knew what 'Dalit' meant.

The peon stuttered in reply. 'No, sahib, I don't. Never heard the word before you mentioned it, sahib.'

'See!' the officer said, turning to me triumphantly. 'I told you! As my *chaprasi* also says, there are no Dalits in our country.'

'Perhaps the word "Dalit" is not used in Pakistan, sir, but they are called *achhoot*s or *kameen*s or Untouchables or low castes,' I responded, suppressing my mounting irritation with the greatest difficulty.

'No, no, there is no caste problem in Pakistan, unlike in India. Our religion teaches equality,' he shot back. 'The Prophet Muhammad said that if a Muslim goes to sleep while his neighbour is hungry, he is not a true believer.'

Before I could reply, the officer heaved himself from his seat and paced up to the wall in front of him. He lifted a framed picture that was hung on it and handed it to me. 'See for yourself, Mr Sikand, this is how Dalits are treated in your country,' he said triumphantly.

It was a photograph of a Dalit child in a Bangalore slum suckling at a bitch's teat, which had been published in a local newspaper. The officer had carefully cut it out and framed it on his wall. I had been warned by a journalist friend that he might show precisely that picture to me. He had done the same to him when he had met him some months ago. Perhaps that was his way of intimidating Indian journalists who wanted to travel to Pakistan. Or, more likely, it was probably his perverse way of asserting his claim of Pakistan's moral superiority over its closest rival.

'So, Mr Sikand,' asked the officer, not concealing his glee, 'what do you have to say about the plight of the Dalits in your own country?'

I hesitated for a bit. I had to admit that the caste system was horrendous and that Dalits were badly treated in India. I readily conceded that Hinduism was inherently and incorrigibly inegalitarian. 'But that's not the whole story about India. And just because Dalits are persecuted in India it does not mean that they fare well in Pakistan,' I protested. I was now almost sure that the man had already made up his mind to refuse me a visa.

'Indian journalists generally write only negative things about Pakistan,' the officer sourly bemoaned. 'Are you sure you won't do the same if I allow you to go there?'

His question rekindled some hope of my actually getting a visa. Perhaps, I thought to myself, he was just testing me.

I assured him that I was committed to fostering friendly relations between India and Pakistan. 'I'll certainly be balanced,' I answered, forcing on a smile.

'Yes, Mr Sikand. There are so many positive things to write

about our country,' he beamed. He sounded positively lyrical now. 'There are the Food Street and the fancy new shopping centres in Lahore, the brand new Karachi airport, the poshest in all South Asia, and the wonderful super highway connecting Lahore with Islamabad, on which even F-16 planes can land!' he excitedly revealed. 'And, in contrast to India, there are no cycle-rickshaws in Pakistan. Don't forget to note that point. You must mention it in your articles when you get back.'

I was in no mood to quibble. I simply had to get the visa. I nodded as he went on.

'Hand over your visa form and passport to my peon and pick it up in the evening,' he said. Then he hauled himself up from his chair and extended me a limp handshake, indicating that the interview was over.

I had passed the gruelling test. I was truly elated.

A week later, the day that I had been impatiently waiting for, finally arrived. Sleep had completely eluded me the night before, the excitement, mixed with trepidation, of leaving for Pakistan having kept me wide awake, fidgety and nervous. The reporting time for the Lahore-bound bus at the Ambedkar Terminus in Delhi was 4 a.m., but I got there more than an hour early, fearing that I might otherwise miss the bus or get an uncomfortable seat in the rear if I were late. It was a frosty December morning, and there was not a soul in sight as I squatted on the pavement of the deserted road waiting for the gates of the terminus to open.

At exactly 4 a.m., I heard the clanking of chains and the shrill blow of a whistle. A guard unlocked the gates, and I headed for the shed reserved for the Delhi–Lahore bus. My backpack was checked cursorily by a yawning policewoman, who appeared bored with her monotonous routine and took

her work as something of an onerous formality. She thrust her
hand in my bag, shook it a bit, and then commanded me to
move ahead. Anyone, I mused, could smuggle almost anything
into Pakistan with such lax checking. I asked the woman to
explain why they had no scanning machine. 'Send a letter to
the Delhi Transport Corporation to find out why and to
complain if you want,' she shot back, dismissing me with a
casual wave of her hand.

I eased myself into a comfortable sofa in the waiting room.
A boy came round with biscuits and tea, which he poured into
stained cups from a lid-less tin kettle. A middle-aged man
walked around handing out his visiting card to bored, bleary-
eyed passengers. 'If you buy cosmetics and clothes in Lahore
you can sell them to me when you return,' he explained. 'You'll
make a good bargain.' No one, however, paid him any attention.

Slowly, more passengers began to trickle in. From their
manner of speaking and their dress they appeared to be largely
from lower-middle class Muslim families. Most of them seemed
to be Muhajirs, migrants from India who had shifted to
Pakistan after the Partition, who had come to India to meet
relatives. And to shop, as was evident from the elephantine
suitcases and bulging cardboard boxes they were carrying,
bursting to the seams with all manner of goodies picked up
from the bazaars of Delhi.

The sleek air-conditioned Delhi Transport Corporation bus,
its sides emblazoned with the Indian and the Pakistani flags
and the logo *Sada-e Sarhad* ('The Voice of the Frontier'),
pulled out of the bus stand and into the dark and deserted
streets of Old Delhi at exactly the appointed time. The smartly
dressed Sikh driver snapped a *gurbani* tape into a cassette
player. The *bhajans*, soul-stirring compositions of the Sikh
gurus, spoke of Ishwar and Allah in the same breath, as being
but two different names of the one Unknowable God, and the
final refuge of all human beings—a fitting way, I thought, to

embark on the journey across the border. I was truly grateful that we were not to be subjected to ear-splitting Bollywood cacophony, but my relief was short-lived for, in a short while, the television screen flickered into life and, for the next three hours, we were treated to Bollywood's latest inanity—a film about two friends who cheated on their wives and entered into multiple affairs with a posse of women. I snuggled in my large, comfortable seat, refusing to glance at the screen, watching, instead, the passing villages and towns come to life in the emerging light of dawn.

Our bus was heralded in front and followed at the rear by smart police vans bearing stern guards brandishing menacing-looking rifles. The vans were fitted with snarling sirens that commanded such fear and authority that the other vehicles on the road veered at once to the side to make way for us. We swiftly hurtled down the highway, and when we slowed down in places where the early morning traffic had already begun to clog the road, curious pedestrians glared at us in consternation. Some of them smiled and even passionately waved out. The 'Lahore–Delhi Bus Service' slogan and the Indian and the Pakistani flags painted on either side of the bus marked us out as passengers heading for what was perceived as 'enemy country'. What, I wondered, did the passers-by looking at us feel? Fear? Hatred? Envy? Curiosity? Or, perhaps, recognition of the fact that, across the forbidden frontier to which we were headed, people must be quite the same as them, despite the religious difference?

We stopped briefly at Pipli, in Haryana, for a hurried breakfast, and then, by noon, at the town of Kartarpur in Punjab for lunch. The passengers piled out of the bus and energetically jostled each other at the buffet table, piling their plates with mountains of rice, meat and vegetables. I prowled around outside looking for a fellow-smoker to beg a cigarette from. It was distressing how few people smoked these days.

The disdainful way that smokers, a seemingly rapidly-declining species, were now treated was simply despicable.

Finally, with much difficulty, I spotted Mr Khan, a genial elderly man who generously rolled a cigarette for me. Like birds of an endangered feather, we two smokers seemed to bond instinctively.

'I'm going to Lahore against my will,' said Mr Khan grimly, as he sucked on his cigarette and let out little curls of smoke from his hairy nostrils. 'I have to meet my relatives there, whom I have not seen for over two decades now. Although I really don't want to go, my wife insists I should, and I know better than to disobey her.'

But why, I asked him, was he so reluctant to visit Pakistan?

'Pakistan has only brought ruin to the Indian Muslims,' he replied. 'The creation of Pakistan has spelt doom for us Muslims in India, who are wrongly suspected as being Pakistani agents and looked down upon by the Hindus. And Pakistan is hardly the truly Islamic country that it claims to be. The entire project of Pakistan is based on sheer hypocrisy, using religion for crude political purposes.'

'Besides,' Mr Khan added, 'Pakistanis, as a rule, are ignorant, crude and slobbery. They're full of hot air, and love to boast about themselves. You just can't have a decent conversation with too many of them, as you are sure to discover sooner rather than later once you get there.'

And, as if to confirm what he had just said, he pointed to our fellow-passengers inside the dining hall. 'See how they are pushing and shoving against each other over food in the lunch room! Like animals! Absolutely pathetic!' he cried out, visibly disgusted. 'After a few days in Pakistan, you'll get so fed up that you'll be pining to come back, I assure you.'

Naturally, I was somewhat sceptical and hesitated to believe Mr Khan. I knew the perils of generalizing about any community and I told him so. All the traits that he had attributed to

Pakistanis, I said, could well apply in the case of many Indians, too. 'I've seen Indians breaking queues and fighting over food, and enough of them who are every bit as slobbery and crude,' I retorted. My feeble protest did not, however, seem to shake Mr Khan's firmly held convictions.

After lunch, the bus headed down the flat Punjab plains, the monotony of glistening wheat fields and acres of brilliant yellow mustard flowers interrupted by onion-domed gurdwaras and the occasional roadside *dhaba* where tired truck-drivers rested on wooden cots. At two in the afternoon, we got on to the by-pass road, skirting the city of Amritsar, and drove down to Attari, the last town on the Indian side, located three kilometres from the border.

As we passed out of Attari and approached the frontier, I spotted the crumbling ruins of an abandoned mosque standing in the middle of an empty field. Evidently, there were no Muslims left in that hamlet, although it must have had a sizeable Muslim population in pre-Partition days. The thought of the tens of thousands of Hindus, Muslims, Dalits and Sikhs, who must have waded through rivers of blood and passed by this now-abandoned mosque in 1947 on their way to the newly created states of India and Pakistan, swirled about in my mind. Who knew, I asked myself, how many thousands of people might have been slaughtered in this very village in that momentous year? I shuddered at the thought, seeking to push it out of my mind, trying to think, instead, of the prospect of crossing the border soon and wondering what awaited me on the other side.

The bus slipped through a heavily guarded gate and ground to a halt at the Customs and Immigration booth. I rushed out of the bus, pushing and shoving and acting quite like the Pakistani passengers of whose behaviour at lunch time Mr Khan had so sternly disapproved, for I had been told that the procedures there could take up to several hours. I hurried up to the counter and presented my passport. A surly officer sitting behind the window flipped through its pages. He turned and looked me up and down suspiciously.

'This is not proper,' he said, bending and twisting my passport this way and that.

My heart sank. Did he mean to say that I could not cross the border? Hesitatingly, I asked him what the matter was. Instead of replying, he gruffly ordered me to wait, 'till further notice', as he put it. 'You may be called shortly,' he grunted as he tossed my passport into a plastic tray behind him.

That last sentence sounded particularly ominous. A wave of fear overwhelmed me, but I told myself that I had no reason to be afraid for my papers were all in order, at least as far as I knew.

Half an hour later, the man at the counter shouted out my name and I nervously approached the window.

'There's no problem, you can go,' he said imperiously, without even glancing at me.

I grabbed my passport and hurried off before he could change his mind. I passed out of the Customs booth and into the waiting area outside. Half a mile ahead, I spied a massive gateway that marked the end of Indian territory. Beyond that, I spotted a similar structure on the Pakistani side. The border, at last! Pakistan! So near, but, yet, it appeared, still so very far!

I walked up to the barbed wire fence that stretched on either side as far as I could see, a short distance behind the border, that had been put up some years ago to keep out possible intruders from Pakistan. Across the fence, although still in Indian territory, Sikh farmers in their tractors worked in fields bursting with a bountiful harvest of wheat. Up and down they bobbed as their tractors climbed and descended mounds of mud that they were levelling. I traced a group of middle-aged Pakistanis trudging down the road, having crossed the border on foot. An Indian delegation walked up towards them. When they finally met, they dissolved into a knot of intertwined bodies, heartily embracing each other and giggling like schoolchildren. I caught snippets of their chattering in loud Punjabi when they passed near where I was standing. Later, I learned that these people had never met before, but had come together to participate in a Sufi music festival at Amritsar designed to revive cultural ties between Punjabis from both sides of the border.

Wagah–Attari border

That display of cross-border camaraderie took me to the mosque at Attari, and then back to the border gates visible in the distance. The gates stood for all that I was viscerally opposed to: national chauvinism, religious intolerance, and the predicating of identities, personal as well as collective, on notions of the menacing 'other'. I cursed the idols of religious exclusivism and nationalism in my mind, to symbolize which I hawked out a ball of phlegm and violently spat it in the direction of the gates. Thoughts of my mother's family loomed before me. They had fled what was now Pakistan in 1947, and some of them must have passed through this route on their way to Delhi. I thought of Mr Khan's relatives in Lahore, who must have undertaken the same journey, but in the opposite direction. I thought, too, of the other passengers in the bus, many of whom must have also been from divided families, each with his or her own gory tale to tell.

The passengers piled back into the bus, which then slowly moved ahead, as if with carefully measured steps, towards the border. A stony silence settled over the bus, and the previously garrulous passengers suddenly turned grim-faced as the gates drew nearer. I sensed a strange mix of the fear and excitement that the allure of the forbidden entails overcome me like a powerful, irresistible wave. Tears welled in my eyes, and my throat went dry as the bus finally arrived at the gate on the Indian side. And there I saw, spread out before me the land of my grandparents, just a heavily barricaded metre ahead.

two

at home in 'enemy' land

The bus slipped through the gate. We had now passed into Pakistan. At last!

A short distance away, the bus pulled in at the Wagah Immigration and Customs Post. The passengers poured out, pushing and shoving at the counter to have their passports stamped. I came out last, carefully meditating on my first step on Pakistani soil, dazed at the thought of having crossed the forbidden frontier at last. I looked about, half-expecting Pakistan to be entirely different from India, which now lay just a quarter of a mile behind. I spotted a battalion of porters bearing ponderous suitcases and boxes on their backs and heads. They looked no different from their counterparts just across in Attari. And, of course, no different, too, were the fields of ripening wheat, the brilliant yellow mustard flowers swaying in the gentle evening breeze, the slobbery buffaloes sunk in ponds with herons perched on their backs, and the cone-shaped thatched huts that stood in the smoky distance.

My passport stamped at the Immigration and Customs booth, I sauntered outside. A flock of sparrows glided across from Indian into Pakistani skies, and I marvelled at the thought that they could come and go across the frontier as they

31

pleased. I headed for the Customs inspection hall, where I presented my luggage for checking. A rotund, officious-looking man, with a carefully combed Hitlerite moustache, drew up to me. Furtively glancing around to make sure he was not being watched, he hissed into my ear, exhaling a cloud of malodorous vapour, 'If you pay me five hundred rupees, sir, you can take your bags without them being checked.'

Shocked, more by the foul stench of his breath than by his outrageous proposal, I curtly replied, 'You can—indeed you must—check my bags. And I am not paying any money for that. That's your work, isn't it?'

The man knitted his brows into a cross. He sullenly rummaged through my luggage and quickly dismissed me. 'Hurry up and move ahead,' he growled.

We filed into the bus, which swerved on to the main road that led from Wagah towards Lahore, thirty-odd kilometres away. We passed a long fleet of trucks, their bodies lovingly decorated with twirling fairy lights, bits of multi-coloured plastic cut into geometric shapes, rows of tinkling copper bells and intricate paintings—of birds in flight, roaring tigers, leaping gazelles, turbaned peasant men, *houri*-like women—and snatches of Urdu calligraphy. These chariots, each a work of art, were driven by rough, hawk-nosed Pakhtun men, whom one might never have associated with such finesse.

I sat glued to the window, trying to observe every detail of what passed by. But, except for the bejewelled trucks, there was nothing that seemed particularly foreign to me. We could just as well have been in any part of semi-rural India. Badly pot-holed, the road was lined for long stretches with unpainted brick houses and electricity poles, weighed under thick serpentine wires, from which hung banners announcing the services of sundry *hakeem*s and extolling the virtues of various menacing-looking political leaders. Hillocks of garbage and pools of stagnant water stretched along the road till it finally wove its way into the suburbs of Lahore.

'Lahore is the Paris of the East!' exclaimed a corpulent Pakistani woman seated in the first row of the bus to no one in particular, and, presumably, to all the passengers in general, as we entered the suburbs of the city. 'So many British colonial officers said so,' she added, to back up her clearly dubious claim. The squalor that spilled out on the road as we sped ahead, and the dull, greying, unfinished buildings that we passed, however, told a vastly different story.

At around seven in the evening, by which time the last flickers of light in the sky had been blotted out, the bus pulled into the parking lot of the diminutive office of the Pakistan Tourist Development Authority in the heart of Lahore. The entire locality was plunged in darkness on account of the regular evening spell of load-shedding. Amidst much pushing and hectoring, I managed to grab my bags and force my way out, to be suddenly assaulted by a battalion of aggressive autorickshaw-drivers offering to take me to my destination. In the darkness, I searched for my host in Lahore, a friend whom I had first bumped into in virtual space—in a yahoo chat room on the Internet—and whom I had met in the 'real' world just once—and that too for a couple of hours—some months before in Delhi. I scouted around the tourist office and on the road outside, but found no trace of her. I began to fear the worst. Perhaps, I thought, she had not come at all. Maybe, I began to think, she had forgotten or, worse still, had chosen to forget. Perhaps, I started to dread, I would have nowhere to go on my very first night in Pakistan. I started making emergency plans. I might go off to the nearest police station. Or else, I thought, I would spend the night in the veranda of the tourist office or look for a Sufi shrine or a mosque that would let me in. I quickly expelled all such ideas, but the prospect of searching for a hotel at that late hour, on a cold wintry night, was far from tempting. In any case, I had no Pakistani money on me, and the money-changers, I found out, had, by now, all closed for the day.

Just as I was close to tears, I spotted my host waving out excitedly. 'Welcome to Pakistan!' she screeched as she rushed up and enveloped me in a tight embrace. I heaved an immense sigh of relief at the same time as I spotted a clutch of men glaring at us in stern disapproval.

My host in Lahore was Sheila, a middle-aged Leftist activist, a truly remarkable woman. Sheila and I had met only once before, but we had been in regular touch by e-mail thereafter. I had felt uneasy about staying with someone I hardly knew, and I had said this to her before leaving for Lahore. But Sheila was not one to take 'no' for an answer. I just *had* to stay with her, she had insisted, when I informed her that my visa had finally come through.

Driving down from the tourist centre to Sheila's house in a new middle-class locality on the outskirts of Lahore, I was jostled between trying to answer Sheila's litany of questions about mutual friends in India and trying to take in every small detail that passed by. What struck me particularly was how identical everything seemed to things back home. It was as if I had not left Delhi at all. I gazed at the cars passing by, driven mainly by clean-shaven men and some even by fashionable-looking women. By all accounts, the people seemed no different, in terms of looks, from fellow Punjabis back in India. There was nothing about them that even remotely resembled the stereotypical Muslim of the Hindu imagination. It struck me—and this I was to remain conscious of during my entire trip—how relatively less common the burqa, beard and skull-cap were here than in most Muslim localities in India. This had probably much to do with the fact that, being a marginalized minority, Indian Muslims were much more protective and demonstrative of their identity. The sameness was, I must admit, somewhat disconcerting, for I had expected to be in a truly foreign country—the utterly alien 'enemy' territory that most Indians imagine Pakistan to be.

That night, Reshma, Sheila's sister who lived with her, had prepared a sumptuous Punjabi meal of *paratha*s, *maa ki daal* and *dahi bhalla*s. There were probably just a few dozen vegetarians in all of Pakistan, and Sheila, Reshma proudly revealed, was one of that rare species. I had been warned that it was next to impossible to get decent vegetarian food in Pakistan. 'Even if you ask for daal, it is likely that you'll find chunks of meat floating in it,' a friend who had travelled extensively in Pakistan had told me before I left. I was a committed vegetarian, and the prospect of spending a month in Pakistan surviving on bread, cheese, chips and the like had been deeply troubling. Quite naturally, then, I heartily responded to Reshma's revelations about Sheila's eating habits, which most Pakistanis would find eccentric, if not wholly 'un-Islamic'.

After dinner, reclining on cushions spread out on the floor in the sparsely furnished drawing room, we chatted about this and that, but mostly about my utter amazement at how everything I had seen so far in the last three hours in Pakistan, from the border onwards, seemed so comfortably familiar. We rued the Partition, cursed British and American imperialists, berated Hindu and Muslim chauvinists, denounced devious politicians, rapacious landlords and insatiably greedy capitalists, all of whom we blamed for keeping our countries apart, and discussed dreams of a South Asian Federation. All these points were to be repeated in conversations with many people I was to later meet throughout my stay in Pakistan, in every town I visited.

I was woken the next morning at the crack of dawn by the mellifluous cry of a *muezzin* that emanated from a nearby mosque. Which was just as well, I told myself, because I wanted to cut down on sleep during my stay, to be able to see and experience as much of the country as possible. There was no knowing, I reminded myself, if and when I would be able to visit Pakistan again.

Was I really in Pakistan, I asked myself, as I threw off the pile of *razai*s that I lay huddled under? Or, was this just a dream and I was actually still in that creaky, uncomfortable cot in the hostel where I lived in Delhi? I looked around the room. No, it was definitely not my room in the hostel, which was barely large enough to contain a bed and a writing table. Compared to that, this one was perversely luxurious: a splendid Afghan carpet covered the entire floor; a smart wooden cabinet held neatly bound volumes whose spines were etched in Urdu calligraphy; and on the walls were displayed a number of Mughal miniatures and framed pictures of hirsute men leading camels over desert sands. I was definitely in Pakistan, I excitedly assured myself.

Sheila was already up and about at that early hour and I joined her for tea. Like me, Sheila was a heavy smoker. Although, the night before, we had promised ourselves that we had had the last cigarette of our lives, that morning, not unexpectedly, we quickly changed our minds. 'We'll never ever give up cigarettes!' she chuckled as she drew out a pack that she had hidden under a cushion to save it from being chewed up by Hemu, her four-year-old Labrador, who, like her, was addicted to tobacco, besides also being a strict vegetarian. We warmed our toes before the room-heater and, over hot, sugary, cardamom tea, puffed away at our cigarettes in a desperate bid to stave off the biting cold.

What was I doing here, in a house in Lahore with two single women whom I hardly knew? How and why had these women so readily agreed to host me, a perfect stranger? So much, I thought, for the stereotypical image of Pakistani women as carefully cloistered creatures who were forbidden any interaction with 'strange' males. But then Sheila was no ordinary Pakistani woman. The third and last child of a feudal lord from southern Punjab, she had rebelled against her family's tradition that forbade womenfolk from even stepping out of their homes unveiled and unescorted by male relatives. In this, she had been encouraged by her mother, who had named her after her best friend, a Hindu woman who had lived in their ancestral village before the Partition, but had been forced to leave for India in 1947. They had never met after that.

Sheila was the only female in her village to have studied beyond high school. She had then gone to a women's college in Lahore and later won a scholarship to do a master's degree in sociology at a university in Australia. There, she got involved with various Leftist groups, seeking to help folks back home by funding small projects in remote villages in Pakistan, as well as galvanizing public opinion against Pakistan's military rulers. It was in Australia that she had met Indians for the first time, fellow Leftists along with whom she set up two informal networks: one, to boost ties between India and Pakistan, and the other, to revive sundered cultural bonds between Punjabis on both sides of the border. It was on the occasion of a conference in Delhi in honour of the Punjabi Sufi poet Baba Farid, hugely popular among Punjabi Muslims, Sikhs and Hindus alike, that I had first met her. Easily the most spirited speaker in the gathering, she had passionately argued the case for a South Asia without or beyond borders, and, for communal harmony, weaving in Baba Farid's vision of universal humanism in a forceful way that I am sure would have made the saint proud.

Like most other committed social activists of her sort, Sheila had faced enormous odds. The landlord she had been married off to against her will had taken a second wife without her consent, ten years after their marriage. Sheila had protested but her husband refused to relent, arguing that Muslim law allowed him that privilege. Unwilling to put up with a second wife in the house and an insensitive husband, Sheila sued for *khula* or dissolution of her marriage. Her husband, eager to get rid of an insouciant wife, willingly agreed but not before he took back the entire *mehr* or dower that he had given her on marriage: a sum of ten lakh rupees.

Sheila's husband did not pay her any maintenance after the marriage was dissolved. Unwilling to go back to her village, she took up sundry jobs in Lahore, working as a translator in a bank, giving English tuitions at home and selling handicrafts produced by women working with a rural development organization. That was how she supported herself, Reshma, her son Iqbal, and her daughter Rani. The little spare time she got from doing chores to earn a living, she devoted to Leftist politics, working in the *kutchi abadi*s or slums of Lahore, and helping out in a school in a remote village up on the mountains in Chitral, in Pakistan-administered Kashmir.

That Sheila had invited me, someone quite unknown to her—an Indian, and, more than that, a male—to come and stay in her house, insisting that I should stay nowhere else while in Lahore, was itself evidence enough of what an intrepid iconoclast she really was.

While Sheila was busy getting ready, I stepped out for a walk. It was still dark outside and bitterly cold. A chill wind swept down from the north. Faint smudges of orange light peeped out from just above the horizon, visible from the gaps between the rows of incomplete houses. A peacock squawked in the distance, hidden behind tall grasses that grew in empty plots ringed with unpainted brick boundary walls. Wires stretched out like lengthy serpents from concrete electricity pillars. The road was patchy and riddled with craters filled with stagnant pools of fetid water. I intently surveyed the surroundings. This could easily have been any run-down lower-middle class locality in New Delhi.

As the sun came up I saw school children in neat uniforms accompanied by their fathers to waiting vans, bearing bags on their backs half their size. Pot-bellied Punjabi housewives hollered out to passing milkmen and haggled with men selling vegetables on wheeled carts over the price of potatoes and onions. Old men hobbled home clutching metal flasks of milk. In a large, neglected patch of grass that served as a public park, boasting a couple of ugly cement benches and a swing long since in disuse, a *mali* turned on a sprinkler. A poster pasted on the wall surrounding the park announced a rally to be addressed by Hafiz Muhammad Saeed, supremo of the Jamaat ud-Dawa, the parent wing of the dreaded terrorist outfit Lashkar-e Tayyeba, which was supposed to have been long since banned by the Government of Pakistan. It was addressed to 'All Islam-Loving Members of the Muslim Community', exhorting them to support the Jamaat in what it called its jihad against the Indian 'infidels' in Kashmir.

I ambled down a muddy path to an eatery a short distance away. It was housed in a thatched hut with stained blue canvas sheets strung together for roofing and encircled by open drains clogged with fresh human faeces, discarded plastic bags and vegetable peels. Outside, an enormous, soot-stained cauldron squatted on a pile of burning logs, sending up spirals of acrid smoke. Bearded old men crouched on broken chairs, their knees lifted up to their chins, puffing away at clay hukkahs and coughing and burping loudly. Vast armies of flies hovered angrily above plastic plates containing bones and bits of left-over meat.

A man boasting a drum-like belly, dressed in a crumpled, heavily stained, shalwar-kameez, stepped out of the hut and swung open the door of a cage that stood on stilts built over a sewer. It contained a dozen or more hens, and he grabbed one by its feet. The bird violently squawked and flapped its wings furiously, as if sensing the fate that awaited it. The man hopped on to a wooden platform and settled on a filthy pillow, fluffing it up to make himself comfortable. He placed a handkerchief on his head and lay the bird down in front of him. Muttering some verses, presumably from the Quran, he lowered a knife towards the hen's neck. I shut my eyes and looked away. The hapless bird let out a series of desperate cries and then suddenly fell silent.

After the gory ritual slaughtering was over—it took several minutes, because, according to Muslim law, it must be done slowly—I turned to the man and asked him if he had anything vegetarian to eat.

'We have spinach with chicken and daal with mutton,' he replied.

I explained exactly what I meant. 'Spinach or daal, without chicken or mutton?'

He shot me a blank, puzzled look. 'No, no, you don't get that sort of food here,' he snorted.

The eatery left a lasting impression on me. Little did I realize then that since I was on a tight budget and had to rough it out, staying away from expensive restaurants throughout my trip, I would be forced to eat in scores of places almost as dingy and filthy as this one, with which Pakistan seemed to abound. Clean and cheap eateries, I was to discover, were an absolute rarity in the country, even in Lahore, which boasted of a supposedly sophisticated culinary tradition.

Tracing my steps back towards Sheila's house, I stopped in an empty square that had been converted into a temporary slum. Desperately poor people lived there, in dozens of tents made of pieces of cloth and plastic stitched together and strung on wooden poles. Unwashed, bare-bottomed toddlers, their hair flaky and yellow with severe malnutrition, played in the sand with broken dolls and deflated rubber balls. Elderly women tended to tin pots set on wood fires, fed leaves to bearded goats, and swung infants huddled in makeshift cradles made of snatches of cloth slung from the branches of trees. Young men joked with each other over a game of cards while puffing away at cheap cigarettes. From their appearance and complexion, these people struck me as being of 'low' caste origin.

'We are from the nomadic Odh caste,' revealed a young man who beckoned me. 'No well-dressed sahibs from this locality ever come to speak to us,' he said as he swept the space about his tent with a broom made of twigs. 'What are you doing here, sahib?' he asked.

I was a visitor from India, I told him, and was staying with a friend who lived close by. He looked me up and down as if I were some sort of museum piece.

'India?' he croaked after a while. 'No, sahib. You must be joking. You look like a real Lahori!'

I drew out my passport from my pocket to convince him.

'Sahib,' he replied, shaking his head, 'we Odhs are illiterate folk. I can't read what's in that booklet.'

Finally, with considerable difficulty, I managed to convince the man about my origins. He grabbed my hand in his and pressed it into the folds of his shalwar. His hands were rough and calloused.

'How soft your hand is, sahib!' he exclaimed, breaking into a boisterous laugh. 'I see you don't do hard work like we do.'

Pointing to the sprawling mansions visible behind a high wall that set them off from the slum, he went on. 'We eat what we earn by our hard labour. Not like those fat sahibs who take bribes, live in fancy houses and even have air-conditioned rooms for their dogs.'

I asked the man to tell me more about his people.

The Odhs, he replied, numbered over a million across Pakistan, and were found especially in southern Punjab and Sindh. Most of them had become Muslim, but there were still several thousands of them who had refused to give up their ancestral animistic traditions and were considered to be Hindus. The two groups retained close ties, bound by memories of their common ancestors. Some Muslim Odhs continued to follow the pre-Islamic practices of their forefathers. Many of them actually knew little about Islam. Some even had Hindu-sounding names and still observed the Hindu practice of *got* or clan exogamy, frowning on cross-cousin marriages, as was common among other Muslims. Traditionally, the Odhs had led a nomadic life, he said, moving from village to village to offer their services as masons and even acrobats. Most of them remained desperately poor, illiterate and landless. The government had hardly done anything for them, he went on.

'We converted to Islam three generations ago, at the time of the Partition,' the man explained. 'Before that, we were Hindus but we were treated as untouchables by the Brahmins and the Banias. In Islam, there is no such thing. Islam teaches equality of all Muslims. That is why we changed our religion. After all, no matter what your caste is, everyone's blood is red, and everyone has finally to go to the grave to meet his creator.'

Listening to the man, I could well understand why almost the whole of Sindh and most of Punjab, where the bulk of the Pakistani population was concentrated, had gone over to Islam over the centuries. It was the hope for escape from the tyranny of the Hindu caste system that had led the oppressed 'low' castes of these regions, who formed the majority of the population, to turn Muslim almost *en masse*.

An old man, bent low on a stick, hobbled into the tent where we were seated. With considerable effort, he lifted the flap that shielded the entrance. He had a heavily creased face, and on his feet I noticed gaping wounds on which sat dozens of flies sipping pale yellow pus.

'Sahib, we Odhs were at one time Rajputs, rulers of a vast kingdom,' he muttered as he settled on the ground. His lizard-like eyes, half shut under the weight of their lids, crinkled with delight at that thought about his ancestors. 'But due to some misdemeanor of one of our forefathers we lost our caste status.' He rolled his head about and clicked his tongue loudly, revealing a set of black, tobacco-stained, almost wholly toothless gums. 'And so we were reduced from dwellers of palaces to builders of hovels.'

'No, *chacha*,' interrupted another man who had just entered. 'I've heard that we are the descendants of the brave Rajput chieftain Dullah Bhatti of Ferozepur, who fought against the invading army of the Mughal Emperor Akbar, but was defeated and forced to flee into the desert to save his life. Since all our lands were seized by the Mughals, we turned into wandering gypsies and took to constructing houses to survive.'

Having been ousted from their thrones, the man continued, the Odhs had taken to constructing mud huts as their caste profession. Till recently, they had moved from village to village across Punjab and Sindh offering their services, setting up temporary shelters on the outskirts of the habitations where they managed to get a few days' work. Now, with increased rural prosperity, village people wanted houses made of brick instead clay and mud, and so, many Odhs had shifted to back-breaking and low-paid work in the brick kilns that dotted the Punjab countryside.

I asked the young Odh if caste and caste-based discrimination were still a reality in Pakistan. I surmised that it could not be half as bad as in India, though, where it received religious legitimacy from the Hindu scriptures.

'We are still treated miserably, sahib,' he complained. 'People shun us, thinking we are thieves and baby-snatchers.' Most Sindhi and Punjabi Pakistanis, as well as the Muhajirs who had come as refugees from India, were, he went on, descendants of Hindus, and many of them still retained their caste identities and prejudices. That was why, he explained, even though the Muslim Odhs could pray in the same mosques as the other Muslims, they were still generally treated as *kammi*s or members of a servile caste.

As in India, the man elaborated, almost all marriages in Pakistan took place within the *biraderi* or caste. That was how the caste system was maintained and continued. Few 'high' caste Muslims would think of marrying an Odh girl, and almost none would be willing to give their girls to Odh men, he said. 'And,' he added, 'there are so many other such Muslim biraderis who, like us, were considered as untouchables by the Hindus and are still looked down upon as low after converting to Islam. While we are recognized as fellow Muslims, power and wealth is largely in the hands of the more powerful biraderis.'

'Of course, all this is completely un-Islamic,' insisted the old man, who had remained silent all the while. 'But,' he asked philosophically, 'how many Pakistanis can be said to be truly Islamic or real Muslims, in the proper sense of the word? If they really were so, we Odhs would not be living in a squalid slum like this, unsure of where we will get our next meal from. After all, our Prophet has said that he who eats well but leaves his neighbour hungry cannot be a good Muslim.'

Sweeping a wide semi-circle with his hand and indicating the ostentatious mansions visible beyond the slum, he mocked, 'If Pakistan were truly an Islamic country, as it claims to be, do you think these rich people would be living in these huge buildings and we in these miserable hovels? Nothing positive has happened for us ever since Pakistan was created, I tell you.'

I stared at the men around me, the poverty, the filth, the squalor and the pall of irredeemable despair and hopelessness that enveloped their miserable slum. Their plight, I wanted to tell the men, was no different from that of most of their fellow 'low' castes, Hindus and Muslims, in my own country. But, I thought, of what use or comfort would that have been to them?

I trudged back to Sheila's house through piles of garbage and concrete waste from abandoned construction sites. My mind went back to the Hindu Odhs I had met years before in Rajasthan, whose living conditions were no less pathetic than those of their Muslim brethren I had just met. They looked the same to me and appeared to live in the same sort of way. Barring their names and their putative religious identities, they seemed, in fact, no different at all. What, I wondered, did religion and nationalism actually mean for such desperately poor people, for the millions of 'low' caste Dalits, in both India and Pakistan? Did it make any difference at all to their pathetic

plight if they were called or called themselves 'Hindus' or
'Muslims', 'Indians' or 'Pakistanis'? In my mind I tried to trace
the complex web between power, religion, caste, class, nation,
and the narrow notions of community identity. I mused on
how 'upper' caste prejudice, both Hindu and Muslim, must
surely have at least something to do with the fact that hardly
any of the literally hundreds of books that had been written
about the trauma of the Partition even touched upon what the
tragedy had meant for the millions of Dalits on both sides of
the border, such as the Odhs I had just encountered. How and
why was it, I asked myself, that Dalits, whether Hindu,
Muslim or other, had virtually no place in official or
'mainstream' Indian and Pakistani historiography, being, instead,
carefully and calculatedly rendered almost totally invisible,
indeed untouchable, by historians?

These depressing thoughts drove me to Sheila's doorstep,
where she was impatiently waiting for me with my brunch—
a stack of steaming hot parathas and a pot of frothy, sweet
lassi.

That first afternoon in Pakistan was spent in Sheila's drawing
room planning a tentative schedule for my month's stay. Sheila
had called over some of her friends, all fellow Leftist activists,
most of them much younger than herself, to join us for tea. She
deputed Irshad to take me to the Punjab University, Salman to
guide me around the Sufi shrines in Old Lahore, Raja to help
me discover the Batras, my distant relatives who lived in the
city, and Heena to accompany me to sundry NGO and activist
meetings. All this was to be done within the next week, she
instructed them. They just could not refuse, even if they

wanted to, for, clearly, they were in complete awe of Sheila, and her every word was a command that simply had to be obeyed. Sheila may have declassed herself to some extent as a committed Marxist, but remnants of her family's feudal past still lingered on in her ability to get things done.

Everyone's work thus assigned, we fell to talking about India–Pakistan relations and about Pakistan's domestic politics. 'There's no difference really between Indians and Pakistanis,' Sheila mused, 'so why do we consider ourselves enemies?' That existential question brought forth a chorus of condemnation from all of us—of politicians, power-hungry *maulvi*s and *pandit*s, of the ruling élite and imperialist powers—and we unanimously decided that our little coterie would settle for nothing less than a visa-free South Asia, with or without separate states.

'I think Bollywood's the best way to bring Indians and Pakistanis together,' suggested Reza, a college dropout who had recently set up a video parlour. 'Pakistanis are glued to Indian television. No sooner is a film released in Mumbai than pirated CDs of it are readily available all across Pakistan. If you ask me, it's not the politicians but the likes of Anil Kapoor and Shah Rukh Khan and Aishwarya Rai, whom every Pakistani and Indian knows and adores, who can bring us together again.'

'What bourgeois *bakwaas*, *yaar*!' screeched Sheila. 'You're just saying that because you want to promote your own video business!'

'There can't be peace between India and Pakistan if the Kashmir issue remains unsettled,' insisted Heena, a student of political science and an activist with a local theatre group. 'If the Indian government's claim that Kashmiris want to be with India is true, why does India refuse to hold a plebiscite in the region?'

I agreed that hers was a pertinent question, though one which the Indian state, for obvious reasons, refused to entertain.

The conversation turned to the subject of Indian politics. 'You chaps are so lucky,' said Kamran naïvely. 'You've never been under army rule. Democracy is so matured in India. So many political parties. Regular elections. Universal franchise. A proper Election Commission. Parties that gracefully exit when they lose at the polls. I wish Pakistan could follow your example.'

'Yes, and your politicians are so intelligent and articulate. Ours are so dumb,' interrupted Heena.

'But, your politicians are so much better-looking than ours,' I joked. 'I think Musharraf is actually quite cute, Benazir was very elegant, although Nawaz Sharif reminds me distinctly of a sloppy buffalo.' On a more serious note I spoke about the grovelling poverty and the vast and rapidly increasing social and economic inequalities in India, about caste oppression and pogroms directed against the country's Muslims, and about India being home to the largest number of poor and illiterate people in the world. 'Bourgeois democracy, even in theory, has its severe limits, and political democracy without social and economic equality is meaningless,' I pleaded. I sounded, I thought, like a boring, wordy professor.

'But it's hardly different in Pakistan, although we do not have the same sort of desperate poverty as in many parts of India,' Heena butted in. 'Minority nationalities in Pakistan look at us Punjabis as a colonial power. Look at how the Sindhis and the Baluchis are being crushed by our state.'

'But what about Muslims in India?' asked Salman, who had till then kept silent. 'We hear about horrendous violence against them, often abetted by agencies of the state. How, then, can India's claims of being this great democracy be taken at all seriously?'

This issue of India's Muslims was to come up in conversations I had with numerous other Pakistanis, even with strangers while travelling on buses and trains or at tea-stalls. I answered Salman, as I later did others who had the same concerns, by being as honest as I could. Yes, I said, that, unfortunately, was true. Muslims were also among the most marginalized communities in India in terms of almost all socio-economic indices. This had, in part, to do with history—with the fact that most Indian Muslims were descendants of impoverished 'low' caste converts whose social and economic conditions had not appreciably changed even after conversion. But, I admitted, neglect on the part of agencies of the state and various forms of discrimination played a major role in reinforcing Muslim vulnerability. I also mentioned that Muslims in India, as in Pakistan—or elsewhere for that matter—were not a homogenous monolith. The Indian Muslims were divided on the basis of caste, class and language, and if, in some places they were impoverished and constantly threatened by Hindu mobs, elsewhere, they had done well for themselves, often despite government indifference.

Zubair, a college student whose parents had fled Delhi for Lahore in 1947 and had narrowly missed being killed by a murderous Sikh mob, interrupted me. 'Minorities in most countries face discrimination,' he said. 'Hindus and Christians in Pakistan also face a lot of problems, including from the state. Some Pakistani laws, instituted in the name of Islamization, have reduced non-Muslim Pakistanis to second-rate citizens in their own country.'

'Oh, the Zia legacy!' moaned Sheila, who had just returned from the kitchen bearing a bowl of steaming onion *pakora*s. 'Zia ul-Haq created havoc for Pakistan, misusing Islam to keep himself in power, firmly backed by the Americans. He introduced all those horrendous laws to curry favour with the *mullahs*.'

'He tried to force his version of strictly literalist Islam down people's throats against their will,' cried Heena. 'In his time, people working in government offices were forced to pray, and many did so just out of fear and compulsion, or simply to please their bosses.' An uncle of hers, who was incorrigibly irreligious, she said, had been appointed as the official organizer of prayers or *nazim-e salat* in his village, a post that he willingly accepted simply because it would make his CV look more impressive.

The discussion veered to the question of whether these purportedly 'Islamic' laws, such as equating the witness of two women to that of a single man, considering the 'blood-money' for a murdered Muslim woman or a non-Muslim to be half that of a Muslim man, and administering capital punishment for blaspheming the Prophet or for apostasy, were really 'Islamic' or not. Husain, the son of a Shia cleric but himself a hardened Marxist, was supposed to be an authority on such matters. He had no doubt in his mind that the sternly puritanical brand of Islam that had been propagated by General Zia, and that continued to be vociferously championed by a host of Islamist outfits had, as he put it, 'completely stultified the Pakistani mind'. 'It's all a matter of interpretation,' he went on. 'If you see Muslim laws in their social and historical context, I suppose one could argue the case that, in today's times, these laws do not represent justice—which is what Islam is said to stand for, and so, ironically, they can perhaps be termed anti-Islamic.'

'But that's not how most of our mullahs and military dictators understand Islamic law,' Sheila protested.

'That's precisely the point,' Husain responded. 'We should be out in the streets, trying to convince people about other ways of understanding Islam, instead of debating all this in your comfortable drawing room.'

'Stop making us all feel guilty and accusing us of being armchair revolutionaries!' Sheila retorted in jest. And all of us broke out into peals of uncontrollable laughter, although we knew that there was some truth in what Sheila had just admitted.

The next afternoon, Sheila had been invited to a meeting of local NGOs to discuss modalities for a forthcoming NGO forum that was to be held in Karachi three months later. She was reluctant to go for the meeting. 'That forum-*shorum* is a complete farce, a jamboree for the do-gooder élite,' she spat out. Many Pakistani NGOs were money-spinning rackets, she said, fronts for funnelling funds from abroad in the name of the poor. 'NGOs have become big business here. It's all part of a grand imperialist–comprador conspiracy. They want to co-opt potentially radical youth and corrupt and then totally depoliticize them.'

It was probably not much different in India, I helpfully added. I had worked for short stints with several NGOs across India but had found that few of them were facilitating any meaningful transformation in the lives of the people in whose names they received vast sums of money. The rest were structured like corporate houses and paid their top-level officers vulgarly exorbitant salaries, in addition to which there were hefty consultancies and regular jaunts abroad, where 'experts' huddled together in cosy conference halls in five-star hotels to discuss the plight of the poor.

'Don't you dare curse me if you find it horrendously boring!' Sheila warned me when she finally consented to go for the meeting and to take me along with her.

The NGO's office, where the meeting was to be held, could

well have been mistaken for the premises of a multinational company. It occupied three floors of a plush, newly constructed building in an upper-middle-class locality. The ground floor served as a lounge. Imitation antique chairs were set around glass coffee tables covered with patchwork spreads in soft pastel shades. High-necked lamps with perforated hand-painted shades made of camel leather were strategically placed in corners, from which streamed pools of soft yellow light. In the centre of the hall was a goldfish pond fed by an artificial brook that glided down a sculpted pile of rocks fringed with bonsai palms. A sleek glass tube-like elevator noiselessly transported us to the first floor, where the office reception was located.

A pleasant-faced woman rose from her seat as we walked in. 'Yes?' she inquired, straightening her dupatta and patting her hair into place. 'Do you have an appointment?'

We have come for the NGO meeting, Sheila replied.

'Please be seated,' answered the woman curtly. She indicated a commodious leather couch at one end of the room that was spread out on the edge of an enormous Persian carpet. 'I'll speak to our CEO and inform him. I won't be a minute.' She sounded as sugary-sweet as a well-trained air hostess.

'*Ting Tong! Tra la la la la! Ting Tong*!' sang a telephone from behind a glass-panelled door that led to the CEO's chamber. A man picked up the phone. I could hear him speak. '*Haan*, send those chaps in,' he grunted.

We pushed open the door and stepped inside an enormous room. It had probably been done up by a professional interior decorator and, obviously, at considerable expense. At one end stood elegant wooden bookcases in which were stacked dozens of brightly hued, neatly labelled box files. A large mahogany table occupied a corner, encircled by a couple of chairs with green velvet seats. Placed on the table was a ponderous onyx vase, from which trailed out flowering tendrils of an assortment of indoor plants. A glass bowl containing a pair of angelfish sat on a stool carved out of an elephant's foot. A collection of African masks decorated a stone pillar in the centre of the room. Behind, on a large stretch of wall, framed posters announced 'End Poverty Now!', 'Drink Pure Water!', 'A Pen in Every Child's Hands!' and so on, in Urdu, Sindhi, Punjabi and English. Another set of posters, on the opposite wall, contained details about the 'five hundred villages' that the NGO had, or so it claimed, 'lifted out of poverty and disease'.

At the other end of the room, behind an immense teak wood desk, surrounded on both sides by computers and piles of papers and files, was the CEO himself—the corpulent, bespectacled Mr Abid.

We exchanged perfunctory *salaam*s. Mr Abid pointed to a sofa placed under a set of gilt-framed Mughal miniatures, and we took our seats. He seemed too preoccupied to talk to us or else did not find us to his taste. We waited, shuffling in our seats and exchanging snide remarks about him in low whispers and about what Sheila termed the 'NGO circus'. Meanwhile, Mr Abid continued to busily tap away at his laptop.

The meeting was scheduled to start at two and we had got there right on time. Half an hour passed but no one else showed up. An hour went by. An hour and a half. Fifteen minutes later, a young man, dressed in a suit and a bright orange tie, joined us, along with a woman in a trim shalwar-kameez. They worked, they told us, with an America-funded NGO that was, so they said, engaged in 'promoting best practices and good governance' in Pakistan. What that meant, I had no idea. Nor, it seemed, did the duo.

Two hours slowly crawled by and only two more people arrived. This, Sheila whispered, was hardly the large assembly that she had been informed would be gathering that evening. I struggled to converse with the men and the women sitting around me. I wanted to know about the work they were engaged in and about how they saw the role of the state and civil society groups in bringing about, or resisting, social change. I was eager to hear them talk about issues concerning women, religious and ethnic minorities, peasants and the urban poor in Pakistan—communities that their NGOs, or so they claimed, were working with. But, with the exception of a bright young man, the rest seemed to have little concern about such matters. They answered my queries for the most part monosyllabically, bent over their laptops and readying power-point presentations for the meeting that showed no signs of starting.

'They are, almost all of them, in it just for the money, for the sake of a job,' hissed Sheila.

'Why don't we start NOW?' Sheila burst out after we had waited for almost three hours. Why had she not thought of saying that an hour or more earlier, I wondered.

Mr Abid who, all this while, had kept aloof from us, working on his laptop and seeming busy, looked up. 'Of course you cannot start,' he shot back, plucking his spectacles off his nose. 'The chairman of today's meeting has not arrived as yet. How can we have the meeting without him?'

The man we were being kept waiting for was the CEO of another large NGO, Sheila whispered. 'A real pain, and horrendously corrupt, too. He and this Abid chap are hand-in-glove in shady deals, pocketing money meant for the poor.'

Sheila hauled herself up from her seat in an angry huff. 'I've had enough of this NGO *nautanki*,' she boomed and dragged me out of the room.

We drove down to the Lahore Press Club and pulled up by a juice bar, where Sheila asked me to wait. The road ahead was blocked by two groups of angry demonstrators. A posse of policemen on horses sauntered about. Others sat on the pavement, wielding shields and batons. Obviously, the protestors were being carefully monitored, and, as an Indian citizen, it was wiser, Sheila suggested, that I stay out.

Sheila rushed off to join the first group—Sindhi Leftists and nationalists, she said they were. A hundred-odd young men held aloft banners and placards in Urdu and misspelt English denouncing the Pakistan government's plans of constructing a massive dam on the Indus River that would divert its waters to the Punjab and turn Sindh into a desert. 'Sindh! Sindh! We love you!' screamed a red, heart-shaped flag pinned across a man's chest. 'It's not just about water, oh Sindh! We'll sacrifice our blood for you!' sang a bunch of men at the rear, raising their clenched fists in anger.

I leaned against a car, sipping a glass of carrot juice, watching Sheila in full form. In the NGO office she had been sullen and silent, clearly feeling out of place. But here she was, the only woman in that crowd of youthful male demonstrators, holding aloft a red flag with a sickle and hammer untidily painted on it, wildly gesticulating at her comrades and at people in the horse-drawn carts and cars that passed by, and letting loose a barrage of revolutionary slogans. *Inquilab Zindabad!* she thundered. 'Long Live the Revolution!' A hundred voices called out after her and a sea of red flags shot up.

Half an hour later, Sheila came back. She had lost her voice. We shared a cigarette and then she trundled off to the park across the road. Two dozen people, more women than men, stood under a clump of gulmohar trees. This group of protestors was Christian. The single largest religious minority in Pakistan, accounting for a little more than one per cent of its population, Christians were among the poorest of Pakistan's poor, mainly converts from the lowest of the Hindu castes. The Christians who huddled together in the park had been driven out from their homes by an irate Muslim mob led by a bunch of mullahs, who had accused them of speaking ill of the Prophet Muhammad, a crime punishable with death in Pakistan. Their miserable hovels had been burnt down and their church destroyed, brick by brick.

A middle-aged woman dressed in a pale grey nun's habit was addressing the group. Sheila rushed up to her, wrapped her in a tight embrace and then joined the others. The group broke out into a song to the accompaniment of enthusiastic clapping. *Hum hongey kamiyab ek din*! they burst forth. 'We shall overcome some day!' I knew the song, popular in Indian Leftist circles, and I joined them in singing it from afar. Yes, indeed, there was so much in the world that desperately needed to be overcome.

three

the mall, the museum,
and the man at the minar

The first thing I needed to do that morning, my third day in Pakistan, was to change some money. Sheila offered to take me in her car to the nearest ATM machine, but I did not want to further impose on her. She was already doing more than enough for me, I felt, although she insisted that I should be completely at ease. I walked down from her house on to a tree-lined road and boarded a crowded bus heading for the famed Anarkali Bazaar, Lahore's major commercial district. Although the bus was jam-packed, I managed to get a seat, and how I managed that is itself an interesting story.

Sheila had remarked that what she called my Urdu (which, to me, was just plain Hindustani) was exceedingly good by Pakistani Punjabi standards. Many Pakistani Punjabis spoke the language in a thickly accented sort of way. I spoke Urdu like a native Urdu-speaking Muhajir, Sheila said, and assured me that I could easily pass off as a Muhajir from Karachi. However, she cautioned, certain words I sometimes used— *dhanyavad* in place of *shukriya* and *bhaiyya* in place of *bhai sahib* and so on—could easily give me away as an Indian.

'Bhaiyya, will this bus go to Anarkali Bazaar?' I asked an elderly man wrapped up in a thick muffler as I boarded the bus.

'*Jee, jee,*' he replied, looking me up and down rather curiously.

'Dhanyavad,' I spontaneously replied.

'Oh, so are you from India?' the man asked.

'Yes,' I stuttered, suddenly remembering what Sheila had said about the words that I had just used. I was not sure how the man would react. I feared that he might even turn hostile.

'Oh jee, welcome to Pakistan!' he beamed, grabbing my hand in his and giving it a firm shake. He removed a pile of packages that was placed on the seat next to his and beckoned me to sit.

The man introduced himself, handing me his visiting card. 'If you have any problem, my son, you must contact me,' he said in an avuncular sort of way, meaning, I felt, every word of it. And then—and this would be repeated in scores of chance meetings I was to have later with many other Pakistanis of his generation—he began to tell me about how and why his family had migrated to Pakistan from East Punjab, now in India, in 1947.

'All of us, Hindus, Muslims and Sikhs, had lived in that village for centuries, as long as anyone could remember,' he said. 'The Muslims in the village were all Jats, as were the Sikhs. In fact, we all belonged to the same Bajwa clan. Being descendants of the same ancestors, we had lived peacefully with each other for centuries.' But things began to change from the 1930s onwards, he went on, when the Hindu Mahasabha established a unit in his village. Its activists went around telling people that in an independent India, Muslims would have to convert to Hinduism or agree to live as second-class citizens. Even many Congressmen believed the same, he said, although they were careful not to openly voice such opinions. That, he went on, was entirely unacceptable to Muslims. Further, as some Muslims began to get educated, they grew increasingly restive in the face of Hindu economic domination and social discrimination. 'They treated us like untouchables. Naturally, we could never agree to live with people like that,' he said. It was this, and not blind religious passion, so he claimed, that had led many Punjabi Muslims to enthusiastically embrace the cause of a separate Muslim state of Pakistan.

His grandparents, the man continued, had been brutally slaughtered by sword-wielding Sikhs who had attacked the train in which they were travelling while fleeing Amritsar for what had become Pakistan. He spoke of the painful trauma of being wrenched from his ancestral home and the fields where his forefathers lay buried, the terror of seeing his grandparents being mowed down before his very eyes, and the struggle to start a new life in a new country as a refugee. His was the other side of the Partition story that was rarely heard in India. Most Indians did not even know of it. Needless to say, the Indian side of that horrific story was also hardly recounted or even recognized in Pakistan.

'But now we must be friends, there is no other way out,' the man went on. 'America and other white powers want India and Pakistan to keep fighting so that they can sell us their weapons and keep us permanently weak.' 'Imagine,' he exclaimed, and now suddenly he sounded hopeful, 'if India and Pakistan were united or at least were good friends, we would together be a veritable superpower!'

I shared the man's enthusiasm, although I told him that his dream might possibly not come true in our lifetime.

'*Inshallah*, it will, some day,' he responded.

'Inshallah,' I added, grasping his hand in a gesture of solidarity.

The bus passed the sprawling grounds of the University of Punjab and drove through well-appointed residential areas with large bungalows hidden behind high walls and guarded by gun-toting soldiers. We turned on to a broad, tree-lined avenue, driving past a row of impressive buildings, relics of the British Raj—clubs, schools, colleges, the courts, various government offices, a park with a massive cannon at its gate. The bus drove on to Mall Road, Lahore's major commercial area, now renamed, as many important roads and buildings across Pakistan had been, after Muhammad Ali Jinnah as the Shah-e Rah-e Qaid-e Azam, 'The Highway of the Great Leader', although few Lahoris referred to it by its new, tongue-twisting name. Most of the grand buildings that lined the road and that now functioned as shops, restaurants and offices, had been built by the city's rich Sikh and Hindu traders before the Partition. Some of them still had the names of their original owners etched above their entrances. Prior to the Partition, there had been just a single Muslim shop in the entire area.

I hopped off the bus at a traffic light. As I stood on the busy pavement, where hefty Pakhtun men, with well-chiselled bodies and dressed in billowing shalwar-kameez, jostled with yuppies in tight jeans and T-shirts emblazoned with pictures of the latest Western pop stars, I tried to imagine how this area must have looked in pre-Partition days, at the time when both my grandfathers had been students at Lahore University. This was meant to be the Lahore that my grandparents never stopped talking about, the Lahore about which many Punjabi migrants in Delhi never ceased raving and wistfully recalling. This was the 'Paris of the East' of their imagination, and as numerous writings by Punjabis on both sides of the border called it. I imagined horse-drawn coaches carrying carefully veiled Punjabi women and white *memsahib*s carousing along the street, Englishmen wearing pith helmets on their heads to keep off the scorching sun, walking sticks tucked under their arms, buying boxes of cigars and chocolates at well-appointed stores that sold goods manufactured back home in Britain, and pot-bellied Bania shopkeepers, their heads buried under tightly wound turbans, sitting behind wooden desks on carpeted floors.

But that, when set against the unmitigated chaos that spilled before me, was a completely unrecognizable picture. The road was choked with unruly traffic, the pavements blocked with milling crowds and stalls selling trinkets and food. This could have been any market back in Delhi. I wondered why Delhi Punjabis, like my own folks, persisted with the myth of a Lahore that had probably never existed.

I scouted around for a place to grab something to eat. The few restaurants on Mall Road were well beyond my budget. I strode into a narrow lane that led off the road, hoping to find something more affordable. A powerful stench of freshly slaughtered animals streamed out from a butcher's stall set up above an open sewer. On either side of the lane were semi-finished, unpainted buildings, enormous piles of rubbish and drains clogged with human refuse. A party of crows feasted on a dead dog.

I entered a grubby eatery, which was housed under tin sheets hammered together. The stall catered mainly to autorickshaw-drivers, artisans and daily wage labourers, who sat on broken plastic bucket seats set before wobbly wooden tables. 'No Discussing Politics Here' warned a tin board hung on the front wall, above framed pictures of Mecca and Medina and a bevy of scantily dressed Bollywood actresses. 'Terrorists Beware, You Are Being Watched' announced a slogan painted on the wall.

Choudhri sahib, the amiable patriarch of the family that ran the eatery, was ensconced at an ornate teak chair, probably a century old, but now badly worn out. Around him were arranged wide-bottomed steel containers filled with raw meat and an assortment of vegetables waiting to be cut. He wore on his head an enormous turnip-shaped turban that was topped with a majestic plume. He puffed away at a hukkah, stopping every now and then to issue instructions to young boys who rushed around or to scold them for no apparent reason.

When he learnt that I was from India, Choudhri sahib firmly refused to accept payment for the cup of tea and packet of biscuits that I had ordered. For him to charge me, he insisted, would be a terrible insult. 'You are our honoured guest,' he said, folding his grubby hands together to make the *namastey*, the Hindu sign of welcome. 'Indians who come to Lahore never eat in humble places such as mine. They eat only in fancy restaurants. You are the first Indian to have ever eaten here, so, how can I make you pay?' he protested. Then, he hollered at a boy to fetch me a glass of sweet lassi, made, he proudly said, from the milk of his own cows.

'Don't leave so soon,' Choudhri sahib commanded as I got up to go after downing the lassi. 'It is rare to meet an Indian, someone from my own land.' He drew a cane stool and sat down next to me. He turned the long stem of his hukkah towards me, and I took a deep drag.

'I was born in India,' he said as I let out circles of smoke that floated up to him. 'You said your grandparents were born in what is Pakistan. But they live in India and I in Pakistan. Strange, is it not?'

Yes, I said, not only was it strange, but tragic, too.

'We are Mula Jats, originally from what is now Haryana in India,' he went on, telling me about his family. 'Jats follow different religions. Some are Hindus, others are Sikhs, and yet others Muslims, and they live in both India and Pakistan. We are sons of the same valiant ancestors, who ruled large parts of India at one time.'

Like a true Jat, I thought, Choudhri sahib seemed to take great pride in his caste identity.

Mula Jats, Choudhri sahib explained, followed Hindu as well as Muslim customs and, till recently, could not easily be classified as either. I had read that British census officials were so perplexed at the religious practices of these people that rather than labelling them as 'Hindus' or 'Muslims', they created a new category for them, appropriately termed as 'Hindu-Musalmans'. Starting in the early twentieth century, Hindu and Muslim revivalist movements began targeting the community, trying to convert them to their respective faiths.

'Some of us became Arya Samajists, others became better Muslims. But many of us remained just as our ancestors had been for centuries,' Choudhri sahib carried on.

Then, in 1947, the Mula Jats were faced with an unenviable choice. 'Hindu mobs attacked our village, seeking to drive us out and grab our lands. They said that we should convert to Hinduism or abandon our lands and flee to Pakistan or else be ready to be killed,' Choudhri sahib said gravely.

Large numbers of Mula Jats were killed in Partition-related violence. Many more, like Choudhri sahib and his family, fled across to the newly created Pakistan. But a small number of them still remained in their ancestral land. Most of these had converted to Hinduism through the Arya Samaj, under duress, hoping thereby to save their lives and lands. Some continued being Muslim, in some vague sense. Some of those who became outwardly Hindu secretly retained their faith in Islam. And there were others who became Hindu for a while but, after peace was restored, turned Muslim again after a few years.

'Their conversion to Hinduism was probably just tactical,' Choudhri sahib commented. 'They later found that, despite their conversion, the Hindu Jats refused to eat or intermarry with them, considering their Muslim past to have rendered them permanently impure.' His eldest brother, he said, decided to convert to Hinduism and stay on in India. He had lost all contact with the rest of the family after the Partition. 'Maybe he's dead now,' said Choudhri sahib softly as tears filled his tired eyes.

I walked back to the bustling chaos of Mall Road, where I hailed an autorickshaw for Anarkali Bazaar where, I had been told, I could change Indian money. The beetle-like vehicle noisily hurtled down through a maze of dirt-strewed lanes that formed the heart of Lahore till we finally got to the bazaar, said to be one of the oldest surviving markets in all of South Asia.

Anarkali Bazaar was touted as one of Lahore's major tourist attractions but I failed to see why. It was just another chaotic market, a pale, run-down, filthier and much smaller version of Old Delhi's Chandni Chowk. It consisted of hundreds of makeshift stalls and shops housed in buildings that dated to colonial times and that were now, like much of the rest of Lahore, in a state of rapid decay. It could be compared to any market in a lower-middle-class part of Delhi or Mumbai, and had no special attraction but for what was said to be the tomb of a courtesan after whom it was named.

Even that claim was questionable, however. Anarkali, local legend had it, was a slave girl whom the Mughal Crown Prince Salim, later to become the Emperor Jahangir, fell desperately in love with. Since she was of 'ignoble' birth, the romance was forbidden by the prince's father, the Emperor Akbar (touted as a 'liberal' and 'enlightened' ruler in Indian history textbooks), who ordered the hapless woman to be buried alive behind a wall. The octagonal building housing her supposed tomb was later used by the French mercenary General Ventura, a top-ranking officer in the Sikh army, after which it was transformed into a church by the British when they occupied Lahore. After Pakistan was created, it was annexed into the sprawling premises of the Punjab Civil Secretariat to house the Provincial Records Office. The vast lawns that had once surrounded the tomb were now occupied by the hundreds of kiosks that formed the bustling Anarkali Bazaar.

Anarkali, recent researches now claim, might never have even existed. According to some scholars, she might actually have been the product of the fertile imagination of an obscure Urdu novelist. I was in no mood to visit the tomb, not having the courage to face the vast crowds shoving against each other as they plodded through dirt-lined narrow lanes of the market. And then, I thought, if it were not really Anarkali's tomb, and if Anarkali did not even exist, why bother to visit it?

I asked around for where I could change Indian money. I was guided to a lane that veered off from the main bazaar, where I spotted stalls selling a range of Indian goods—CDs of the latest Bollywood films, blow-ups of Bollywood stars in various states of undress, gaudy mirror-work *ghagra cholis*, piles of heart-shaped paan leaves, bottles of Dabur Amla hair oil, stacks of Lijjat *papad* and tubes of Fair and Lovely face cream. The foreign exchange bureau was hardly what I had expected it to be. It consisted of a broken plastic table and a steel chair chained, to prevent it from being stolen, to an electric pole planted beside a clogged drain. The unfriendly proprietor, whose protruding belly was firmly stuck between the desk and the chair he was sitting on, grabbed the Indian money I had in my hand, did some quick mental calculations and handed me a thick wad of Pakistani notes in different colours and sizes, all of them embossed with pictures of a morose-looking Muhammad Ali Jinnah. I exchanged enough Indian money to last me for a month, but, as I was to later discover, I was hardly able to spend half of it. Wherever I travelled, my Pakistani friends and acquaintances simply refused to let me pay for almost anything.

Lahore's museum, located at the far end of Mall Road, opposite the old University Hall, was said to be one of the richest and largest in the whole of South Asia. The sprawling cluster of buildings that formed the museum was itself an architectural marvel, a fine blend of Gothic, Victorian and Mughal styles. The museum was established to commemorate the Golden Jubilee of the reign of Queen Victoria, Empress of India, in 1887. The foundation stone was laid three years later by Victoria's grandson, Prince Albert Victor, Duke of Clarence, notoriously infamous as the alleged 'Jack the Ripper'. John Lockwood, father of Rudyard Kipling, served as curator of the museum for several years, and Kipling's hugely popular novel *Kim* was set in the museum's vicinity.

The museum boasted the usual curiosities that one could find in most Indian museums of comparable size. There were artifacts from Pakistan's pre-Aryan, Buddhist, Jain, Hindu and Sikh past—statues of an assortment of gods and goddesses, coins and amulets made of precious metals, multicoloured votive flags, carved wooden doorways decorated with multi-limbed deities, fraying embroidered silk robes, and portraits of bearded rajas and veiled ranis sporting in bathing pools and flower-filled gardens. The pride of place was occupied by the famous fasting Siddharth, a delicately chiselled sculpture of the Buddha silently absorbed in meditation, his deer-like eyes sunk deep into their hollows, his stomach stripped of every bit of flesh by stern austerities, and yet, despite or perhaps because of all this, a hint of a smile faintly shimmering on his lips. He appeared supremely indifferent to the fact that his body had completely wasted away and had turned into a bag of bones, over which serpentine veins intertwined like knotted creepers. An adjacent chamber exhibited findings from the five-thousand-year-old Indus Valley Civilization that long predated the invasions of the Aryans—clay toys, pottery shards, seals and votive tablets from Moenjo Daro and curly-haired deities, painted beads and roughly hewn stone weapons from Harappa.

An eerie silence hung over the poorly lit corridors of this section of the museum. Slim shafts of sunlight filtered in through crannies in the walls and slits in the shut windows, bringing in streams of dust that hung in the air as if in suspended animation. The massive stone Hindu and Buddhist statues that lined the walls cast long, eerie shadows that spilled across the cold granite floor, as if seeking desperately to reach out to each other in an expression of solidarity.

The museum boasted an enormous collection of exhibits relating to the country's Muslim heritage: miniature Mughal paintings, turbans and frocks that had belonged to a series of Sultans, carved Central Asian maces and muskets, hand-written copies of the Quran and Persian Sufi tomes yellowing with age. All this, as well as the pre-Islamic exhibits, would have been entirely familiar to a visitor from north India, where many museums stocked almost identical items, albeit with some minor regional variations. But what, to me as an Indian, was definitely distinctly Pakistani about the museum was the hall dedicated to the 'Freedom Movement' that occupied almost its entire upper floor.

Modern museums, as institutions set up and funded by governments, are not meant simply to store a motley collection of ancient artefacts. Rather, they have a distinctly political purpose—to construct and present a certain notion of national identity and culture, and to make the tenuous claim that the modern state truly represents a people's past and hence must be obeyed, feared and, indeed, almost worshipped. All this, the unsuspecting visitor is expected to imbibe. That cynical political role was precisely what the 'Freedom Movement' section of the Lahore museum was intended to play. Through a range of artefacts and images, it sought to project a particularly skewed version of South Asian history, from medieval times till our own, that aimed to confirm official Pakistani nationalism, or what was called the 'Ideology of Pakistan' or, also, the 'Two-Nation Theory'.

The Two-Nation Theory, speaking out against which constituted a punishable crime in Pakistan, was based on the premise that the Hindus and the Muslims of South Asia, despite having lived together for centuries and notwithstanding the Hindu roots of most South Asian Muslims, were actually two distinct, indeed completely antagonistic, 'nations'. According to this bizarre theory, the Muslims of South Asia had constantly struggled not just to maintain their own separate cultural and religious identity but also to establish their own political realm, a struggle that finally culminated in the creation of Pakistan in 1947. The state of Pakistan, then, supposedly represented what the forefathers of the citizens of the nation had, throughout the centuries, all along dreamed of and fought for against a host of opponents, particularly the 'wily' Hindus. In this reading of history, the creation of Pakistan was projected as a natural corollary and logical consequence of a long chain of events that went back as far as Islam's first contact with South Asia, in the seventh century. These events were presented as a foreshadowing of or as a prelude to the cataclysmic event of the coming into being of the new, distinctly Muslim state of the 'Land of the Pure'—that was what the word 'Pakistan' meant—in 1947.

Fading watercolour portraits of the eighteenth-century 'Tiger of Mysore', Tipu Sultan, unsheathed sword in hand, astride a ponderous elephant and leading his army against invading British forces, hung from nails driven into the wall. Siraj ud-Daulah, Nawab of Bengal, nudged against him, looking comically effeminate in a flowing silken gown, surrounded by a host of hirsute turbaned ministers. The last Mughal Emperor, Bahadur Shah, was relegated to a diminutive corner of the panel, lying limp on his deathbed, his tired, haunted eyes, like pools of darkness, staring into nothingness, faintly hinting at his valiant, but ultimately futile, resistance against the British.

But what, one could ask, did these figures have to do with the modern-day state of Pakistan? Pretty much nothing at all, as far as I could discern. The northern-most tip of Tipu Sultan's realms, which lay in the far south of India, was more than a thousand miles away from the closest part of what was now Pakistan. And then, Tipu Sultan had not sought to establish an exclusivist Muslim state, as the museum appeared to suggest, but, rather, to protect his own kingdom that had been remarkably non-communal for his times. Somewhat the same could be said for Siraj ud-Daulah as well, and for Bahadur Shah Zafar, too. But since the aim of the 'Freedom Movement' section of the museum was to put forward the specious claim that the desire for a separate Pakistan had burnt in the hearts of every zealous South Asian Muslim for centuries— and that the country was not simply, as was actually the case, a twentieth-century creation—these heroic figures had been conveniently appropriated and their struggles selectively interpreted to make an entirely different argument, one that, I supposed, would have made these revered figures shudder in horror had they heard of it.

The portion of the museum devoted to the 'Freedom Movement' that covered twentieth-century Indian Muslim leaders was equally revealing. I had not seen pictures of, or references to, these figures in any Indian museum, although I had read about some of them, mostly in works by Indian authors with a distinctly anti-Pakistani bent. Museums in India served the purpose of promoting official Indian nationalism, which had no room for these heroes who, in their own ways, and sometimes for perfectly legitimate reasons, challenged the hegemonic, heavily Hindu-influenced nationalism that the Congress Party and the Hindu Mahasabha stood for. This was partly because these parties had refused to accommodate genuine Muslim concerns, forcing many Muslims to back the Pakistan scheme. Consequently, many of these Muslim heroes, several of whom had played key roles in the anti-colonial struggle, were never mentioned, let alone commemorated, in Indian museums. Peering at the portraits of the men that decorated the hall—the pioneers of the Khilafat struggle, the early stalwarts of the

Aligarh movement, the war-like Hurs, dedicated disciples of Pirs from the desert sands of Sindh who had engaged in several skirmishes with the British, the fierce, freedom-loving Frontier Pakhtun tribesmen who had harried the British decades after the Raj had subdued the rest of India, and, most notably, the architects of the Muslim League—provided me with a different perspective on the anti-colonial struggle in South Asia, one that was constantly and consciously blacked out back in India.

Adjacent to this panel of pictures was a large collection of photographs pasted on the wall, grouped together under the label 'Atrocities on Muslims by Hindus and Sikhs'. These exhibits displayed gory images of the unspeakable violence that had accompanied the Partition which had witnessed the death of over a million people and caused the displacement of more than twenty million from their ancestral homes—images of flames leaping out of train coaches, of slain burqa-clad women lying outside destroyed huts, their entrails spread out around them, of a mob of sword-wielding Sikh marauders hurtling towards a group of Muslims huddling in the corner of a burnt-down mosque, of a long train of bullock-carts moving past the Attari railway station and into what had just become Pakistan, bearing dozens of dispossessed, poverty-stricken Muslim families fleeing east Punjab.

Horrifying images indeed, and they continue to haunt me. But even as they depicted one side of the brutal truth about the orgy of violence that had accompanied the Partition which was rarely recognized in India—that Muslims had suffered as much as Hindus and Sikhs—they told only the partial truth. It was as if Muslims alone had been victims of the Partition-related violence and as if Hindus and Sikhs alone had been its perpetrators. It was, in other words, as incomplete a truth as was the standard Indian view of those barbarous times.

The public transport system in Lahore, as in most Pakistani cities, was woefully inadequate. There were no government-owned buses in the city, or, for that matter, in almost the rest of the country. All the buses and vans that plied the streets of Lahore were privately owned. Most of them, so I was told, belonged to a single person—a powerful minister, someone said, or a minister's minion, according to another source.

One of those fearsome dragons on wheels suddenly swerved round the corner, coughing out voluminous clouds of black smoke behind it, and screeched to an abrupt halt at the bus-stop. The driver stuck his head out of the window and squirted out a stream of blood-red paan liquid. The conductor kept up a rhythmic banging on the side of the bus, crying out the names of the places where the bus would stop. I could not recognize any of these, but as the bus revved up to go I rushed towards it and leapt through the front door.

I struggled up the steps as the bus hurtled ahead, and then, as I turned to grab a seat, I was greeted with a loud collective gasp—from a posse of women who scowled at me, angrily sizing me up and down and hurriedly drawing their dupattas over their faces, as if I were an unwelcome intruder. And that, I was informed by the furious driver, I certainly was. Didn't I have any shame, he barked, barging into the ladies' compartment of the bus like that? Was I out of my mind? Did I want to be thrashed and have my legs broken with a hockey stick?

I froze. I had been informed about separate sections for women and men in Pakistani buses, but it had completely slipped my mind. My head began to spin violently. A sudden wave of fear rushed through my belly and up my head. I wanted to retch. I imagined the driver, a burly, muscular Pakhtun, grabbing me by the collar and banging my face into a pulpy mess.

'Brother!' I gasped pathetically, 'please forgive me. I've just arrived from India, where we don't have separate sections for women, and I didn't know about this rule here.' I turned to the women and murmured, not daring to look them in the eye, 'I am really sorry.'

All at once the driver's angry visage underwent a complete transformation. He burst into a smile and his pale green eyes lit up. He let loose a loud, hearty laugh that made his ample belly jiggle with mirth. 'Arey bhai! No problem at all! Welcome to Pakistan!' he said as he lustily swung his leg up, causing his shalwar to swell up into a balloon, and then jammed it on to the brake. The bus spluttered to a halt. 'We have this rule in our buses, so please use the back door, which is reserved for men.'

I glanced at the women, who were now looking at me with unconcealed amusement. 'Don't worry, son. This happens sometimes,' said an old woman sitting in the front row. Her forehead was cobwebbed with creases. As she spoke, she shot out jets of spittle through the gaps in her remaining teeth. 'What is this Pakistan? What is this India? To me, the entire world is one,' she looked up to the roof of the bus and muttered aloud, addressing no one in particular.

I rushed down the steps and entered the bus from the rear door into the section reserved for males. The conductor grabbed my hand and gave me a friendly wink. 'Don't worry, brother,' he said, patting me on the shoulder. 'He is our Indian guest!' he called out, commanding the standing passengers to make way for me. A young boy in a school uniform got up and offered me his seat.

I sank into the seat, overwhelmed by what had just transpired. The bus swung into motion and hurtled down a narrow lane. Next to me sat a corpulent, middle-aged man dressed in a turquoise blue shalwar-kameez. In one hand he clutched a bag of groceries. The index finger of his other hand was kept suitably occupied deep inside his nostrils. Every now and then he would draw out his finger, carefully inspect it, curl the mucous that smeared it into a ball and fling it out of the window.

'So, are you from India?' he turned to me and asked as he jabbed his finger into his nose again and furiously shook it about. 'How are conditions in India?'

'I don't quite understand your question, brother,' I responded. 'It depends on what or whose conditions you mean.'

'The conditions of Indian Muslims, of course,' he shot back. 'You are a Muslim, aren't you?' He twisted his eyebrows into a menacing knot. I could feel several pairs of eyes riveted on me—of passengers who already regarded me as some sort of oddity.

This was the first time in Pakistan that I had been asked my religion and I did not how to respond. The man's reaction would, I knew, depend on what answer I gave. I could hardly tell him that I was not quite sure what I was—sometimes an agnostic and occasionally even an atheist, but that is what I did.

The man drew out his finger from his nose. I glimpsed a spot of orange-coloured muck on its tip. He grabbed my hand in his. I shuddered but did not dare withdraw it.

'Muslims are badly treated in India, is it not? The new Untouchables they have become,' he said, loud enough for all the other passengers to hear. 'Very, very sad indeed,' he cried out.

I tried to be as honest as I could. 'In some parts of India, conditions are bad and are getting even worse. But it is difficult to generalize for the whole country,' I stuttered.

'Do Hindus still consider Muslims as untouchables?' inquired an elderly man seated behind me. 'When we were young, here in Lahore, Hindus would refuse to drink water touched by us. They had separate water pots at the railway stations and all Muslims, even rich landlords and high-born Syeds, were forbidden from entering their homes.'

'Bloody tyrants the Hindus are!' thundered an angry-looking man with a long scar that ran down his cheek like an exclamation mark.

I ached to tell the men that not all Hindus were bad, and, for that matter, not all Muslims were good. Such wild generalizations could not be made about any community, I wanted to explain. And what, I wished I could have asked them, about Muslims who slaughtered fellow Muslims in Pakistan, Muslims who belonged to rival political parties or warring sects and ethnicities, and who cared nothing of throwing bombs into mosques full of worshippers? What about the stories that I had heard of Pakistani Hindus, a small, scattered and insecure minority, being kidnapped and forced to convert to Islam? Surely, I wanted to tell them, oppression and tyranny knew no bounds or religion, community or nationality—a trite point, but one which the passengers did not seem to realize, just as many Hindus back home in India would refuse to admit it, considering Muslims as the cause of all the world's woes. But, I wisely chose to keep silent. I had already created enough controversy by entering the women's section of the bus.

'Our hearts go out to hapless Muslims of India,' the man seated next to me went on. He slung his arm around me, and I quivered under its weight and the overpowering stench of sweat that emanated from his armpits.

'Cut the crap out!' I wanted to scream. If Pakistan, I wished I could have asked him, were truly so concerned about the plight of Indian Muslims, why were Pakistani jihadist outfits, some of them fully backed by the Pakistani state, spreading terror and creating mayhem in India, which had further hardened anti-Muslim sentiments and helped no one at all but Hindu fascist forces, who thrived on fanning hatred and mob violence directed against the hapless Indian Muslims?

I cursed the man in my mind but, of course, kept silent. I even managed to stick a fake smile on my face.

'Are Muslims allowed to pray in India? Can they call the *azan* from their mosques? Can they slaughter cows? Does the Indian government allow madrasas to function?' He rolled off a volley of questions, not waiting for me to answer.

He continued, unconcerned about whether I was listening to him or not. 'We hear that things are so bad for Muslims in India that some of them, for fear of the Hindus or wanting to win their favour, marry their girls off to Hindu men and adopt Hindu names.' He let out an angry snort and inserted his finger back into his nostril. He carefully rotated it and drew out a blob of mucus. 'We are lucky,' he said triumphantly, twirling the ball with his fingers and flicking it out of the window. 'Pakistan is an Islamic state, and here we Muslims can strive to establish Islam in its entirety, something that the Indian Muslims can never dream of.'

I had heard Muslim friends of mine back in India complain about Pakistanis who considered themselves as superior or better Muslims than them because, while Pakistanis were almost wholly Muslim, the Muslims of India were a marginalized minority. Many Pakistani Muslims saw themselves as martial, warlike, strong and sturdy, as able to stand up to Indian or Hindu 'tyranny'. As a popular Pakistani saying went, *Hans ke liye hain Pakistan, ladke lenge India*. (We took Pakistan with a laugh, and now we'll fight and conquer India.) For these Pakistanis, Indian Muslims were an effete lot, who had all but lost their martial spirit. 'Oppressed', 'meek' and 'cowardly', they were unable to confront the 'effeminate', 'grass-eating' Hindus or to even demand their basic human rights, being so put down, so the argument went, that they now had to grovel before the 'infidels' simply to be allowed to exist. Even that right, it was alleged, was now brutally denied to them. Listening to the man go on, I understood exactly why my Indian Muslim friends felt so upset about this patronizing attitude. But I also understood that there was some merit in what the man was saying. The creation of Pakistan had certainly meant liberation from the shackles of 'upper' caste Hindu domination for many Muslims who had lived in or chosen to shift to the country, even though it had been replaced by an equally oppressive domination by fellow-Muslims.

The sun turned into an enormous red ball as it slid behind the forest of half-built clay and brick houses that sprang out from the main road where the bus finally stopped. This was the *Andrauni Shahr*, the 'Inner City' of Lahore, immortalized in travellers' accounts, by Mughal scribes and British colonial officers, by nostalgic Hindu refugees now living in Delhi, and in pamphlets meant for gullible foreign tourists that quaintly described it as 'renowned for its nabobs and kebobs'. They gushed eloquently about its myriad Mughal-period mosques with their graceful breast-shaped domes, its Persian-style perfumed gardens, in which peacocks carelessly strutted, and flocks of deer gracefully sauntered about amidst singing fountains, its many sprawling marble tomb complexes of mystics and saints, where devotees fell into a trance to the sound of soul-stirring verses sung by itinerant *qawwals*, its dark-eyed dancing girls, whose one glance was said to be enough to drive men to madness, and its splendid Mughal Fort and the adjoining Badshahi Mosque, the largest in the East, which stood at the heart of this wondrous city.

But, standing at the bus-stand below the ramparts of the Fort, I recognized nothing that even remotely corresponded to that exotic image of Lahore's Old City. Spread out before me was an enormous, chaotic swamp of humanity. Little boys perched on balding donkeys that nervously clip-clopped along the road, struggling to avoid a speeding army of autorickshaws. A circle of cars, coming from two opposite directions, surrounded a camel-cart that had got stuck in the middle. The wild gesticulations and angry abuse of the drivers seemed to have no effect on the droopy-eyed dromedary. She peered down imperiously at the men, who had by now rolled up their sleeves and were readying to come to blows. Enormous trucks, some laden with sacks of wheat and fresh vegetables, others carrying bearded goats and half-sleeping buffaloes headed for slaughter, halted behind the cars, their drivers furiously honking and hollering out. On either side of the road, the pavements were clogged with peddlers hawking cheap underwear, plastic shoes, dog-eared second-hand books, plastic toys and pens from China, and an assortment of religious icons. Plumes of purple smoke whirled out of makeshift roadside barbeques, where bits of meat were being roasted on pale blue charcoal fires. A pack of beggars, high on dope, squatted outside a Sufi shrine, rattling tins before passers-by and sucking at clay *chillum*s. Children milled around a man selling home-made ice-lollies on wooden sticks that were calculated to cause a range of illnesses, or so I imagined. Behind where I stood, ran a narrow open sewer that was laden with little brown sausage-like wedges—that afternoon's consignment of human refuse.

I strode up to the Fort but was informed by a smart uniformed guard who stood outside that it had closed for the day. I wound my way across the road to the Minar-e Pakistan (also known as the Yadgar-e Pakistan, 'The Pakistan Memorial'), a massive, erect phallus-like tower that dominated the Lahore skyline. It stood in the middle of the sprawling grounds of the Iqbal Park, marking the place where, on 23 March 1940, the Muslim League had passed what was known as the

Qarardad-e Pakistan or Pakistan Resolution, calling for a separate homeland or homelands for Indian Muslims in the regions where they were in a majority. The day is now celebrated as Pakistan's Republic Day.

Minar-e Pakistan

This gigantic monument, a symbol of Pakistani nationhood, had none of the grace and beauty characteristic of Mughal buildings although Pakistan saw itself, in some sense, as the successor to the Mughal Empire. It stood on a vast stone platform, grew into what appeared like a lotus-shaped bowl, and then shot up like a rocket 60 metres high till it turned into a cone-shaped pinnacle made of stainless steel and dotted with bits of coloured glass. Minor concessions had been made to the Mughal tradition by incorporating a corridor pierced with arches at regular intervals, snatches of calligraphic verses from the Quran, and marble plaques embossed with the ninety-nine names of Allah in gold. The overall feel, however, was distinctly 'modernist', as that term was then understood in 1960s Pakistan, when the monument was constructed—gigantic squares of unadorned marble were stuck on high walls, the pillars that were scattered about were shaped like factory smoke-shafts, and the jagged-edged stone balconies that ringed each floor were bereft of even minimal decoration. The tower even had an elephantine elevator that could contain over two dozen people. Till recently, visitors were allowed to climb up, by stairs or lift, to the balcony of the top-most floor, from where a panoramic view of the city would spread out before them at their feet. A sudden spate of people ascending the tower not to delight in that beatific vision but, rather, to hurtle down to their deaths had forced the authorities to ban that practice.

Commemorative plaques were carved into the inner walls at the base of the tower. I paused to read them. Most of them were excerpts from speeches by Muhammad Ali Jinnah and the poet Muhammad Iqbal, calling for a separate Muslim state, stressing the claim that the Muslims and the Hindus of India were two different 'nations', and, therefore, entitled to their own separate nation states. The largest of these, embossed in bold letters in English, Urdu and Bengali, contained the full text of the Lahore Resolution that laid down the manifesto for a separate state for Indian Muslims, which was born seven years after the Resolution was passed at that very spot.

Curiously, the Resolution did not specifically mention the word 'Pakistan', although it called for the creation of independent, sovereign Muslim 'states' (as opposed to the single state that Pakistan, with its east and west wings, separated by a thousand and more miles of hostile Indian territory, was to become, lasting till the emergence of Bangladesh in 1971) in Muslim majority regions of the subcontinent. It declared:

> No constitutional plan would be workable or acceptable to the Muslims unless geographically contiguous units are demarcated into regions which should be so constituted with such territorial readjustments as may be necessary that the areas in which the Muslims are numerically in majority, as in the North-Western and Eastern zones of India, should be grouped to constitute independent states in which the constituent units shall be autonomous and sovereign.

As numerous historians have argued, this represented a major break from what Muslim League leaders had till then been demanding—provincial autonomy and guarantees for Muslim rights within a loosely federal united India. Had the League's earlier proposals, some of which made eminent sense, been accepted by the 'upper' caste Hindu-dominated Congress and the virulently anti-Muslim Hindu Mahasabha, it could possibly have saved India the blood-soaked Partition, the numerous wars that followed between India and Pakistan, and the seemingly endless tension between what became two permanently hostile neighbours. But Hindu intransigence, including dreams of establishing an unfettered Hindu Raj—which would have meant doom for the Muslims of India—drove leaders of the League, many of whom, like Jinnah himself, had hitherto been firmly committed to Hindu–Muslim unity, to press the demand for a separate, sovereign Muslim state, interpreting the Lahore

Resolution in a manner that those who had drafted it might not have actually intended. Clearly, it struck me, as I studied the writing on the plaques, Pakistan might not have come into being, and India could still have been one, had genuine Muslim demands been accommodated by the Hindu leadership. That is a reality that has continued to be rudely denied back home in India, where the blame for the Partition was apportioned entirely on the Muslims.

four

searching for kin and a sufi saint

One morning, a week after my arrival, Sheila decided that I had gadded about town quite enough and that I now needed to get down to locating my distant relatives, the branch of my maternal grandmother's family that had stayed behind in Lahore after the Partition. I had deliberately kept this off for later, fearing that if I met them too early on in my stay I might be taken under their wing and carefully sheltered, not allowed to discover Lahore on my own. But I agreed with Sheila. It was about time.

Sheila sent for Raja who, she said, would help me trace the family. There was a special reason, she explained, why she had appointed Raja as my guide for this purpose. Raja's paternal grandmother had been a Hindu, the daughter of a wealthy Khatri cloth merchant, one of the richest men in pre-Partition Lahore. Courting the wrath of her clan, she had married a Muslim from the Kumhar or potter caste, defying multiple barriers—of caste, class and religion. Her irate father hired a notorious dacoit to slit her throat, and that of her husband, too, but the couple fled to Chitral in the far north, where they stayed right till the Partition. In August 1947, her parents fled across to what had become the independent state of India. It was only then that she and her husband managed to return to Lahore. Although the woman had died some years earlier, Sheila felt that her son, Raja's father, might know of others in Lahore who had earlier been Hindu but had converted to Islam at the time of the Partition. Perhaps they might, through their network of contacts, be able to help us locate my relatives.

I had with me the last letter sent to me by Aunty Mohini, my Nani's cousin's wife with whom I had once been in regular touch with, posted some twenty years ago. It mentioned her address—a location in Gulberg, home to Lahore's hyper-rich. Raja took me there in an autorickshaw, through wide, tree-lined lanes, on either side of which stood massive monument-like mansions set behind heavily guarded walls.

A fierce Pakhtun brandishing a Kalashnikov squatted on a stool inside a wooden box-like guardhouse outside the house whose address Aunty Mohini had written on her letter. He looked at us oddly as we piled out of the autorickshaw. Few, if any, people in this posh enclave probably travelled in this plebian mode of transportation or received visitors who did. A spanking new Benz and a racy sports car were parked in the porch of the mansion, visible through a half-opened gate.

'Whom do you want to meet?' the guard snapped.

The Batras, we told him.

The Batras had left the house several years ago, he replied. He had no idea where they were now.

We rang up Sheila. She had been almost as excited as I was that morning as we set off for Gulberg, as if it were some long-lost relatives of hers, rather than mine, that we were going to meet. The phone rang just once before she picked up the receiver. 'So, Yogi! How does it feel to have found them at last?' she giggled excitedly like a schoolgirl. I gave her the news. Her voice softened and she let out a gasp, but then she collected herself. There was no cause to worry, she said. She had some good news for me. She had just heard from a colleague that a Batra woman worked in an NGO she was familiar with. It was likely that this woman was related to Mohini Batra—perhaps her daughter or maybe a daughter-in-law. After all, she said, there could surely not be too many Batras in Lahore, and, in any case, since all Batras were related to each other, members of the same small clan, she must be related to Mohini, and, through my grandmother, to me, in some remote way.

Sheila instructed Raja to take me to the NGO where the Batra woman worked. It was located in a village on the outskirts of Lahore, a journey that would entail a change of two buses and then a thirty-minute walk. I suggested we call the NGO before embarking on what seemed an arduous journey. Raja did so, but only to be informed that the woman had quit her job several months ago.

I had been in Lahore for a week, and although I had not yet visited any of the dozens of fine Mughal monuments that crowded the Old City, Lahore's star tourist attraction, I badly needed a change. I decided to head for Kasur, a town some sixty kilometres to the south-east of Lahore, to visit the shrine of Baba Bulleh Shah, a seventeenth-century Sufi poet and saint who was deeply revered by Punjabis, irrespective of religion and on both sides of the border.

But there was one major hitch. My visa did not mention Kasur in the list of places I was permitted to visit. That probably, therefore, meant that I was forbidden from travelling there. But, was that really the case? I had heard conflicting reports from friends. One had said that he was definite that I could not go to any places other than those specified in my visa. Another, however, had a different opinion. She suggested that I could not spend the night in any places other than those mentioned in the visa, but short day trips to nearby places were permitted. That meant, so she surmised, that I could indeed go to Kasur although I needed to return to Lahore the same day. A third friend suggested I get the approval of the concerned ministry—she was not sure which one. Perhaps the ministry of the interior? Or maybe the ministry of external affairs? Or was there a special department concerned with monitoring the movements of visiting Indians? But, then, all these offices were located in Islamabad, which would have meant a five-hour drive to the north, a journey that was effectively ruled out because my visa did not permit me to visit that city. A fourth friend eventually decided for me. 'Yaar,' he said, 'why are you making such a big hue and cry about this small thing? There's nothing strategic about Kasur, so even if your visa doesn't allow you to go there, if you get caught nothing will happen. Just go!'

'But that might land me in jail!' I retorted. The thought of the numerous Indians who continued to languish in Pakistani prisons for years without any legal recourse (as also Pakistanis who faced a similar plight in Indian jails) flashed before my eyes.

'Don't be silly, yaar,' he retorted. 'What are we here for? We have all the right contacts in all the right places, and we can easily fix that if it happens!' That's how things worked in Pakistan, he explained—that is, for people who had the 'right' contacts and were politically connected, like himself.

I decided to head for Kasur in any case. The bus terminal— if it indeed could be called that—consisted of a series of rundown sheds covered with giant metal sheets. Garbage littered the open gutters, spilling out in enormous heaps on their embankments, over which people gingerly stepped, carefully lifting up their shalwars to their knees. There were no sitting arrangements, no decent eateries, not even a toilet in sight. Naked bulbs hung from wires that climbed out of gaping holes in the roof. A policeman sat stolidly on a stool with his legs wide apart, caressing the wooden baton that he held in his hand and looking bored. He appeared to have no function at all save to preside like a silent mummy over the unimaginable chaos that spread before him. Gaily painted buses angrily elbowed each other as they swung into the terminal and out of it. A resounding cacophony of dozens of horns simultaneously blowing, some set to Bollywood tunes, others sounding like stern military commands, drowned out the voice emanating from a diminutive loudspeaker strung on an electric pole that announced arrivals and departures. Agile conductors, mostly rough, unshaved young men, leapt out of moving buses, waving their arms about furiously and hollering out the names of the places where they were heading to.

'Sargodha! Sargodha!' a conductor cried out. He was perched halfway up the steps at the rear of a bus leading to the roof. His face was only faintly visible from behind a huge cloud of poisonous black smoke. On the roof, a dozen or more men squatted around mountains of luggage—giant tin boxes, plump gunny-sacks, a cycle, a clutch of hens. One of them, a rustic patriarch with a splendid pair of whiskers that curled up to his ears, clutched a goat in his lap. 'Hu! Hu! Hu! Hut! Hut! Hut!' he boomed, spanking the animal's bottom and commanding it to behave itself.

Sargodha! Giroth, Nani's ancestral village, was in Sargodha district, I remembered. Perhaps the bus would pass by the village. Even if it did not, I thought, perhaps I could take another bus from Sargodha town to Giroth, if there were one.

'Arey brother!' I called out to the conductor, who was

engaged in a heated argument with an irate passenger. He beamed down at me from his perch. Yes, he said, when I asked him, the bus would pass through Giroth. Inshallah, that is. 'There's a bit of space up there,' he said, indicating a tiny wedge between the patriarch with the goat and an elderly man wearing an onion-shaped turban on his head and bent double with arthritis.

I was thrilled. For just a moment, though. The bus would take at least five hours to reach Giroth, the conductor said. That would mean that I would not be able to get back to Lahore the same day and that I would have to spend the night in Giroth. But where would I stay in Giroth? I knew no one there. There were no members of the Batra clan left in the village, I was sure. And since Nani's ancestors had probably been oppressive landlords, I doubted that even those denizens of the village who remembered the family would be willing to take me in for the night. There was no lodge or hotel in Giroth, the conductor told me. 'You might possibly be able to spend the night in the village police station or in the army camp close by,' he suggested—advice which, of course, I would not dare act on.

Thus was I forced to abandon my plans for visiting the village of my ancestors.

I went back to my original plan and boarded a bus heading for Kasur. In a short while, we were bumping along a road pitted with yawning craters and lined on either side with drab-looking factories and brick-kilns, out of which dribbled enormous ribbons of smoke that trailed up into the clear blue sky.

'Kasur! Kasur!' the conductor cried out, some two hours later. I stuck my head out of the window but saw nothing even remotely resembling a bus terminal, which the place was actually meant to be. I scampered off the bus, found directions to the *dargah* of Baba Bulleh Shah and sauntered down a maze of passageways. Several buildings that lined these lanes dated, so it appeared, to the Mughal period. Decorated *jharoka*s, carved balconies pierced with latticed stone screens, peeped out of the flanks of crumbling mansions. Women from wealthy families, kept heavily cloistered in their homes, must have sat behind them for fresh air and for a passing glimpse of life in the streets below. But, as in Lahore's Old City, whatever little else I saw of Kasur—the filth, the squalor, the utter chaos of it all—indicated an almost total lack of civic concern as well as absolute governmental neglect.

Kasur had not always been like that, however. According to Hindu legend, the town was founded by Kasur, also known as Kasu or Kush, son of the Hindu hero Ram, whose other son, Lav, so the Hindu version of history has it, had built Lahore, which was said to have been named after him. According to another account, Kasur was established by a Pathan clan in the reign of the Mughal Emperor Akbar as a fort, or *qasr* in Arabic, whence its name. Under the Mughals, Kasur emerged as a flourishing centre of commerce and trade. And of Punjabi Sufism as well, when Abdullah, who later adopted the name of Bulleh Shah, shifted to the town in the early eighteenth century, spending several years there writing his provocative, soul-stirring *kafi*s or mystical refrains that were considered to be gems of Punjabi literary heritage.

Born in 1680 in a village in southern Punjab, Bulleh Shah was the son of a Syed, a putative descendant of the Prophet Muhammad. As a child, he received an education that befitted the scion of a Syed family of those times, studying the Quran, Arabic and Persian from traditional maulvis. Not satisfied with mere 'external' knowledge, he hankered after an experiential understanding of the Truth. That led him to become a devoted disciple of a noted Sufi of the Qadri order, Shah Inayat. The relationship between the two men raised a major furore, for Shah Inayat was a 'low' caste Arain.

Following in the path of numerous Punjabi Sufi and Bhakti saints before him, Bulleh used poetry as a powerful medium for communicating his message—a bitterly iconoclastic one that thundered at cantankerous mullahs and rapacious pandits alike. He fearlessly mocked religious externalism and meaningless ritualism, denounced all distinctions of caste and religion, and overturned deeply rooted social hierarchies. For our own troubled times, Bulleh Shah has particular relevance.

I passed through a narrow lane that ended at the entrance of the vast complex that housed Bulleh Shah's tomb. Outside, a cluster of stalls set up under canvas awnings stocked standard pilgrim memorabilia: silver-coloured *taweez* boxes to ward off evil spirits, loops of yellow and red threads for good fortune or for curing illnesses, wide-bottomed jugs with elongated snouts for ablutions, glass phials containing rose water and perfume, green silk sheets embossed with verses from the Quran, and hand-woven saucer-shaped wicker baskets bearing bunches of roses strung together and packets of sugar shaped like popcorn.

From the architectural point of view, the shrine was an unrelieved disappointment. Bulleh Shah himself would have sternly disapproved of the massive mausoleum that had come up over his simple grave. It was topped with an enormous dome that was shaped like an inverted teacup and lined on all four sides by squat, stump-like marble pillars. Behind the shrine towered a new mosque that looked like an enormous pumpkin. There was absolutely nothing traditional, or even remotely suggestive of Bulleh Shah's Sufi world view, about the eminently ugly monstrosity.

But that is not to say that Bulleh Shah is no longer a living reality for millions of Pakistanis. That, I was to discover—to my sheer delight and relief—when I returned to Lahore that evening. Sheila, whom I had not told that I was going to Kasur for fear that she might dissuade me, called me shortly after I got back. 'We've got tickets for a play this evening,' she said. 'It's *Bulleh Shah*, by the activist Ajoka group.' She gave me directions to the Alhamra theatre where the play was being staged.

I was delighted. This, for two reasons. Firstly, because of the central character of the play and the uncanny coincidence of having visited his shrine earlier that day. Secondly, because the play was being staged by Ajoka, an immensely popular Pakistani theatre group.

Ajoka was the brainchild of a brilliant couple who were among the most well-known cultural activists in Pakistan—Shahid Nadeem, who had earlier worked with Pakistan Television and later joined Amnesty International, and his wife Madeeha Gauhar, a noted writer. A pioneer in developing street theatre as a tool for political activism and mobilization in South Asia, Ajoka had been launched at the peak of the decade-long spell of army rule under General Zia ul-Haq who, with American and Saudi backing, had sought to impose a strictly puritanical version of Islam in order to buttress his rule and to quash all opposition. That move had galvanized a host of conservative Islamist forces as well as traditionalist mullahs, fired with their own dreams of power and grandeur, to fiercely back the brutal dictator. At the same time, however, Zia's brand of Islamic rule gave rise to widespread discontent, particularly among ethnic and religious minorities, the working classes and women, who were among the worst-hit by some of the harsh laws that he promulgated in the name of 'Islamizing' the country.

Ajoka was a product of, and a forceful response to, those troubled times, when any expression of dissent could have meant instantaneous imprisonment, a hundred lashes in public or even death by hanging or stoning. To do socially meaningful theatre and to contribute to the struggle for a secular, humane, just and egalitarian society in Pakistan, was Ajoka's principal aim. The group's first play, staged in 1984, a year after it was formed, was a trenchant critique of dictatorship that had been scripted by a noted Leftist writer from India. Since then, Ajoka had been continuously performing socially meaningful plays across Pakistan and abroad as well, particularly in India—plays that denounced women's oppression, critiqued religious bigotry and spoke out against feudal lords and political bigwigs, plays that celebrated communal harmony and dared to dream of peace and solidarity between Indians and Pakistanis.

I got to the Alhamra an hour before the play was to start. Stone buildings dotted the campus, which was framed with neatly laid out flowerbeds and plants in enormous brass pot-holders. A clutch of young men—the arty sort, sporting unkempt beards and dressed in T-shirts with Che Guevara logos and torn jeans—loitered about, smoking hand-rolled cigarettes. A faint smell of hashish hung in the air. A middle-aged woman in a peach-coloured silk sari entered, tip-toeing on a pair of slender stilettos, boldly tossing her shoulder-length hair about her as she passed through the door. Behind her trailed her richly embroidered *pallu*, like a peacock's tail. A whiff of sandalwood perfume floated by as she daintily clip-clopped past me. Another woman, considerably younger, rushed up to greet her. She looked clumsy, even bohemian—perhaps that was the in-thing in those circles. Her hair, which she had snatched up into a topknot, was streaked a pale red. She balanced a slim pair of spectacles on the tip of her nose. She wore thick wooden clogs on her feet, and from her ears dangled two enormous heart-shaped earrings.

'Sameera darling!' this latter woman squealed with what struck me as feigned delight as she rushed to wrap the sari-clad woman in a tight embrace. 'Long time no see, sweety! I thought you were still in DC!'

'Nahin, nahin, Rehana!' gushed Sameera. 'Saleem recently

got a job with a UN agency, and now we've shifted to London! He's a development consultant there.'

'Ooh! Hai, you lucky thing!' Rehana cooed like a dove in the throes of an orgasm. 'London! I'd do anything to be back there! I'm really, really jealous! Tell Saleem to fix me a job there, na!' I noticed a streak of envy flashing across her eyes as she pressed her painted lips into a pout and then into what clearly seemed a forced smile.

A socialites' evening it was going to be then, and Sameera and Rehana seemed to know many of the men and women who were scattered around the hall. 'The dreadful NGO circuit, completely counter-revolutionary,' croaked Sheila when I caught up with her, but she also pointed out some individuals who, she said, were passionately committed to what she called 'the cause': a young painter who was active in the Pakistan–India People's Forum for Peace and Democracy; a lawyer who was fighting the case of a Sindhi Hindu family whose daughter had been kidnapped by a feudal lord; a divorcee and mother of four, who had set up a shelter for battered and discarded brides. 'Some nice people in here, but these ugly arty-farty sort want to capture our space,' Sheila bemoaned.

The curtains went up, the lights were turned off, a hushed silence fell on the hall as the seated socialites ceased their chattering and the play began. By the time it got over, an hour or so later, my opinion about what I had imagined to be the sorry state of the legacy of Bulleh Shah in contemporary Pakistan had been completely overturned. The brilliantly executed play, certainly the most provocative theatrical production I had ever seen, had churned within me the full range and depths of emotions, subtly evoking them without sounding preachy—uncontrollable rage, fear and foreboding, hope amidst deadening despair, an unconquerable passion for life, boundless love, and sheer exhilaration. The play seemed to directly speak to me, addressing the many questions that buzzed around in my head—questions about religion and nationalism and the role of human beings in constructing them, about self-righteous Hindus and smug Muslims and Bible-thumping Christians deluded into believing that they alone had privileged access to God, about chauvinist Indians and ultra-nationalist Pakistanis, about imperialist America and Zionist messiahs who were scheming to send the world hurtling towards Armageddon. To all of these, Bulleh Shah had a bold NO to scream into their faces, and he had already won a willing convert and accomplice in me.

Such a powerfully iconoclastic play could possibly never have been staged in India, I said to Sheila as we remained sunk in our seats waiting for the hall to clear before we could leave. Numerous films, dramas, street-corner plays and art exhibitions had been brutally vandalized by irate goons in India in recent years, and a play even remotely similar to a Hindu version of Ajoka's *Bulleh Shah* might easily have been attacked by Hindutva hoodlums and even by the police, who were generally in cahoots with them. The play had forcefully questioned some of the foundational tenets of Islam as many traditional Muslims understood them. It fearlessly mocked the mullahs and derided their obsession with external rituals and rules. It passionately challenged the notion of Muslim superiority and Hindu 'otherness'. It roundly denounced Muslim political authorities as being willing accomplices of the mullahs in seeking to enforce an utterly dehumanizing dispensation in the name of Islam that Bulleh Shah spent his life boldly protesting against. All this and more Bulleh Shah had done through his personal example and his soul-stirring poetry, not as an unbeliever or an atheist but as a different sort of believer, developing his own form of liberation theology, to use a modern-day phrase, which had earned him the wrath of the mullahs and the love of millions of Punjabis, irrespective of religion and caste. The play had an immediate relevance for contemporary Pakistan—for the world in general, in fact—which was not lost on the audience, as was indicated by the thunderous applause and standing ovation that it received.

Bulleh Shah's legacy, I was pleased to discover—in contrast to what I had witnessed at his shrine in Kasur—was still alive and throbbing, at least in some quarters in Pakistan.

five

---

an evening with a
wine-bibbing islamist

More than a week had passed since I had arrived in
Pakistan, and I was beginning to get a sort of feel of the
country. The initial excitement of arrival had begun to wane
somewhat, and questions that I had kept firmly repressed in my
mind at first began raising their heads. The officer I had met
at the Pakistan High Commission in Delhi had complained
that Indian journalists visiting the country rarely, if ever, wrote
anything nice about it, and I had promised him that I would
be different. I sincerely wanted to look at Pakistan in a
different sort of way. During my first few days in Lahore, I
consciously scouted around for images and impressions that
I could recount on my return to counter the standard view of
Pakistan as a 'failed state', a country racked by bomb blasts and
sectarian blood-letting, looming under the very real threat of
being taken over by wild-eyed religious radicals and hurtling
towards an uncontrollable chaos and complete lawlessness.

Although not without some effort, I did manage to locate
sufficient evidence that might qualify, if not somewhat
undermine, those pessimistic prognostications. Yet, nagging

doubts kept tugging at the corners of my mind. I had desperately sought to shut my mind to evidence that might actually reinforce widely held Indian stereotypes about Pakistan, but, as the days passed by, I noticed subtle changes within me. I was not being true to myself, I knew, and the struggle to try to be politically correct and abstain from making unfavourable comparisons with India was becoming somewhat stressful. Nor was I being true to the reality of Pakistan as I was experiencing it. Maybe, I began to feel, Mr Khan, the Indian Muslim man from Delhi whom I had met on the bus to Lahore, was right after all. He was travelling to Pakistan much against his will, on the orders of his wife. He hated it there. 'I can't stand those foul-mannered, blockheaded Punjabi bumpkins. Lazy, good for nothing, fit only for eating all day and whiling away their time ceaselessly chattering. They saunter around, puffed up with pride, like overfed buffaloes in heat,' he had bemoaned, quite oblivious to the fact that he was addressing another Punjabi. 'I hate their smug self-righteousness,' he had gone on. 'And look what they've done to the country that they created in the name of Islam! It's a filthy mess!' he had groaned in unconcealed disgust.

'I assure you,' he had carried on with his heated harangue, unmindful of the Pakistani passengers who sat nearby, 'you won't be able to have a decent conversation with almost anyone in the country. The universities are all defunct. Academic discourse is pathetic. And most people you will meet will just go ranting about themselves, caring a damn for whether you are interested in their cock-and-bull or not.'

In the initial flush of enthusiasm of simply being in Pakistan I had shut Mr Khan firmly out of my mind. He must definitely be wrong, unnecessarily alarmist, unduly pessimistic, I had told myself. But then, a week later, I started seeing visions of him. Yes, maybe, after all, he was not entirely incorrect. I was beginning to change my opinions. I was getting bored. Irritable. Exasperated. Fed up. Suddenly, I wanted to flee back to India!

It was not that I had encountered anything unpleasant personally. On the contrary, everyone I had met had been exceedingly courteous to me. Many of them had even gone considerably out of their way to help. Sheila, on her part, had been a perfect hostess, although she did not have to be. Yet, as the days passed by, I began making insidious comparisons between India and Pakistan. In most cases, the latter fared unfavourably by a wide margin. Much of Lahore was a chaotic mess. Traffic appeared to follow no rules whatsoever. The ATM machine nearest to where I was staying was an hour's bus ride away, and even that had been out of order for a week or more. The autorickshaw-drivers were gruff and rapacious, and their cramped vehicles, which were fed on cooking gas cylinders, vomited out clouds of poisonous black smoke that filled the entire town with smog and stench. There were no decent affordable eateries, and good, wholesome vegetarian food was almost unheard of. Only Hindus ate such insipid *ghaas-phoos*—grass—I was told. The only food available at the grubby street roadside stalls I frequented, and that I could eat, was insipid boiled eggs, probably cooked the previous day, and soggy slices of bread. Most men on the streets looked scruffy and unwashed. Even among the middle class, the standard of English was pathetic. I had not had a decent conversation in English since I had arrived. Hardly anyone spoke the refined courtly Urdu that I had imagined they would. Questions in that language were almost invariably answered in incomprehensible Punjabi. The list went on ... No, most definitely not, Lahore was not 'just like New Delhi', unlike what many Pakistanis insisted on and wanted to believe.

And then there were the standard conversations that were now proving unbearably tiresome and inane. Most people I had met were exceedingly polite, but they rarely cared to probe further than asking when I had arrived, what I thought of the country, and how long I planned to stay, although some of them mentioned in passing aspects of the cultural heritage shared by the subcontinent's peoples. Admittedly, only a few responded by ignoring me altogether or appearing openly hostile or indifferent. In order to elicit a different sort of reaction, in some cases I had tried to pass off as a Muslim from India, and then there would be the expected queries about the many problems that Indian Muslims faced, expressions of sympathy for their plight, sometimes bitter harangues about 'Hindu oppression', and lengthy diatribes against alleged global conspiracies launched by sundry 'anti-Islamic forces' against the entire worldwide Muslim *ummah*.

With the exception of her 'inner circle' of Leftist comrades, even the people Sheila introduced me to made boring conversationalists. After we had been introduced, a brief question–answer session would follow that seemed to conform to, so I gradually discovered, a set pattern:

Question 1: How do you like Pakistan?

Answer 1: Hmm. Nice. Interesting. I'm glad to be here.

Question 2: Which part of *Eendeea* (that was how most of them pronounced it) are you from?

Answer 2: I'm a Punjabi, born in Calcutta, now living in Delhi but my family is in Bangalore.

This would be met with a short spell of silence, during which the questioner tried to figure out what exactly that meant.

End of question–answer session.

No more questions would follow. Instead, what inevitably ensued was an uninterrupted monologue that touched upon a vast range of subjects: the possible causes of the Partition, the role of cunning white imperialists in stoking rivalries in the subcontinent, the rapaciousness of political bosses and feudal lords, the latest gossip about Bollywood, and, depending on the ideological position of the person on the Hindu–Muslim question, the incredible similarities or the stark differences between Hindus and Muslims.

An hour and three cups of tea later, the man (they were almost all men—I met few women) would still exhibit no signs of halting his banter. I would begin to look this way and that in a muffled effort to shut him up. That was no easy matter, however, as he would have his eyes carefully transfixed on mine. If this trick did not succeed (as it generally did not), I would violently clear my throat or shuffle around in my pockets for a kerchief or a cigarette—any motion that might disturb that never-ending torrent of words that gushed forth and swarmed round in my head like an army of angry wasps.

But, I soon realized, these stratagems rarely, if ever, worked. More high-handed tactics were urgently required. I had been subjected to two dozen or more such deadly verbal avalanches since my arrival, and my patience was fast running out. So was my time, for I had only a few days left in Lahore and I had hardly seen anything of the town as yet. Henceforth, I decided, even if it seemed rude I would stand up when it got simply unbearable and think of a reasonable enough excuse to be permitted to leave.

It took a while to learn the trick but, after a couple of halting efforts, I was adept at it. The first time I tried it out was at the residence of a wealthy industrialist. Sheila knew Mr Shaukat vaguely, and when he heard that she had an Indian guest he insisted that she bring me over. She was not too keen on it, though, primarily because he was a sympathizer of an Islamist outfit that she described as 'a fascist formation, the Pakistani equivalent of the Indian Vishwa Hindu Parishad', although, she added, he was not known for his personal piety. I begged her to take me along. I wanted to see a different sort of

Pakistani, a wealthy Islamist, not quite the sort of person in whose company Sheila and her comrades wanted to be seen. She grudgingly relented, and one evening we bundled ourselves into an autorickshaw and headed to a heavily barricaded leafy suburb of Lahore.

Mr Shaukat lived in a sprawling mansion, surrounded by a high wall topped with metal spikes and shards of broken glass designed to keep robbers and other unwanted intruders out. From under a bower framed by flowering creepers, a cobbled path led into an enormous, carefully tended lawn. Its elliptical circumference was decorated with beds of roses, magnolias, pansies and chrysanthemums in various stages of bloom. It was pierced at the four cardinal points with Japanese-style pools, in which stood enormous fountains made of onyx in the shape of semi-nude bathing beauties. Jets of water shot out from the pots that they bore on their heads. These 'singing fountains', I was told by their proud owner as he ushered me inside his house, had been specially designed for him by a firm in China. They could 'sing' five different tunes, he boasted, including two numbers from a 1960 Hindi film. In the middle of the garden, a variety of flowering cacti and assorted stunted shrubs imported from Africa and Latin America flourished under the watchful eyes of a battery of three malis. A pair of white peacocks, recently smuggled from Myanmar, strutted about, and a giant painted stork, balancing on one leg, meditated on its reflection in a fish pond.

Inside, the mansion appeared no less vulgar and intimidating. The entire building was centrally air-conditioned, and its floors, made of marble imported from Italy, were draped with delicately patterned *killim*s from Iran, silk carpets in soft pastel shades from Kashmir, and red and black rugs from Badakhshan. Costly looking curios brought from a number of countries— for Mr Shaukat was a widely travelled man—lay scattered all over the hall where we sat. An ornate chandelier made of

Venetian crystal and dating back to Mughal times, or so Mr Shaukat claimed, hung from an enormous hook on the ceiling, shedding soft pools of light across the room. Two liveried servants, dressed in costumes reminiscent of the Raj, stood to attention at the entrance of the hall, ready to receive and act on their master's orders. Our host was obviously a hugely influential and immensely wealthy man.

Sheila and I shifted about uncomfortably on the leather sofa into which we had sunk. We waited for Mr Shaukat to start speaking, which he did after he finished penning his signature to a fat bundle of files that had been brought to him by a servant on a silver tray. 'Okay, so you are Sheila's Indian guest, are you?' he looked me up and down and said. I smiled, but before I could say anything, he continued. 'India. Hmm. We have so much in common. So, so very much indeed.'

That trite observation was suddenly interrupted with the arrival of a middle-aged man who boasted a cauldron-shaped belly and a massive clutch of hair so carefully plastered with oil that it appeared like a single thick stroke of black paint. Our host introduced him as Mr Mallik, a 'renowned intellectual of Lahore'. But before Mr Mallik and I could greet each other, Mr Shaukat resumed what he appeared to believe were his acute observations on the similarities between the peoples of India and Pakistan.

'So, as I was saying, we have so much in common,' he went on. 'We speak the same languages, look the same, eat the same sort of food, listen to the same sort of music, dance the same way. We share the same water, the same air, the same sun, the same moon.'

Then followed a long, winding lecture about corruption in high places, about the insatiable greed of Pakistan's feudal lords in league with top-level bureaucrats and army officers, about soaring crime rates in the country and about the crass insensitivity of Pakistan's élite to the plight of the country's poor millions. I looked about me, at the marble floors and the carpets that were spread over them, at the thick velvet curtains that were drawn across the French windows that opened out on to the lawns outside, at the heads of a pair of leopards and a tiger displayed on the wall facing me—animals shot by his father, Mr Shaukat said, in the 'good old days when *shikar* was legal and plentiful'. I shuddered. The hypocrisy of it all! Shut up! Stop it at once! I wanted to scream.

Without being prompted in any way by the silent trio before him, our host, after having tired of roundly berating the social class to which he himself belonged, decided to transfer his attention to more esoteric matters. 'Islam has all the answers, you see,' he announced. I did not quite see what Mr Khan had seen. I didn't see Islam in quite the same way as had the late Maulana Sayyid Abul Ala Maududi, Mr Shaukat's ideological mentor, the founder of the Jamaat-e-Islami, of which Mr Shaukat was said to be a passionate sympathizer. Maududi had interpreted Islam as a total, indeed totalitarian, ideology, with supposedly premeditated, permanent and fixed answers to almost every conceivable question. He considered as authentic Muslims only those who agreed with his eccentric understanding of Islam. And, like other radical Islamists who saw the world in starkly Manichaean terms, he believed that humankind was divided into two antagonistic camps: 'true' Muslims, people of his ilk, whom he termed 'the army of God', and the rest, foot soldiers of what he called the 'army of Satan'. Mercifully, not many Pakistanis agreed with Maududi's version of Islam, as evidenced by the humiliating drubbing that the Jamaat had invariably received in successive elections—that is, whenever they were allowed to be held in the country.

Sheila, looking visibly ill at ease, sat silently, fiddling the ends of her faded kameez. We let Mr Shaukat go unchallenged. And so he went on, for the next hour or more, elaborating on the theories of Maulana Maududi, of how he had allegedly 'restored to Muslims their lost pride', of how he had 'shaken the roots of imperialism and communism alike', and of how he had 'proven that if Muslims were to rule the world, all its many problems would be solved'. He took down a tome, bound in expensive Moroccan calf leather—as he made a point to inform us—from a shelf that stretched out above a mock fireplace. A volume of the late Maududi's writings, it was about the concept of the 'Islamic state', Maududi's pet theme. 'You see!' he excitedly burst out as he read a portion from a chapter that he randomly selected, 'An Islamic state, of the sort whose blueprint Maududi Sahib has worked out for us, is the solution to all our ills.' The chapter enjoined the killing of apostates, discriminatory laws for non-Muslims, and strict seclusion for women. It referred to Muslims—that is, those who championed the version of Islam that Maududi envisioned—as being perpetually opposed to the rest of humanity. In short, it was a form of religion that was wholly and viscerally opposed to that practised by men like Bulleh Shah and such gentle mystics.

'That, as I said, is the solution to our problems,' repeated Mr Shaukat earnestly. 'Only in this way can Muslims take on the West.' He launched on to a lengthy diatribe about what the West was doing to Muslims the world over—funding Israeli crimes in Palestine, bombing Afghanistan and Iraq back to the Stone Age, and silently supporting India in what he called its 'illegal occupation' of Kashmir. Sheila scribbled on a chit and slid it to me from under the table. 'His own children study in the States. That's also where Maududi, who had spent his entire life berating the West, went for medical treatment and died,' it read.

'Arey, Mallik Sahib!' Mr Shaukat suddenly interrupted himself and said to his friend, 'Have you brought the stuff?'

Mr Mallik hurriedly thrust his hand inside his waistcoat and drew out a package. Mr Shaukat grabbed the package and began unpacking it. This took some time, as the item was wrapped in three layers of newspaper. Mr Shaukat's face lit up with delight as he unravelled the last wrapper. A black metal cap poked out, like a turtle's head protruding from its shell. The wrapper fell to the floor and a bottle of pale purple liquid rolled into his hands. '*Waah* yaar!' he exclaimed wide-eyed, as he admired the bottle. 'Real French wine! Ages since I last savoured it.'

Mr Shaukat slapped Mr Mallik on the back, grinning with unconcealed glee. He held the bottle up, as if brandishing an Olympic trophy. I felt positively nauseous. I wanted to scream at the thought of it all, at this ardent admirer of an Islamist outfit who spoke passionately about the poor but lived like a *pasha* and who thought nothing at all of consuming alcohol, and that, too, in public.

All at once, and even without thinking, I stood up. 'Gosh! My head's bursting to the seams! I've had just about enough! I can't take a word more from this man!' I boomed.

Sheila turned to me in shock, but a moment later I spied a glint in her eyes and a faint smile struggling against her tightly pursed lips. Mr Shaukat's arm remained suspended in the air, clutching the bottle. Mr Mallik's eyes flitted between Mr Shaukat and me. He looked visibly embarrassed.

'Sheila-ji! *Chalo*! Let's go!' I burst out.

Sheila gathered the folds of her kameez, jerked herself out of the sofa and together we stomped out of the room. We passed through the garden with its singing fountains and its wondrously shaped plants, ducked under the bower of flowering creepers, and drew up on to the road, where we hailed an autorickshaw to take us back to Sheila's home.

the fading delights of old lahore

I was woken the next morning by Sheila bearing an enormous mug of vanilla-flavoured milk and a plate of steaming *samosa*s. I shuffled in my razai. Outside, the thick blanket of mist was gradually lifting, but it was still dark.

'You poor, poor boy,' clucked Sheila as she handed me the milk. 'You must be really worked up about last evening's *hangama.*' Before I could respond, she went on. 'Mr Shaukat isn't unusually self-centred. Most Pakistani men are like this. So full of themselves. They couldn't care a damn about others. It's all to do with exaggerated Pakistani machismo,' she expounded. 'Somehow, these men think that to be really male one must necessarily be nasty, bossy and controlling.' She had seen the worst of it, she went on. Her husband had treated her shabbily, and when he had married another woman without her consent she had been told that she had better put up with his decision or else be out on the streets. She had chosen the latter course.

'Perhaps it's the feudal set-up. Perhaps it is something to do with the way in which Islam is commonly understood, as inseparable from domination, whether over non-Muslims or Muslim women. Perhaps it's the remnant of ancient tribalism.

I don't really know,' she mused as she lit up her first cigarette for the morning. The call to the morning prayer wafted in from a mosque in the distance, a plaintive wail that lifted higher and higher, as if seeking to draw out, inch by inch, the sun from the veil of darkness that had shrouded it.

'Perhaps it's also about the way Pakistanis imagine their history,' Sheila went on. 'Pakistani history, as it has come to be written, is, by and large, simply a chronicle of wars and conquests. To be male has come to be seen as being a conqueror, being stern and rugged, nasty and brutish, imposing one's will on others, on women as well as other men, and refusing to ever compromise, for that is considered effeminate.'

'*Apa*!' screeched Reshma from behind the door that separated my room from hers. 'Not at five-thirty in the morning! For heaven's sake! Stop lecturing and hectoring poor Yogi!'

Reshma scolded Sheila playfully as she joined us. 'It's all your fault. Yogi's come to see Pakistan and there you are, forcing him to hang around with your oh so horribly boring friends!'

Sheila looked on the bed sheepishly as Reshma went on. 'Mr Shaukat is simply disgusting. As for that journalist friend of yours, Shehzad, whom you dragged Yogi to meet the other day, he doesn't let anyone speak at all. And that horrendously boring Shahid who looks and croaks like a frog. The less said about him the better. And that awful Salma, with her constant blabber about her finishing school in Switzerland, the dancing women who were specially flown down from Beirut for her cousin's wedding, and her incessant whining about how she cannot get the right sort of mushrooms and pasta in Pakistan.'

Sheila muttered something about Salma being a 'real bitch, a total one', and hastened to clarify that the people Reshma had mentioned were not her friends but, rather, merely 'very remote acquaintances'. Reshma paid no attention to her, however. She stood in front of the tall gilt-edged mirror in the corner of the room and peered into it. 'Hai! My hair looks like a vulture's nest! Disgusting!' she shrieked as she ran her fingers through her matted locks. She grabbed my mug of vanilla milk and tossed down a gulp, leaving a moustache of cream round her lips. 'Apa!' she protested. 'Poor Yogi's been subjected to too much, to all these nerds. Now let him have a break, will you?'

'Okay baba! Okay!' Sheila cried, twisting her lips and crumpling her forehead in mock anger. 'I know you're jealous of my friends because you don't have any.' She stomped out of the room but shortly returned and thrust a book into my hand. A glossy guide to Old Lahore, it listed over two hundred mosques, tombs and Sufi shrines that dotted the city, dating to Mughal times and even earlier. 'I'd hate to let you go about town on your own,' she said, 'but I know this is what you want.'

Legend has it, so the guidebook said, that Lahore was founded by Lav, son of Ram, hero of the Hindu epic Ramayana. Possibly one of the earliest extant historical references to Lahore is to be found in the *Geographia* of the celebrated astronomer and geographer, Ptolemy of Alexandria (83–168 C.E.), who mentioned a city called Labokla, situated on the route between the Indus and Palibothra—Pataliputra, or modern-day Patna—in a country called Kasperia, or Kashmir. The anonymous author of the late-tenth-century Arabic text *Hudud al-Alam* ('The Boundaries of the World') referred to Lahore as boasting 'impressive temples, large markets and huge orchards'. Few other references to Lahore exist for the period before its capture by Sultan Mahmud of Ghazni in the early eleventh century, after a long siege that resulted in the virtual depopulation of the city. Mahmud appointed his Turkic slave and lover, Malik Ayaz, as governor, who resettled the city and ordered the construction of various buildings, some of which still survive, although in various stages of dilapidation.

Mahmud continues to be reviled in India as a bloodthirsty Islamic iconoclast, who sacked numerous temples. In Pakistan, however, he is lionized as a Muslim hero, who was supposedly driven by an irrepressible religious zeal against the 'infidels'. The fact that Mahmud had numerous Hindus in his army and that he even minted coins depicting Hindu deities clearly indicates that he does not quite fit either of those contrary descriptions. A more humanistic portrayal of the Sultan has been provided in the works of numerous Sufis, who extolled his love for Ayaz as the epitome of devotion and as symbolizing the Sufi's total dedication to God. The passion that bound the Sultan to his slave was also seen as a paragon of Islamic egalitarianism, and was best encapsulated in the well-known couplet of Muhammad Iqbal, Pakistan's national poet:

Ek hi saf mein khade ho gaye Mahmud-o-Ayaz
Na koi banda raha aur na koi banda nawaz

Mahmud and Ayaz in single file stood, side by side.
Then there was no servant, no master, nothing did them divide.

The rule of the Ghaznavids, descendants of Mahmud, in Lahore, proved short-lived. After them, the town came under the control of various Turkic and Afghan dynasties, including the Khiljis, Tughlaqs, Syeds, Lodhis and Suris, till it became part of the Mughal Empire in the mid-sixteenth century. During this long period, Lahore witnessed feverish building activity that completely changed its landscape. Mughal power began to crumble by the late eighteenth century, when Lahore bore the brunt of numerous invasions by the Afghans, till it was turned into their capital by the Sikhs, who also added numerous buildings to the city, a pattern that the British replicated when they captured it some decades later.

I spent the next few days trundling through Lahore's Old City, doing a quick round of selected Mughal monuments that my guidebook recommended. There were far too many for me to see them all, and I necessarily had to be selective. Lahore's star architectural attraction was undoubtedly the Shahi Qila or the 'Royal Fort', located adjacent to the Minar-e Pakistan, on the dusty banks of the stony bed of the River Ravi that had once flowed below it. The history of the fort goes back to pre-Islamic times, but various Muslim rulers had added structures behind its imposing yellow sandstone walls, which were now a UNESCO World Heritage site: the Sheesh Mahal, almost every inch of its walls covered with tiny mirrors; the marble-floored and richly embellished Diwan-e Khas, where emperors held court and received visiting foreign guests; the small but exquisite Naulakha pavilion, topped with a marble roof shaped like an umbrella, from where could be had a panoramic view of the bustling town below; and the unpretentious-looking Moti Masjid, a simple mosque with graceful, pencil-like minarets. Overall, however, compared to the Mughal Fort in Delhi, the complex had a shoddy, dour appearance. The fountains had run dry, the flowerbeds were almost empty, and in the sprawling gardens in which the royal structures were set, pale yellow grass grew in scattered, mangy clumps. Pictures of Hindu deities and of the Sikh ruler of Punjab, Ranjit Singh, that decorated some walls had borne the wrath of vandals, who had rendered them headless, as if symbolically executing and thereby excising them from public memory. The only eatery in the vast complex was a dark, one-roomed building. Paint had peeled off from its soot-stained walls in large strips. Bones and left-over bits of meat lay strewn on tables, on which feasted battalions of flies. A powerful stench of kerosene oil hung in the air.

I trudged across the fort to the expansive Hazuri Bagh lawn below, to the modestly sized Moorish-style tomb of Pakistan's national poet, Muhammad Iqbal. Pakistanis consider him one of the ideological fathers of their country, although he had died some years before Pakistan came into being. This Cambridge graduate, who is also ranked among the pioneers of Islamic 'modernism' in South Asia, was among the first to suggest that the future of the Muslims of the north-western part of British India, where Muslims formed a substantial majority, lay in the creation of a separate sovereign state. Scores of major public buildings, roads and institutions across Pakistan are named after him, a privilege that he shares with the founder of the country, Muhammad Ali Jinnah.

As befits a man who was something of a Sufi—although, at the same time, a bitter critic of what he regarded as world-renouncing and un-Islamic mystical tendencies—Iqbal's grave is a simple marble structure. It lay buried under a heap of marigold and rose garlands—the offerings of a steady stream of visitors, for whom Iqbal is something of a blessed saint. About me dozens of men and a lone woman stood in various poses of supplication, some sitting, others kneeling, yet others standing, all with their hands cupped in front of their faces and whispering silent prayers.

Iqbal's mausoleum stands at the base of the grand Badshahi Masjid or 'Emperor's Mosque', whose towering minarets can be seen from miles around. Built in 1673 by the Mughal Emperor Alamgir Aurangzeb, the mosque is a fine specimen of Indo-Islamic architecture, similar in appearance to, but somehow more awe-inspiring than, its counterpart in Delhi, the Jamia Masjid, that had been built by Aurangzeb's father, Shah Jahan.

Capable of holding over fifty thousand worshippers, this is the largest mosque in Pakistan after the Faisal Mosque in Islamabad.

I washed myself in the *wazu khana*—a marble-rimmed pool in which swam shoals of well-fed goldfish—in the centre of the vast courtyard of the mosque, and then strolled around, overwhelmed by the thoughts of the tumultuous waves of history that this monument must have witnessed: the glory of the Mughals, the sacking of the town by Afghan hordes not long after Aurangzeb's death, the Sikh takeover, when the mosque was used as a stable by Sikh troops and Muslims were banned from announcing the call to prayer in much of Punjab, and then the British capture of the town, after which, for some years, the mosque was used by British soldiers for military practice and as their residential quarters. They were said to have even sawn off enormous chunks of its walls to sell as building material to make a quick buck.

Climbing into a corridor along the perimeter of the mosque, I turned to the chaos of the Old City that spread out below. Here, at the foot of the mosque, once lived large numbers of Hindus and Sikhs who, till 1947, formed a majority of the town's population. My mind travelled to the bloody massacres of that fateful year to which the richly embellished red stone walls of the mosque, the delicately frescoed panels of its inner chambers, and its graceful, pear-shaped domes bore mute testimony, the wounds of which would probably never heal.

I climbed up a narrow, dimly lit flight of stairs that led to the mosque's modest-sized museum. Displayed in giant glass cases were numerous relics—genuine or, equally possibly, spurious—of the Prophet Muhammad, including a frayed pale green coat, a pair of loose trousers, a blanket, a long bolt of cloth that might have been used as a turban, a pair of leather sandals, a single strand of hair and the purported footprint of the Prophet embedded in a slab of stone. Also on display were rusted swords, knob-ended staffs, calligraphed books and a

variety of costumes attributed to various other venerable
personages, including the Prophet's son-in-law Ali, the Prophet's
daughter and Ali's wife Fatima, and several noted Sufi saints.
Awestruck visitors stood transfixed before the cases, some of
them murmuring silent prayers, others offering loud-throated
salutations to the Prophet and his descendants. The cases were
heavily padlocked. Stern-looking guards lounged around the
room. Four years ago, one of them said to me, a pair of slippers
that was said to have belonged to the Prophet had been
purloined from the museum.

Badshahi Masjid and the adjacent gurdwara

From the mosque I walked down, barely fifty metres ahead, to the large, neatly whitewashed Gurdwara Dera Sahib Panjvin Padshahi. Lahore, seat of the mighty Sikh Empire under Ranjit Singh, the 'Lion of the Punjab', and his successors, once boasted of a large Sikh community and numerous imposing Sikh gurdwaras. Following the Partition, all but three of the city's Sikh families had been either killed or forced to flee to India. Those remaining families now looked after the three functioning gurdwaras in Lahore, including this one, the largest. Located just outside the wall that encircled the mosque, with its Mughal-style gilded domes and slender minarets, it could easily be mistaken for yet another Muslim monument. It stood on the spot where the fifth Sikh guru, Arjan Dev, was martyred in 1606 on the orders of the Mughal Emperor Jahangir, and was named after him. It also contains the *samadhi* of Ranjit Singh, and his wives and concubines who committed sati on his death, leaping to their gory deaths on his funeral pyre. The construction of the complex was begun by Ranjit Singh's eldest son and successor, Kharak Singh, in 1839. It was completed by another of his sons, Maharaja Dalip Singh, the last Sikh ruler of Punjab, in 1848, a year before the Sikhs were defeated by the British. Then just twelve years of age, Dalip Singh was forced to relinquish his throne. Four years later, he converted to Christianity at the bidding of his British guardians and sailed to England, where he married an Englishwoman. He reconverted to Sikhism in the last years of his life and breathed his last in Paris in 1893.

At the entrance I was stopped by a uniformed guard. Only Sikhs and Hindus, he said, could enter the shrine. Was this for fear of attack by militant Islamist groups, I asked him? He did not reply, but a Sikh passing through the gate nodded in my direction. I showed the guard my Indian passport and he let me in, instructing an elderly man to take me around.

The man, dark and bent, spoke no Urdu or Punjabi but he

chattered away excitedly. From what he said I made out that he
was a Hindu from a town in Baluchistan, where he worked as
a sweeper. He led me through the gurdwara's guest house and
charitable medical clinic and into the main hall of the shrine,
where an aged *granthi*, a Sikh elder, sat under a domed pavilion
reading in a sonorous drone from a copy of the Guru Granth
Sahib, the holy book of the Sikhs, which rested on a platform
before him. Behind him stood a handsome young Sikh dressed
in a white knee-length frock and blue turban, waving a yak's-
tail fly-whisk. From the hall, a narrow passageway led through
several chambers, their walls richly decorated with fading
frescoes, ending in a room where, under a gilded canopy, was
a marble urn carved in the shape of a lotus. This was the
samadhi of Ranjit Singh. Placed around it were smaller urns
that contained the ashes of his four wives and seven concubines,
who are said to have taken their own lives following his death.

Outside, Sikh and Hindu families spread out on the neatly
trimmed grass of the expansive lawns, some asleep in the
warmth of the soft sunlight, others eating their afternoon meal,
which they had carried from the enormous *langar khana*, the
free community kitchen run by the gurdwara. Most of these
families were from Sindh and the North-West Frontier Province.
Some of them had come to Lahore on work, others on
pilgrimage, and yet others were on their way to India to meet
relatives.

I emerged from the gurdwara and settled on a bench on the
lawn. A while later, a middle-aged Sikh man drew up and sat
next to me. We exchanged pleasantries. He introduced himself
as a trader from Peshawar, and we began talking, our
conversation centring on the conditions of Pakistan's miniscule
Sikh population. The community had now dwindled to less
than 50,000, he said, their largest concentration being in the
North-West Frontier Province, mainly in Peshawar and nearby
towns. That lawless region had been conquered by Ranjit

Singh in the early-nineteenth century and incorporated into the vast Sikh Empire which, at its zenith, had stretched from Delhi to the borders of Afghanistan and Tibet. During Sikh rule, a large number of Sikhs from Punjab had settled in the Frontier Province, as traders, soldiers and government officials. In addition to these Punjabi-speaking Sikhs was a smaller number of native Pashto-speakers, converts to Sikhism from among the warlike Pakhtuns.

'Many Pakhtuns respect us because, like them, and unlike the Hindus, we Sikhs are a martial race,' the man said, beaming with evident pride. 'In contrast to the Hindus, it is rare for Pakistani Sikh girls to be abducted or raped.' Because the Sikhs were treated better than the Hindus, in recent years, a number of Pakistani Hindus had converted to Sikhism, he added. There were several wealthy Sikh merchants in Peshawar, and some of them had relatives across the porous border in neighbouring Afghanistan where, till recently, they had controlled the money market. There were hardly any Sikhs in government service, the man said. They preferred to be economically independent, and then, like other non-Muslims in Pakistan, they faced various forms of discrimination in securing government jobs. Recently, he said, a nineteen-year-old Sikh lad had been appointed as the first Sikh officer in the Pakistan Army. So, he surmised, things might change for the better for the community in the future. He fell silent and looked about. 'But perhaps they won't,' he added, as an afterthought.

In recent years, he went on, the Pakistan government had been trying to woo its Sikh population. While, for most Pakistanis, Sikhs, rather than Hindus, were the epitome of anti-Muslim hatred—memories of Muslims fleeing east Punjab in 1947 being hewn down by Sikh mobs still remained fresh in the minds of many—things began to change in the 1980s, when the Khalistan movement emerged in Indian Punjab. The

Pakistan government actively backed the movement as its way to take revenge on India for its role in dismembering Pakistan in the 1971 war that had resulted in the creation of Bangladesh. Money and arms were supplied by the Pakistanis to Khalistani militants, some of whom now lived in exile in Pakistan. In order to liaise between the Pakistani government and the country's Sikhs, the Pakistani Shiromani Gurdwara Prabhandak Committee (PSGPC) was set up some years ago, charged with the ostensible purpose of managing Pakistani Sikh affairs. Instead of a Sikh religious scholar, the Pakistani government had thought it fit to appoint the former director of its notorious Inter-Services Intelligence, Lieutenant General Javed Nasir, as its president. He had presided over the Pakistani secret service agency's financing of terrorist groups in Afghanistan, Kashmir and Indian Punjab. The actual purpose behind Nasir's appointment was made clear shortly after he had assumed his post, when he declared that the creation of the PSGPC would provide a fillip to the separatist movement in Indian Punjab.

Various forms of support to Khalistani ideologues and terrorists provided by the Pakistan government had been accompanied by seemingly generous overtures to Pakistani Sikhs, the man related. Funds had been allotted for the renovation of some derelict gurdwaras, for instance. But all that was largely symbolic, he complained. 'There are almost 130 major gurdwaras scattered across Pakistan, and most of them remain unattended or have fallen into disuse. Some of them are even used as schools and cowsheds.' Many of them had vast amounts of land attached to them which, following the mass exodus of Sikhs to India in 1947, had been taken over and administered by the Waqf Board, a government body whose major responsibility was to care for Muslim endowments. Corruption was rife in the Waqf Board and, despite the vast revenues that it generated from the properties of the gurdwaras under its control, it spent little money on their upkeep.

From what the man said, it seemed that Pakistani Sikhs did have at least some freedom to practise their faith but, as he indicated, the rise of violent Islamist groups had begun to make things increasingly difficult for them in some places. 'These self-styled custodians of Islam think they are God's chosen people, and that non-Muslims are enemies of God whom He will send to Hell,' he sniggered. In some parts of the Frontier Province, he said, Sikhs had to pay a sort of tax, akin to the medieval Islamic *jizya* levy, to tribal chieftains in return for safety. But the situation was not half as bad as in Afghanistan, he said, where the Sikh and the Hindu population had fallen by more than half after the Taliban, backed by Pakistan, had captured Kabul and set about enforcing laws that heavily discriminated against the country's religious minorities. Many of Afghanistan's Sikhs had since migrated to India, and a fair number of them had also shifted to Pakistan. America's invasion and continuing bombing of Afghanistan had unleashed yet another wave of Sikh refugees fleeing the country.

'What's the use of bemoaning our plight, brother?' the man then said, throwing up his hands in despair. 'Muslims in your country are oppressed, and non-Muslims in my country face the same fate. Maybe minorities all over the world face the same predicament.'

We remained silent for a while. A party of Sikh men passed us by. They washed their feet in a pool of water at the bottom of the flight of stairs leading to the gurdwara and then filed into the shrine. The evening *kirtan* had started, and the Gurbani, the holy word of the Gurus, sung to the accompaniment of a *tabla* and a harmonium, wafted from the building.

'Baba Nanak had the right solution,' the man lowered his voice and said, interrupting the silence. His eyes were firmly shut and he swayed gently to the music floating out of the gurdwara. 'Five hundred years ago, Baba Nanak discovered and declared: "There is no Hindu, there is no Musalman,'" he whispered. 'If only people would listen to him.'

I was woken the next morning by the cry of the muezzin that emanated from the neighbourhood mosque. It was still dark outside, but a pale half-moon peered out from behind a thick blanket of fog. Through a broken window pane a bitterly cold wind swept into the room. 'God is the Greatest! God is the Greatest!' the muezzin chanted, his voice piercing the stillness. 'Come to prayer! Come to prayer! Come to success! Come to success!' he continued, stirring the faithful out of their beds. 'Prayer is better than sleep! Prayer is better than sleep!'

Changing three buses later that morning, I arrived at the sprawling mausoleum of Lahore's most famous Sufi saint, the eleventh-century Syed Abul Hasan bin Ali al-Hujweri or Data Ganj Bakhsh ('the Giver of Treasures') or simply Data Sahib, as he was more commonly known. He was the author of the *Kashf al-Mahjub* ('The Unveiling of the Veiled'), the earliest extant Persian treatise on Sufism. A group of rag-clad stragglers squatted in a concrete traffic triangle in the middle of the road at the foot of the shrine. Necklaces made of colourful beads and brass medallions dangled from their necks, and on their fingers they brandished rings bearing red and green stones, the size of birds' eggs. One of the men, who sported an enormous parrot-green turban that looked like an untidy pile of laundry, furiously tugged at a clay pipe. He let out a stream of sweet-smelling smoke through his nose, which quickly dissolved in the surrounding fog. A younger man seated cross-legged next to him grabbed the pipe as he lifted it to his lips, causing him to burst into a fit of rage. The two men flung off the filthy patched quilts wrapped round their bodies and, jumping to

their feet, began raining blows on each other. Their companions
shrieked with laughter and goaded them on.

I climbed up the marble stairway that led into the shrine.
Already, at this early hour, large crowds had assembled inside,
pushing and shoving in order to enter the inner chamber where
Data Ganj Bakhsh lay buried under a latticed marble canopy,
his grave draped with green silken sheets richly embossed with
Quranic verses. I paid my respects at the shrine and, weaving
my way through the crowd, headed for the grave of Data
Sahib's Hindu disciple who had converted to Islam at his
hands. Slumped against a carved pillar at the entrance to the
room that housed the grave, squatted an enormous middle-
aged man. His head was buried under a woollen monkey-cap

Data Ganj Baksh dargah

that stretched over his ears and down to his beefy neck. In one hand he held a bunch of peacock feathers, with which he patted visitors on their backs as they emerged from the grave complex. The other hand rested on his enormous drum-like belly.

I sat down at his feet and asked him to tell me about Data Sahib's Hindu follower.

'Oh, he was a very big saint in his own right. That is why Data Sahib made him his disciple,' he explained as he tapped his peacock-feather whisk on the head of a man who emerged from the grave complex and walked backwards, out of respect for the buried saint. 'His Hindu name was Rai Raju, and he was an important chieftain in Lahore. He was known as a powerful worker of miracles. Lahore was then under the Ghaznavids, having been conquered by Sultan Mahmud of Ghazni. When Data Sahib came to Lahore and started converting many people to Islam, Rai Raju's jealousy was provoked and he plotted to silence Data Sahib by defeating him in a spiritual contest.'

The man interrupted the story to stretch out his palm to receive some money from a pilgrim. 'So, as I was saying,' he continued, tucking the wad of notes that he had just received into the breast-pocket of his kameez, 'this contest was organized and a large number of people flocked to the venue to see who was more powerful, the Hindu chief or the Muslim saint. Rai Raju used his miraculous powers and flew up like a bird into the sky, but Data Sahib remained unperturbed. Taking Allah's name, he flung his shoe into the air. It travelled even higher than Rai Raju, and started beating and banging his head, forcing him to fall back to the ground. Rai Raju was suitably humbled. He had witnessed the truth and superiority of Islam and at once accepted the faith. Data Sahib took him as his disciple, blessing him with the Muslim name of Shaikh Ahmad Hindi.'

The many historical treatises that I had read about Punjab had not mentioned this supposed spiritual battle, and it was obvious to me that it was a fanciful tale. The story of a Sufi saint defeating a Hindu miracle-worker, leading to the latter's conversion to Islam, was a common trope in Indian Sufistic hagiographical writings. I was also familiar with Hindu stories about alleged miraculous encounters between Hindu *jogi*s and Muslim *faqir*s that ended with the predictable defeat of the latter.

'Hmm,' I said to the man, 'very interesting,' not believing the story at all. As I stood up to leave, he grasped my hand, brushed my back with his peacock-feather whisk and implored for a payment.

Outside in the pale sunshine, the courtyard was buzzing with activity. Large crowds made their way to the enormous mosque at the far end, an ugly, newly constructed concrete structure that had none of the charm and grace of the centuries-old tomb structure of Data Sahib. It was squat and stolid, like a giant cement block. Olive-green glass panes ran along the length of the building, which boasted towering missile-shaped minarets at all four corners. Outside the entrance of the mosque, rows of bearded men bent in genuflection behind an elderly man, an *imam* who sported an Afghan-style turban and a richly embroidered waistcoat. A dozen men squatted on square slabs of marble at the edge of a pool performing the *wazu*, ritual ablutions before their prayers. Groups of women sat cross-legged in the colonnaded balconies that ran along the inner walls of the shrine, some moving back and forth as they read out from copies of the Quran placed on wooden stands before them, others twisting beads between their fingers and invoking the names of God. Yet others spread out sheets and opened out their picnic baskets or stretched out to sleep in the warm sunlight that entered in bold, thick shafts through carved pillars against which they rested their heads.

I climbed down the steps of the shrine and walked through the narrow lanes behind, lined with ancient *havelis*, now fast crumbling, and mountains of garbage that gathered in giant, neglected heaps. I hailed an autorickshaw and headed for the dargah of another of Lahore's many acclaimed Sufis, the seventeenth-century Sain Mir Muhammad, more popularly known as Mian Mir. There was a special reason why I wanted to visit the dargah. Mian Mir had laid the foundation stone of the holiest of Sikh shrines, the Harminder Sahib at the Golden Temple at Amritsar, and I considered him an icon of intercommunal ecumenism.

That morning I had fixed an appointment with the custodian of the shrine of Mian Mir, whom I had met by chance almost ten years before in London. Makhdum Syed Chan Shah Qadri immediately recognized me when I contacted him on the phone, and we agreed to meet at the dargah where, he said, he would show me around, after which he insisted that I lunch with him at his home.

Makhdum sahib seemed to have aged not a whit since I had last met him. He still appeared like a character straight out of the pages of the Old Testament. He wore a white turban tightly wound round his head, somewhat in the Sikh fashion, and a loose white gown that stretched to his ankles. He sported an enormous white beard that reached down to his belly, and a carefully trimmed moustache.

'Puttar!' he exclaimed as he entered the compound of the shrine and wrapped me in his arms in an avuncular embrace.

A descendant of Umar, the second Sunni Caliph, Mian Mir belonged to the Qadri order of Sufis, whose putative founder was the renowned Islamic scholar and mystic, Abdul Qadir Gilani of Baghdad. Renowned for his piety and scholarship, Mian Mir had attracted a vast number of followers, including members of the ruling Mughal family. The Mughal Emperor Jahangir met him in 1620 and, in his memoirs, the *Tuzuk-e*

Jahangiri, described him as 'a noble personage', 'a great gain' and 'a delightful existence'. Jahangir's son and successor, Shah Jahan, paid the saint three visits. Dara Shikoh, Shah Jahan's eldest son, was a disciple of Mulla Shah Badakhshani, one of Mian Mir's closest followers. Noted for his Sufi proclivities and his close relations with Hindu *sadhus*, which greatly angered many leading Muslim clerics, Dara was credited with a detailed biography of Mian Mir and his disciples. It was because of his fame as a Sufi that Mian Mir was honoured by the fifth Sikh Guru, Arjan Dev, by being requested to lay the foundation stone of the Golden Temple at Amritsar.

I begged Makhdum sahib to tell me more than what I already knew about the relations between Mian Mir and the Sikh Gurus, part of a long-standing and deep-rooted bond between Sikh and Muslim saints that later political developments had almost completely occluded from popular memory.

When Mian Mir came to Lahore, Makhdum sahib explained, he befriended the fourth Sikh Guru, Ram Das, who also lived in the city. Like the Sikh Gurus, Mian Mir believed in the doctrine of *wahdat-al wujud* or the unity of all beings. He often visited the Guru's home to listen to his discourses and to discuss spiritual matters. At this time, the Sikhs were not a separate, well-established community. Rather, in line with the teachings of Guru Nanak, they were a loosely organized group of Hindus and Muslims united in the quest to travel on God's path.

Guru Ram Das had purchased a plot of land in Amritsar, where he constructed a large tank, Makhdum Sahib went on. He was said to have forecast that a shrine would be established there and that its foundation stone would be laid by one whom he described as the noblest person of the time. He was succeeded by his son Guru Arjan Dev, who decided to build the Harminder Sahib, or what is now popularly called the Golden Temple, on that spot. In accordance with his father's

wishes, he requested Mian Mir sahib—whom he considered a
devout Sufi—to lay the foundation stone of the shrine.

Jealous of his growing popularity, bigoted Muslim mullahs
(or scheming Brahmins, according to another version of the
story) instigated the Mughal Emperor Jahangir to execute
Guru Arjan Dev. He ordered the Guru to be placed on a hot
iron plate and had burning sand poured over his head. Mian
Mir is said to have rushed to his rescue, saying, 'My friend, just
give me one word and I shall cause the thrones of Delhi
and Lahore to come crashing down,' but the Guru stoically
replied, 'This is the will of God, and I must give an example
to the people, or else how will they know what true martyrdom
is?' On Mian Mir's intervention, Makhdum Sahib said, the
torture was stopped, but a few days later, the Guru breathed
his last.

'In short,' Makhdum sahib concluded, 'the notion that Sikhs
and Muslims are sworn enemies, compelled by their respective
religions to hate each other, is completely misplaced.' Political
interests and compulsions had led to brutal wars between
certain Mughal emperors, Hindu rajas and some of the Sikh
gurus, he said, but many renowned Sufis, the most pious of the
Muslims, had consistently supported the Gurus and their
mission.

It was obvious from what Makhdum sahib recounted
that the history of intercommunity relations in Punjab had
been far more complex than the widely held theory of Sikhs
being the 'martial arm of the Hindus' and 'inveterate foes of
Islam' suggests. And in this complicated history, of which
competing narratives provide widely diverging, indeed
diametrically opposite, perspectives on relations between Punjabi
Hindus, Muslims and Sikhs, all knit together by a common
ethnicity and language, the Sufi saints had a major role to
play.

But what relevance, I asked Makhdum sahib, did Sufism

have for intercommunity relations in our times, and for the increasingly strained relations between India and Pakistan?

The Quran, he replied, taught that God had sent prophets to all the peoples of the world, and they all preached the same basic faith, which in Arabic was called *Islam*. This simply meant 'submission'—that is, to God alone. 'India is such a huge country, and so how could it be that God did not send any prophets here? He must surely have, and that is why some Sufis believe that perhaps the Buddha might have been a messenger of God,' Makhdum Sahib explained. 'So, we must respect men of God of all communities. That is what the Sufis also did.'

'The Quran also tells us,' he continued, 'that the Prophet Muhammad had been sent by Allah to fulfil, and not to negate, the teachings of the previous prophets and to correct the wrong beliefs and practices that had crept into the religion of those who claimed to be their followers.' This understanding of universal revelation, he believed, provided a firm foundation for interreligious and intercommunal dialogue. Yet, sadly, he added, few organized efforts were being made by Sufis in this regard today. If Makhdum sahib were to be believed, there were hardly any living Sufis left.

It was now time for the afternoon prayer. Makhdum sahib rose and headed towards a nearby mosque. Meanwhile, I slowly circumambulated Mian Mir's dargah, wondering at the momentous life of the enigmatic saint who lay buried within its hallowed precincts.

Half an hour later, Makhdum sahib returned. 'I've kept you hungry. You can't feed yourself simply on stories from the past,' he chuckled. 'It's well past lunchtime. Come, let's go home.'

We wove our way through a maze of lanes and then on to a broad road choked with traffic. An hour later, we drew up beside a modestly sized house. Half a dozen men emerged from the front door. Each took his turn to kiss Makhdum sahib's hand and receive his blessings, bending their heads low as he patted them on their heads or their backs.

After lunch, Makhdum sahib made a couple of phone calls. 'I'm calling over some people you would love to meet,' he said. An hour later, a young man entered the room, lifting the curtain that separated it from the waiting chamber on the other side. He drew up to Makhdum sahib and bent low, with his hands folded. 'Live long, my son,' Makhdum sahib greeted him, and turned to introduce him to me. He was Naeem sahib, a direct descendant of Bhai Mardana, Guru Nanak sahib's first and closest disciple.

I clasped his hand, and placed my lips on it. The man removed his hand from mine and gently placed it on my head in blessing. He drew me close, and pressed my chest against his. 'Remain happy, brother. May Allah bless you,' he whispered.

Relatively little has been written about Bhai Mardana, although he was a key figure in Sikh history. I asked Naeem sahib to tell me what he knew about his venerable ancestor.

Guru Nanak and Bhai Mardana were born in the village of Talwandi, not far from Lahore, Naeem sahib began. Bhai Mardana was a Muslim from the Mirasi caste, whose ancestral occupation was singing. Although he was ten years older than Guru Nanak, they were inseparable companions. He accompanied him on his various missionary travels, playing the *rabab* and singing the verses that the Guru composed. They also travelled together to Arabia for the Haj, the Muslim pilgrimage, and then to Baghdad, the resting place of many great Sufi saints and the seat of the Muslim Caliphs.

Bhai Mardana was recognized by the Sikhs as the first of their *rababi*s, musicians who sing the verses of the Guru Granth Sahib, the Sikh holy book, in the gurdwaras. Some of his compositions had also been included in the Sikh scripture.

Naeem sahib cleared his voice and shut his eyes. Gently

swaying this way and that, he sang a verse by Bhai Mardana, in a soft, plaintive voice, which he later translated for me:

> *The barmaid is misery, wine is desire and man is the drinker.*
> *The wine-cup filled with worldly desire is wrath and is served with pride.*
> *The company is false and desirous, ruined by excessive drink.*
> *Instead of this, make good conduct your ghee and modesty your meat.*
> *Such things, O Nanak, are obtained by God's favour.*
> *By partaking of them, sins depart.*

'Guru Nanak sahib did not intend to found a new religion,' Naeem sahib explained when I asked him if, having been such a close disciple of the Guru's, Bhai Mardana had abandoned Islam. He had remained a Muslim till the end, he said, although, like Guru Nanak, he understood his religion in an expansive way that transcended narrow communal boundaries. Even today, he added, many Punjabi Muslims continued to hold Guru Nanak in high regard, believing him to have been a sort of Sufi. In the beginning, the word 'Sikh' had simply meant 'disciple' of the Guru, and the early Sikhs included people who had been born into Hindu as well as Muslim families. 'The Guru wanted people to recognize the one God of all and the universality of humankind,' Naeem sahib said.

All Bhai Mardana's living descendants now lived in Pakistan and, although they were Muslims, they still deeply revered Guru Nanak. Only a few of them continued with their ancestral tradition, though, being occasionally invited to sing in the few remaining gurdwaras in Pakistan. Naeem sahib's father, Ashiq Ali sahib, had been a famous singer of Sikh hymns, and he had taught his sons several verses of the Guru Granth Sahib when they were children. But since there were now few Sikhs left in Pakistan, that tradition was rapidly disappearing. Most members of his family, Naeem sahib said, were poor, and singing, their age-old profession, no longer sufficed to make ends meet. He himself now worked as a travelling salesman. 'Sadly', he lamented, 'in India, too, Sikh organizations do not seem to feel the need to preserve our family's heritage.' Some members of his family, he said, had visited Amritsar some years ago in the hope of being able to sing at the Golden Temple, but the authorities there had reportedly turned down their request on the grounds that they were not Sikhs in the conventional sense of the term.

While Naeem sahib was talking, a wiry, bespectacled middle-aged man joined us, silently listening to our conversation. Naeem sahib got up to leave, and I walked with him to the door. When I returned, Makhdum Sahib introduced me to the new visitor. 'Zahoor Khan, seventh-generation descendant of Ghani Khan and Nabi Khan, two close companions of the last Sikh Guru, Gobind Singh-ji,' he announced.

The man handed me his visiting card. On it were printed precisely the words that Makhdum sahib had used to introduce him. From that I presumed that he considered his link with his seventeenth-century forefathers as his primary identity. I asked him to tell me about the two Pathan men, about whom I knew nothing except that they had played a crucial role in Guru Gobind Singh's life.

When Guru Gobind Singh was being pursued by the forces of the Mughal Emperor Aurangzeb, Zahoor Khan related, he reached a place called Machhiwara. There, he was surrounded by the Mughal army, but managed to escape with the help of the two brothers, Nabi Khan and Ghani Khan, who disguised him in a blue robe and passed him off as a Muslim saint, the Pir of Ucch. Carrying him in a heavily curtained palanquin, they slipped through the Mughal lines. The Mughal commander, Dilawar Khan, questioned the Guru but was not convinced that he was really the Pir of Ucch. He ordered a *qazi*, a learned

Muslim judge, from a neighbouring village, to verify his identity. The qazi advised Dilawar Khan not to stop the Guru, whom he reportedly described as 'a great and holy man', a 'saint in union with Allah'. Satisfied with the qazi's assurance, Dilawar Khan let the Guru pass through untouched.

Since the two brothers had helped save his life, the Guru presented them with a *hukum namah*, which Zahoor Khan claimed to have in his possession. 'In the letter,' he went on, 'Guru Gobind Sahib wrote, "Whoever among my followers loves and protects these two brothers loves me, too."' In recognition of the services rendered to the Guru by the two men, Ranjit Singh, the founder of the Sikh kingdom in Punjab, had granted their descendants a large estate in Mandara, a village in present-day Indian Punjab, where Zahoor Khan and his family had resided till 1947 when, during the Partition riots, they were forced to flee to Pakistan.

But why, I asked, did they abandon their ancestral village? Surely, in accordance with the Guru's hukum namah, they would have been safely protected by their Sikh and Hindu neighbours from marauding mobs?

Zahoor sahib sat still for what seemed a long while. Then, drawing a deep breath, he spoke softly, 'At that time, my son, the whole of Punjab was up in flames. Hindus and Sikhs in western Punjab and Muslims in the eastern half of the province were being massacred in thousands and driven out of their homes. In eastern Punjab, Muslims accounted for more than a third of the population, but they were all killed or else forced to flee to Pakistan.' Much of the violence against the Muslims was the handiwork of Sikhs, he added. 'Yet, because of the hukum namah of the Guru, the Sikhs of Mandara pleaded with my father and other relatives not to leave. But we had to, so terrible was the situation then.'

Zahoor Khan was a young lad of fifteen when Punjab was partitioned. 'We left everything in our village and escaped with just the clothes on our backs,' he said, choking with emotion. 'It was impossible to go back, although I often thought of our village and pined to return at least once before I died.' As his luck would have it, he was recently able to travel to India at the invitation of an Indian Sikh organization, and he took the opportunity to visit his ancestral village. There, he was given an enthusiastic welcome by the denizens of Mandara.

'I don't know if I'll ever get to visit my village again before I die,' he went on, his eyes now clouded with tears. 'Life here is just not the same as it had been there.'

Later that day, I did a hurried round of the remaining monuments that I wanted to visit. On the other side of Lahore, straddling the River Ravi, is one of Lahore's finest Mughal monuments—the mausoleum of the seventeenth-century Mughal Emperor Jahangir. Set in an attractive walled garden, it is entered through enormous yellow sandstone gateways that lead into a massive square, criss-crossed by four canals that have long since run dry. The mausoleum itself is modest in size by Mughal standards, but that only enhances its attractiveness. In contrast to other Mughal tomb-structures, it lacks a central dome, but this is made up for by four elegant minarets, each over thirty metres high, built of flanks of red sandstone and slender carved slabs of marble. The colonnaded corridor that trails along the sides of the mausoleum pierced with scalloped arches, its inner walls richly embellished with elegant mosaics cleverly pieced together to form flowers, buds, leaves and tendrils set in frames that encircle verses of the Quran crafted out of bits of polished black stone. The elevated sarcophagus inside the mausoleum is made of pale white marble, the sides of which are decorated with semi-precious stones set in floral and geometrical patterns.

If Jahangir's mausoleum recaptures something of the lost glory of the Mughals, the decaying ruins of two other Mughal-period tomb-structures located in the vicinity stand as mute testimonies to the tragic fate that was to meet that dynasty. The tomb of Noor Jahan, 'Light of the World', the twentieth and favourite wife of the Emperor Jahangir, is now in a crumbling shambles. A board nailed to the entrance to the complex explains that this once-fine structure had suffered extensive damage at the hands of marauders after Lahore passed into Sikh hands. All of its many treasures and the precious tiles and coloured stones that decked it were looted and carted off, to be used to adorn various Sikh buildings, so the board claims.

Even more desolate, and now attracting almost no visitors, is the adjacent mausoleum of Asaf Khan, Noor Jahan's elder brother and father of Mumtaz Mahal, wife of Jahangir's son and successor, Shah Jahan. All that remains of it is its bare, skeleton-like brickwork frame, the layers of fine marble and turquoise blue and pale yellow coloured tiles that had once adorned it having long since been stripped off, again by Sikh looters. An army of bats had made the crumbling central dome of the structure their home, hanging upside down with their black, leathery wings tightly wrapped around their stomachs to keep out the cold, lying inert and motionless, like bizarre trapeze artists. Purple pigeons flitted about, the frantic flapping of their wings breaking the eerie silence which hung like a shroud that drapes the now-bare grave of this once-powerful Mughal nobleman, which is splattered with a thick coating of avian excrement. Impenetrable cobweb curtains—the product of the ceaseless, patient toil of who knows how many years—stretch across carved alcoves built into the walls, holding in their throttling embrace moths and dragonflies and hairy black spiders the size of birds. An overpowering stench of human excrement, mixed with ammonium fumes that emanates from fetid pools of stagnant water outside, envelops the tomb. The extensive lawns that had once surrounded the tomb are now a vast dumping ground for construction waste. The narrow mud track that cut across from the far end and led to the mausoleum has almost completely disappeared under a jungle of weeds and knee-high grass.

'This man inside the tomb was an evil Nawab, who sucked the blood of the poor,' said the mali, an old, dark man with a deeply creased forehead, when I asked him why the mausoleum and its surroundings were in such a pathetic state. 'Maybe this is God's way of punishing him for his sins.'

seven

with maulvis in gujranwala

After several days in Lahore, I decided that I had had just about enough of the city. I had seen most of its major monuments, leaving out numerous minor ones—scores of mosques, madrasas and mausoleums which, I supposed and hoped, would not be exceptionally noteworthy or different in style and form from many of the structures I had already visited. Then, the head-spinning boredom of many of the conversations I was forced into—mostly extended monologues while I pretended to be attentive—had taken a heavy toll on my patience. And, there was also the fact that, although Sheila had been a wonderful hostess, going completely out of her way to make me feel at home, I had begun to feel guilty about taking further advantage of her goodness. I decided, therefore, to head for Gujranwala.

My host in Gujranwala, Ammar Nasir, was a young Deobandi maulvi who ran a madrasa in the town, and whom I had never met before. We had been corresponding by e-mail regularly, for the past two years, after I had chanced upon the website of his institute, the Al-Shariah Academy, in the course of working on a book about Islamic education. He had translated some articles of mine and published them in his journal, although they had been critical of some aspects of traditional madrasas. When he learnt of my visit to Pakistan, he had insisted that I should spend some days in Gujranwala with him and his father, a well-known Pakistan *alim* or Muslim religious scholar.

And, there was another reason why I wanted to visit the town—Nani was born and brought up there, and had lived there till she got married and followed Nana to Ooty in the Nilgiri Hills, more than three thousand miles away, in the early 1930s.

Sheila was aghast when I told her about my plans for visiting Ammar and staying in his madrasa. 'No way!' she burst out. 'Are you out of your mind or what?' She, like her Leftist comrades, had a visceral hatred of 'mullahs', as she derisively referred to them. And, to make matters even more complicated, Ammar and his father were dyed-in-the-wool Deobandis, the latter being a senior leader of the Jamiat-e Ulema-e Islam, a religio-political outfit that made no bones of its ardent support for the Taliban.

'They might kidnap you. Poison you perhaps. Bump you off, like the Islamists did to Daniel Pearle. There's no telling what they might do,' she warned. 'I'm not letting you go, and that's final.'

But, I had made up my mind and was adamant that I had to leave Lahore. I called up Ammar, somewhat hesitatingly. What if Sheila was right, I wondered, as the phone rang. What if the mullahs decided that I was a spy or an ill-intentioned Indian up to no good?

'*Asalaam Aleikum*,' said the voice that answered the phone. 'Who's that, please?' He sounded the very epitome of gentleness.

'Ammar-ji!' I screamed excitedly. 'It's me, Yogi, from India. I'm speaking from Lahore.'

'Yogi-ji!' he exulted in response. 'When are you coming to Gujranwala? Come right away, if you can.'

There was no way now that I would not go to Gujranwala.

We agreed that he would come later that morning to Sheila's house to pick me up.

An hour or so later, the doorbell rang. Sheila hurriedly threw a scarf over her head and went down to open the door. 'Yogi!' she whispered as she placed her hand on the door-handle. 'You still have time to change your mind. Don't blame me if you get into trouble.'

'It's all in God's hands, Sheila-ji,' I shrugged.

A delicately built man in his late twenties, with deep-set eyes and a wispy beard, stood at the door. He wore a white embroidered prayer cap on his head, and was dressed in a neatly pressed pistachio-green shalwar-kameez. An enormous smile spread over his face as he peered over Sheila's shoulders and our eyes met. '*Asalaam Aleikum wa Rahmatullah wa Barakatuhu*, Yogi-ji! At last we have met! At last!' he burst out and pressed me in a tight embrace, as if we had been long-separated friends.

We sat down to chat in the drawing room, and in a few minutes Sheila underwent a dramatic transformation. She was now bubbling with excitement, laughing uncontrollably and chattering away like a schoolgirl. 'Beta Ammar, eat this', 'Beta Ammar, drink that', 'Beta, try these nice-nice hot-hot *alu pakoras*', 'Beta Ammar, tell me more', she went on and on. The 'mullah' she had so dreaded before meeting him was now, she had decided and announced, like her very own son. Ammar had won my heart, too. Here, at last, I felt, was one Pakistani whom I could really relate to. He was a patient listener and spoke little, but when he did it was not about himself, nor about his own achievements, which I knew were many. He had an almost encyclopaedic knowledge of almost everything I wanted to know about Pakistan: its economy, its education system, its politics and, most of all, given my own personal interest in the subject, its religious schools and organizations. Sheila was mesmerized by him, and so was I.

'Yes, Yogi, of course you should go to Gujranwala with Ammar beta,' Sheila insisted. She was adamant that I must and that there were no two ways about it.

We drove to the Al-Mawrid Institute, at the heart of Lahore, where Ammar did part-time work, translating Islamic texts from English into Urdu. The building that housed the institute was a minor architectural marvel, a Moroccan-style palace transported into a lower-middle Lahore locality. I was ushered into a room to meet the director, Javed Ahmed Ghamidi, reputed to be among the few modernist Islamic scholars in Pakistan. Behind a massive mahogany desk sat the bespectacled Mr Ghamidi, his silvery hair neatly pushed back, revealing a large, clear forehead. A massive leather-bound volume lay in his lap. The desk was cluttered with files, bundles of papers and books. On the walls behind it were polished wooden racks bearing stacks of books, neatly arranged, that reached almost till the ceiling. Many of these were collections of classical Arabic texts that ran into several volumes. The room seemed to have been decorated by a professional interior designer. A green carpet covered the entire floor. The soft lighting was just appropriate. Leather stools lay before a carved wooden table, and tasteful artefacts lay scattered about in just the right places.

We exchanged pleasantries, and Mr Ghamidi told me briefly about himself and the work of his institute. He had a degree in English literature from Lahore University, and had studied Islam under the late Amin Ahsan Islahi, an émigré from India, one of the founding members of the Jamaat-e-Islami, Pakistan's most well-organized Right-wing Islamist outfit. Islahi had stayed with the party for seventeen years, being one of its major intellectuals, and serving as a member of its central governing council till he resigned in 1958 following serious difference with its founder and chief ideologue, Sayyid Abul Ala Maududi. Ghamidi saw himself as inheriting, preserving and promoting Islahi's legacy, which he expressed as 'approaching and deliberating on the Quran directly in order to present its teachings in their pristine form and applying them in the current circumstances'. In this way, he seemed to suggest, Islamic thought could be made more relevant in today's fast-changing world, stripped of the burden of medieval interpretations. This, he elaborated, was in accordance with Islahi's understanding of Islam as a 'comprehensive world view' that 'provided positive solutions to the problems faced in every field for every age—law, politics, society, the economy, international relations—everything.'

His institute published several journals, Mr Ghamidi said, and had brought out numerous books, most of which he himself had penned. It also organized regular lecture series in colleges, and Mr Ghamidi had a regular talk show on a local TV channel. 'Our aim is to present Islam in an idiom understandable to the modern mind,' he explained. This work entailed treading on treacherous ground, revisiting traditional notions, ardently championed by conservative mullahs, on a host of issues: politics, economics, education, women's rights, relations with non-Muslims, and so on, all geared to promoting what Mr Ghamidi saw as a 'contextually relevant' and, at the same time, 'authentically Islamic' response to the myriad challenges that modernity had forced Muslims to confront.

Shortly after, Mr Ghamidi excused himself. He had an important meeting to attend, he said, handing me a bundle of copies of his monthly English magazine *Renaissance* as a gift. I skimmed through their contents. Many of the articles consisted of short commentaries on selected verses of the Quran, such as could be found in any other Islamic periodical. But certain other articles, on issues about which heated, inconclusive debate continue to rage, caught my attention. Several dealt with the doctrine of jihad, persuasively arguing against its cynical misuse by radical Islamists and hardened Islamophobes alike. A piece on music, deemed wholly un-Islamic by conservative mullahs, sought to argue that 'only music and songs which stimulate vulgar emotions are prohibited'. Another article critiqued the notion that a woman could not aspire to become the head of state of a Muslim country, based on a report or *hadith* attributed to the Prophet. 'This hadith,' it boldly argued, 'is against the Quran. It is the purport of the Quran that anyone who enjoys the confidence of the majority is eligible to become the ruler of the Muslims. Nowhere does it exclude women from this general principle.' In response to a query about the gender of God in the context of Allah being referred to as 'He' in the Quran, another article stressed that 'Allah is a neutral, genderless term.'

It was apparent that on a host of issues Ghamidi and his team had made a radical departure from the tradition associated with the mullahs, although in several respects they still remained within a decidedly conservative framework. Yet, considering the particular Pakistani context in which they operated, where open defiance of radical Islamists and mullahs could easily invite death, their halting progressivism struck me as bold, and, in many ways, innovative.

Ammar emerged when the early afternoon prayer got over and took me into his cabin. From a bundle wrapped up in cloth he drew out a steel tiffin-carrier.

'Since you are from India, I supposed you would be a vegetarian, and so I asked my mother to make a special vegetarian lunch for you,' he said as he opened the lids of the containers inside the tiffin-carrier. He ladled out a curry made of beans and potatoes, deep-fried bits of eggplant, a mash made of pumpkin and cottage cheese, and a mound of rice, into a large steel plate, from which we both ate together, in traditional Muslim style. I had visited several Pakistani homes by now, but nowhere, except in Sheila's house, had the hosts ever thought that I might be anything but a diehard carnivore, and so I had been forced to make do with plain rice and salad, much to my embarrassment and that of my hosts as well. But this bearded maulvi, who Sheila and, I admit, I myself, had imagined might well be a raving, firebrand fanatic, had turned out to be nothing of the sort at all. His kind gesture completely overwhelmed me. At that moment, there was nothing more that I wanted to do than give him a tight hug, which was precisely what I did, unmindful of the men piling out of the prayer-room and passing by.

After the sumptuous meal, we got to Lahore's main intercity bus-station—if it could at all be called that. An enormous knot of vehicles of various kinds—trucks, buses, cars, autorickshaws and horse-drawn carts—blocked the entrance. The vehicles shoved this way and that to unscramble themselves. Showers of abuse gushed out from irate drivers and irritated passengers. Frantic neighs and grunts burst forth from frightened donkeys yoked to carts three times their size, bearing mounds of stones and bricks and enormous piles of hay.

A *shamiana* painted in bright rainbow colours strung on bamboo poles set up on the pavement caught my eye. Wrapped around it was a banner in bold Urdu letters announcing, 'Earthquake Relief Camp: Help Us, in the Name of God'. Painted on both sides of the slogan was the image of a raised fist brandishing an AK-47. It was a camp for gathering donations for victims of a killer quake that had recently struck Kashmir, organized by a deadly Islamist terrorist outfit, the Lashkar-e-Tayyaba.

I leapt off the autorickshaw, telling Ammar that I would meet him at the bus-station, where he was to purchase our tickets for Gujranwala. I wound my way through the traffic and approached the shamiana. A corpulent young man with a pill-box cap on his shaven head, a straggly unkempt beehive-like beard and a pencil-thin moustache, squatted on a plastic stool, crying out to mostly indifferent passers-by, imploring for donations for the hapless quake-hit victims. 'Allah will reward you, my brethren! Help those in need. It is your Islamic duty as believers.' There was something strangely wolf-like about him, with a broad jaw that jutted out of his face, with his flat, blubbery nose, his dark, shifty eyes that darted this way and that, and his leathery purple lips that opened and closed in quick succession like a mechanized toy. 'Yes, my brother,' he beckoned me, sweeping his hands in the air about him, 'help our fellow Muslims suffering in Kashmir.'

A mound of pullovers and jackets, some of them patched and badly faded, lay at his feet—donations by the kind-hearted. Although the Lashkar-e-Tayyaba was feared and even hated by many Pakistanis for its extreme radical views, it had, so newspapers reported, provided relief on an impressive scale to literally thousands of people stranded in the mountain fastnesses of Pakistani-administered Kashmir in the wake of the deadly quake. Its team of volunteers, armed with tents and bags of food and clothes, besides their guns, had reached inaccessible hamlets miles from the nearest road where even the Pakistani Army had not dared to venture.

But all that undoubtedly noble work came at a considerable price. It was obviously being aggressively used, as many Pakistani newspapers had suggested, as a handy tool for the Lashkar's vicious propaganda machine. Two large tin cans with slits in their lids, placed on stools under the shamiana, bore stickers with the image of an open book—presumably the Quran—surrounded by a pair of unsheathed swords, below which a slogan cried out, 'Oh! People of the Faith! Join the Jihad Against Infidel India'. A board nailed to a pole that held the shamiana up warned passers-by, 'Feminism is a Ploy by the Enemies of Islam to Destroy Muslim Society'. Spread out on a plastic sheet on the pavement were dozens of books in Urdu, some slim leaflets, others, voluminous tomes. Several of these were standard religious texts—about methods of prayer, the duties of spouses and the appropriate style of facial hair and so on—but others were of an altogether different genre—angry diatribes against followers of the Sufi saints, who were summarily dismissed as 'grave-worshippers', against 'heretical splitters', a contemptuous term reserved for Shias, and their 'utter falsehood', and against 'fake Muslim Deobandis', who were, they alleged, 'crypto-Sufis, trying to pass off as Muslims'. In short, in the Lashkar's eyes, so these books suggested, the vast majority of the Muslims of Pakistan had strayed far from the narrow and beaten Islamic path. Then, there was a number of titles of a third genre: devoted to the specific purpose of promoting what it called 'armed jihad' against sundry 'enemies of Islam', including the Hindus of India, Zionist Jews and Christian 'Crusaders'.

Just then, my cellphone rang. It was Ammar. 'Hurry up, bhai! The bus is about to leave!' he hollered. I flung back a book on the pavement from where I had picked it. It was curiously titled *And At Last India Was Sandwiched*.

The bus bumbled along the road to Gujranwala, after spending almost half an hour trying to negotiate itself out of the chaos that stretched from out of the bus-stand till as far as I could see. The grubby suburbs of Lahore fell back as we drove northwards and turned onto the Grand Trunk Road, possibly the longest, and certainly one of the oldest, roads in the world. It stretches a distance of over 2,500 kilometres, starting in Sonargaon in Bangladesh, passing through several states in eastern and northern India, and then, via the Wagah border, into Pakistan and all the way up to Peshawar, on the Afghan frontier. According to some scholars, the road was first built by the Mauryans, who ruled over vast tracts of north India in the centuries immediately after the Buddha. It was renovated almost two thousand years later, by the sixteenth-century Pathan ruler of much of north India, Sher Shah Suri, who bestowed on it the honorific title of *Sadak-e-Azam* or 'The Great Road'. Under the Mughals, the road was further extended to Kabul, via the treacherous Khyber Pass, a major engineering marvel.

The stretch of the Grand Trunk Road that connects Lahore with Gujranwala is just under 70 kilometres long, a bus journey of two hours. We passed by thoroughly unremarkable countryside. Large stretches of what must have till recently been fertile wheat fields, had been cut up into little squares by low-level brick walls, creating plots to be sold to urban dwellers, as Lahore and Gujranwala—already bursting at the seams—continued to expand rapidly. 'Farm houses' of Lahore's hyper-rich—nothing rustic about them, notwithstanding what they were called—occupied vast tracts of land, their ugly mock-Tudor mansions ringed by leafy trees and designer pools and guarded by heavily armed sentries. Burly turbaned peasant men aloft tractors bumped up and down, levelling their fields, driving their vehicles like battle tanks. Then followed a long string of factories that stretched almost till we finally reached Gujranwala, belching out massive clouds of poisonous smoke. This is one of Pakistan's major industrial belts.

Darkness fell as the bus sped past a row of bungalows sheltered behind high walls, the homes of Gujranwala's rich: industrialists, landlords and army officials. As we travelled further into the town, vast herds of sheep, goats, cows and buffaloes lined either side of the road. A dozen camels trotted around a clump of mangled trees, straining their necks to gnaw at their thorny branches. Sturdy peasant men, dressed in long kurtas and sarong-like *lungis*, sauntered around with long wooden poles slung across their shoulders, hollering at their animals and administering sharp whacks to the recalcitrant beasts. Makeshift tents had been set up in the fields abutting the road, outside which old men crouched on wooden *charpai*s sucking their hukkahs. The Muslim festival of Eid ul-Azha, when animals are slaughtered in vast numbers, was a few weeks away but feverish preparations had already begun. The literally thousands of animals sequestered there would soon meet with a gory end.

Gujjars with sheep and camels

Gujranwala's main bus-stand was just a long cement platform, an island in a bay of fetid water fed by open gutters. Compared to it, the Lahore bus-station appeared positively plush. We waded through the water, wound our way through the narrow lanes of a crowded bazaar and turned round a corner to Ammar's house—a modest two-storey building in a lower-middle-class locality. Just ahead, Ammar pointed out, behind a locked iron gate stood a row of crumbling pillars sheathed under a thick carpet of moss—the *baradari* or royal pavilion of Ranjit Singh, the Sikh ruler of Lahore, who was born in Gujranwala in 1780. In the aftermath of the destruction of the Babri Masjid in Ayodhya in India in 1992 by Hindu goons, an irate mob had vented its anger on this structure, although it had no religious significance, and had torn down its roof. A Hindu temple nearby, locked up since 1947 after the town's Hindu inhabitants had fled, had, however, escaped the same fate.

I followed Ammar up a narrow column of stairs dimly lit by a bare bulb that hung from a string suspended from the ceiling. He knocked on the door and deliberately coughed loud enough for the women of the house to hear him and move into the separate women's chambers, where no men but close relatives could enter. I heard the quick shuffling of feet and then a woman's voice coming from the inner recesses of the house, informing Ammar that we could now come in.

The drawing room was simple, indeed austere, yet, in its own way, elegant. A large, glass-paned, wooden cupboard occupied much of the space, its three racks neatly stacked with Arabic and Urdu tomes. A laminated picture depicting the Prophet's green-domed mosque in Medina hung on the front wall, before which swirled thousands of devout pilgrims dressed in the white robes that *hajis* must don. Thin mattresses were strewn on the floor, on which were placed neatly folded piles of razais and velvet-covered bolsters. On one of these mattresses rested a slimly built man with a towel-like turban wound round his head. He seemed to be in his late fifties or thereabouts. '*Abba Huzoor*,' announced Ammar softly as we entered the room, 'our guest has come.'

Maulana Zahid ul-Rashdi got up from his bed, stretched out his arms and drew me into a hearty embrace. 'Welcome, son, it is such a pleasure to have you with us,' he said as he gently kissed my forehead. 'Come, come, it is icy outside. Snuggle under a razai before the cold gets to you.'

I settled on a mattress next to Maulana sahib, huddled under a fluffy razai, my toes, already wrapped in two pairs of woollen socks, against a heater to warm out the numbness. Ammar left to help his mother cook dinner, and for a while the room was silent. Maulana sahib had been doing his *zikr*, remembrance of Allah, when we had disturbed him, and he went back to finish counting the beads of his *tasbih*, his eyes shut, his lips moving silently. Suddenly, a wave of fear and uncertainty rushed through me, beginning like a sharp, shooting ray that emanated from deep in my guts and spreading through my entire system, like a bursting cluster bomb. I wanted to retch. What was I doing here, in the house of an unknown Pakistani mullah, I asked myself? What if Sheila's initial fears proved true? Would I at all be able to get out of here alive?

Maulana sahib finished his evening zikr, having recited the specified incantations a certain recommended number of times. Cupping his hands before his face, he made his *dua*, supplication to God, bending his neck backwards slightly and turning his half-closed eyes heavenwards. His lips quivered as he silently addressed His Maker. At that moment, it struck me, he seemed strangely ethereal, like some mendicant fervently in love with his creator and totally submitting to Him every particle of his being. There was something profoundly otherworldly about him, a bit of the angelic, or so I imagined. But, as I gazed intently at him, it struck me that this man, like the rest of the leaders of the political party with which he was associated, was probably an ardent supporter of the Taliban-style 'Islamic' rule that was based on a brutal medieval code, and which upheld a stern, even Manichaean, view of the world, one that was starkly divided between those who, in their pathetic self-righteousness, regarded themselves as Allah's valiant vanguard, and the rest of humanity, whom they considered to be Allah's enemies, meriting everlasting perdition in hell.

A short while later, his lips stopped moving. He opened his eyes, rubbed his hands on his face, moving them down to his neck and chest, and then turned to me. 'I've done dua for you also,' he said, giving me a disarming, avuncular smile. At that moment, I knew that, despite the vast chasm that divided us on numerous matters of faith and culture, this was a man of honour, in whose presence I could be perfectly safe.

Maulana sahib began to tell me about himself and his work. His family was known for its tradition of Islamic learning, he said, and his father, Maulana Muhammad Sarfaraz Khan, had been a leading Muslim religious scholar. He had studied at the prestigious Dar ul-Ulum in Deoband, now in India, today probably the world's largest traditional madrasa, where he had been a disciple of the famous Maulana Husain Ahmad Madni, a fervent opponent of the Muslim League and the Partition of India. After the Partition, he had taught at various madrasas in Pakistan and authored almost fifty books.

Following in his father's footsteps, Maulana Zahid ul-Rashdi had received a traditional Islamic education in a madrasa in Gujranwala, and had been teaching for several years now at the madrasa attached to the Jamia Masjid, the town's major mosque. In addition to his scholarly work, he was associated with a leading religio-political party, the Deobandi Jamiat-e Ulema-e Islam, in which he had occupied various senior posts. But he had left active politics some years ago and had decided to occupy himself with intellectual pursuits instead. For this purpose, he had set up an educational centre in Gujranwala called the Al-Shariah Academy which, he explained, aimed at promoting reforms within madrasas as well as stimulating debate among the ulema community on a host of issues of contemporary import. Besides this, he wrote regular columns in two leading Pakistani Urdu newspapers.

Our conversation turned to the much-debated issue of reforms in the madrasas. Western governments and international NGOs were haranguing the Pakistani government for dragging its feet on reining in the country's madrasas. They claimed that Pakistan's madrasas had become hotbeds for training 'terrorists', a wild generalization that mistook a relatively few extremist religious schools as representing all the madrasas in the country. The ulema of the madrasas, quite naturally, saw the Pakistan government's feeble calls for madrasa reforms as highly suspect and as being dictated by its American benefactors.

Maulana sahib had written extensively about madrasa reforms. His own stand was, he explained, that the present system of the madrasas should be preserved and their autonomy should not be tampered with. But, at the same time, he stressed, the madrasas should appreciate contemporary demands and make such changes in their curricula and pedagogy as would enable would-be ulema to understand the needs and challenges of the times and to represent Islam in modern terms.

Another charge against Pakistani madrasas was that many of them were actively engaged in fanning intra-Muslim sectarian strife which, in parts of Pakistan, had taken on wildly bloody forms, resulting in bomb blasts and serial killings, in which literally tens of thousands had so far been killed. Many Deobandi mullahs and their madrasas were deeply complicit in this seemingly unending violence, their major targets being Shias, whom they branded as heretics and clearly outside the pale of Islam, as well as Barelvis who, like the Deobandis, were Sunnis, but upheld certain beliefs and practices associated with popular

Sufism that the Deobandis considered to be deviant. What, I
asked Maulana Sahib, did he, as a leading Pakistani Deobandi
scholar and political activist, feel about all this?

'As far as the links between madrasas and sectarian strife are
concerned,' he frankly confessed, 'the situation is not at all
encouraging.' In the vast majority of madrasas, he went on,
students were systematically trained to rebut other sects and to
engage in heated polemics. This, he felt was 'pathetic and
destructive'. His solution to the problem was for madrasas to
familiarize their students with the beliefs of the different
Muslim sects and to encourage them to engage in peaceful
intersectarian dialogue. 'Sectarian differences cannot be
eliminated, least of all by force, as some radical groups stupidly
believe,' he admitted. 'They have to be accepted, and can be
possibly reduced only through peaceful interaction. There's
simply no other way.'

Finally, and with some trepidation, I came to an issue that
I felt might be particularly sensitive to broach. What, I asked
Maulana sahib, did he feel about radical Islamists in Pakistan,
some leading Deobandis among them, who preached visceral
hatred of Hindus, Christians, Jews and other non-Muslims,
branding them all together as inveterate foes of Muslims and of
God as well? My mind flashed back to the Lashkar-e-Tayyaba
camp I had seen in Lahore earlier that day—the slogans and
stickers that called for jihad against the 'infidel Hindus' and the
book that proclaimed that India had at last been 'sandwiched'.

'To consider all non-Muslims as enemies and to seek to stir
up hatred against them,' the Maulana unhesitatingly replied, 'is
absolutely wrong. It is completely un-Islamic.' Contrary to
what numerous radical Islamists believed, he said, most non-
Muslims were not inherently anti-Islamic. 'Many of them are
willing to hear about Islam. They have the same concerns and
problems as we do, but Muslims have not bothered to reach
out to them. It's our fault, really. We have to try to reach out

to all people of goodwill, not alienate them by arbitrarily branding them as enemies.'

And that goodwill was amply evident in the warmth that the Maulana exuded, in his simplicity and kindness, and in the overwhelming hospitality of his family. That night, Ammar's mother had prepared an enormous special vegetarian meal: two types of rice, a bean curry, several vegetable preparations and home-made sweets, and this was to be repeated three times a day over the next three days that I spent in Gujranwala.

The next morning, I rang up Nani, who was then in Delhi, and told her where I was.

'Are you really in Gujranwala or are you joking?' she excitedly burst out.

'Oh, then you must look up the haveli where we grew up. Ask anyone, no problem at all. Everyone in our time in Gujranwala knew my father, Rai Bahadur Udai Bhan Batra. His sprawling mansion was among the biggest in the whole town. Even English officers, who would otherwise never enter Indian homes, considering it a terrible disgrace, would come to our haveli for a meal occasionally.'

I suppressed a snigger.

'And, yes,' she continued, 'take lots of photographs of the house. God knows what those Muslim wretches, who looted everything we possessed, have done with it.'

I asked Ammar's father if he knew anyone in town who might have heard of Nani's father, who had worked as a civil surgeon in Gujranwala in the 1920s and '30s. Nani claimed that he had been a notable *rais* or landlord and that he had saved the town from being taken over by a sudden epidemic of plague, for which he was rewarded by the British with the

honorific title of 'Rai Bahadur'. Were it not for him, Nani
boasted, perhaps the whole population of Gujranwala would
have perished.

Maulvi sahib shook his head emphatically. No, he had never
heard of him. Nor had the several elderly men who came to his
house that morning. Ammar made some telephone calls to
people who he thought might know better, but without any
luck. Clearly, the Rai Bahadur had not been even remotely as
reputed as Nani had made him out to be.

Later that day, Ammar took me to a half-built house where his
father's Al-Shariah Academy had its offices. The Academy,
explained a board placed at the entrance, was attempting
pioneering work in the area of madrasa reforms. It had set for
itself an impressive range of ambitious objectives: conducting
research and providing guidance on various issues facing
Muslims; promoting a spirit of ecumenism among the different
Muslim sects and schools of thought; countering the ideological,
social, economic and political challenges from the West; and
encouraging awareness among the clerics of contemporary
developments and the importance of mass media.

Ammar arranged for me to interact with the students of the
Academy—all madrasa graduates in their late teens or early
twenties, who had spent eight years or more in traditional
Deobandi madrasas and were now enrolled in the Academy to
study subjects that they had little or no familiarity with before:
English, elementary computer applications, a bit of world
history and geography, the basic teachings of other religions.
They were dressed in loose-flowing white shalwar-kameez, and
on their heads they wore the distinctive Deobandi-style round
skull-caps. They seemed a cheerful, chatty bunch.

Ammar introduced me to the students, and announced that I was to deliver a lecture shortly after. On what, I asked Ammar, completely taken back, not having been informed of this earlier. 'On anything you like,' he answered.

I gathered my thoughts for a while and then decided to speak on a subject on which I had done some research, and in which, I thought, the students might be interested—initiatives by Indian Muslim clerics to promote interfaith dialogue. I talked about the desperate need for intercommunal harmony as well as better relations between India and Pakistan, and of what role I felt religious leaders could play in that regard. Somewhat hesitatingly, I also critiqued the role of Right-wing Hindu and Muslim groups in fanning intercommunal violence and terrorism, although I feared that here I might be intruding into sensitive territory.

I rambled on for a good part of one hour, after which I was plied with a long spate of questions. 'Since you know so much about Islam and Muslims, have you converted to Islam?' asked one student. I had been confronted with that question innumerable times before by Muslim acquaintances in India, and I knew what reply to give. 'My faith is an entirely personal matter, between the Ultimate and myself,' I replied.

'No, religion is also a public thing and has a communitarian dimension,' the student shot back.

Sensing my embarrassment, Ammar quickly interrupted and cut him short, asking other students to raise their queries.

This they did, and with an eagerness that surprised me. They were curious to learn about Muslims in India and my research on the Indian madrasas. They wanted to know about India's achievements in the fields of science and technology, about efforts to promote harmony between different Muslim sects in India and between Hindus and Muslims, about movements in India that sought to challenge Western imperialism, and about the menace of Hindutva fascism.

One of the students, a plump buck-toothed boy who was evidently the class jester, winked naughtily and asked, 'And what, sir, do you think of Aishwarya Rai?'

My answer to that—that I did not watch Bollywood movies—was met with a loud collective gasp.

'How can that be, sir? In Pakistan, almost everyone is obsessed with Indian movies!' the lad exclaimed in disbelief.

This batch of would-be Muslim clerics seemed far more keen on discussing issues with me than the middle-class 'comrades' and NGO workers that Sheila had introduced me in Lahore, most of whom had asked me no questions at all. Those three hours of friendly exchange with them easily made the most lively, enriching and absorbing conversation I had during my entire trip. The students enthusiastically replied to my many queries, even those that, I felt, might be particularly sensitive. No, they said, they did not believe that all non-Muslims were 'enemies of Islam'. Radical Islamists who believed otherwise, they insisted, were wrong and their knowledge of the Quran, faulty. Nor did they agree with some fellow Pakistani Deobandis who called for the indiscriminate slaughter of Shias. All forms of terrorism, they averred—whether in the name of Islam or Hinduism, or perpetrated by the 'Imperialist Americans', 'Christian Crusaders' and 'Zionist Jews', or even by Muslims themselves—deserved to be sternly condemned. Yes, they felt, reforms were long overdue in the madrasas, and they pointed out the work of the Al-Shariah Academy as a major step in that direction. Yes, too, they heartily agreed, relations between India and Pakistan must improve. All of them insisted, however, that this could happen only if Kashmiris were allowed to determine their own political future.

The next two days that I spent in Ammar's house were well-deserved, sheer bliss: wonderful food, a warm bed in which I lazed under a mountain of razais, skimming through past issues of the Al-Shariah journal, and delightful company—that of Ammar, his father and a string of their maulvi colleagues who streamed into the house from early morning till late into the night.

On the evening of my last day in Gujranwala, I ambled through the bazaar that spread out in the warren of crooked lanes behind Ammar's house. The lanes were clogged with shoppers even though the bazaar was drowned in darkness as the electricity supply had been cut off. I hurried to an eatery at the end of the lane in order to flee the enveloping filth, stench and gut-wrenching chaos.

That was where I met Umar. An attractive young man dressed in a parrot-green sweater, he had a hawk-like nose, pale blue eyes and an almond-shaped, heavily freckled face. A thick mop of deep brown hair hid his forehead. He seemed to be in his early thirties. He sat alone at a table in a corner of the grubby room, whose walls were lined with thick, grey curtains of cobwebs. The other tables were all occupied and so I asked if I could join him. He smiled and pointed to the plastic chair in front of him, indicating that I could.

Shortly, a boy emerged from the kitchen and asked me what I wanted to order. He rattled off, with practised ease, a list of items that were available—a dozen varieties of kabab, chicken biryani, beef pulao, mutton and daal mix, curried lamb's liver, goat's hooves cooked with spinach and potatoes. No, he replied, looking quite taken aback when I asked, there was no vegetarian dish on the menu. The only thing that I could settle for, then, was tea.

Umar put down the newspaper he was reading. 'Pardon me,' he said, in impeccable English. 'I've never met a Pakistani vegetarian before. Are you from Gujranwala or elsewhere?'

I answered his question, wondering how he might react.

'India,' he excitedly burst out. 'I don't believe it!' He stretched his hand across the table to give me a firm handshake.

'Yaar,' he exclaimed, 'I'm from Srinagar, Kashmir!'

'Arey!' I screeched, unable to control my excitement. 'I know Srinagar well. I go there at least twice every year. I have loads of friends there.'

'Hey Raja!' Umar called out to the boy, who was disappearing into the kitchen. 'Fetch this brother an extra-special tea with lots of cream, and don't add any water to the milk.'

Umar kept my hand firmly clutched in his as we continued to talk. In a short while, it seemed as if we had long been the best of friends, meeting after a separation of many years. We spoke in English, which none of the men sitting in the room, who glared at us intensely, seemed to understand.

I drank my tea and Umar finished his dinner. 'It's best to talk elsewhere,' he lowered his voice and said, 'even though the men here may not understand what we are saying.'

We walked over to a dimly lit park close by, and Umar began telling me about himself. He had been born and brought up in Srinagar. The only son of his parents, he was in college when, in 1989, a group of Kashmiri youths had crossed over to Pakistan to receive armed training and returned to launch an armed struggle against Indian rule. Soon, it seemed, dreams of independence had fired the imagination of almost all Kashmiri Muslims, long suffering from what they saw as 'Indian imperialism'. Along with some of his friends, and without informing his parents, Umar had escaped to Pakistan. 'I could not take Indian atrocities any longer. I could not sit back and watch my people die,' he related. This was two years after the outbreak of the armed conflict in Kashmir, when state repression had reached brutal heights. He was then a lad of just eighteen.

For three months, Umar had stayed in a training camp in

Pakistan-administered Kashmir, learning to handle weapons that he was supposed to use after being sent back across the Line of Control. But, soon enough, his initial enthusiasm began to waver. 'I saw around me how some leaders, who were calling on the Kashmiris to sacrifice their lives for the cause of independence, were themselves leading lives of unimaginable luxury. Their own sons and daughters were kept carefully sheltered away in America and England, and it was us poor Kashmiris who were getting killed. Many of them used Islam just as a tool to serve their own interests,' he said. Then, one night, under cover of darkness, he had escaped from the training camp and fled to Islamabad.

Since then, Umar had taken up several odd jobs to scrape an existence. When I met him he was working as a travelling sales agent for a hosiery company. 'I came here to fight for freedom for Kashmir and now I am selling undergarments in Gujranwala! Can you imagine?' he said, his eyes brimming with tears. 'I've ruined my life completely.'

Umar had little complimentary to say about Pakistan, where he had spent almost fifteen years. 'Pakistan's claim of being an Islamic state and defender of Islam is absolute nonsense. In many ways, it is much worse than India,' he spat out. The country's educational system was pathetic, he said. 'Even Kashmir University, which was never among the better-known Indian universities, is far better than Punjab University in Lahore, Pakistan's premier university.' Pakistani politicians, he complained, were thoroughly corrupt. They had bartered the country to America, which he described as 'the greatest enemy of Islam'. Economic conditions in Pakistan-administered Kashmir, he went on, were miserable, barring the few pockets of prosperity that had emerged as a result of remittances from immigrants who worked in sweatshops in Britain, and as construction labourers and taxi-drivers in the Gulf. And Pakistan's proclaimed commitment to the Kashmir cause, he added, was 'as empty a hoax as India's'. 'They both want our land and aren't at all bothered about our people,' he said.

Fifteen years had passed since Umar had left Kashmir, since he had last seen his parents. Freedom for Kashmir seemed as remote a prospect as before, but, like most other Kashmiris I knew, the hope that one day their land would be independent still remained burning deep within him. 'It's best for all, for us Kashmiris, of course, but also for India and Pakistan, that Kashmir be free,' he mused.

Umar pined to go back to Kashmir. 'I've vowed that I won't die in Pakistan,' he said as a torrent of tears spilt out of his eyes. I took his hand in mine and pressed it against my chest. 'Brother,' he choked as his wet cheeks turned a pale red, 'I want to live and die for my own suffering Kashmiri people. How long can I carry on like this, travelling like a tramp, selling hosiery items? This isn't why I came to Pakistan.'

But, going back to Kashmir, he knew, was almost impossible. He had crossed over to Pakistan without a passport, and so he could not legally return to India. If he tried to slip back into Indian-administered Kashmir, he said, there was no guarantee that he would not be killed—shot dead by Pakistani or Indian soldiers or even by Kashmiri militants, who might treat him as a renegade.

'Brother, think of a way to help me get back home, back to my parents,' he stuttered and burst out sobbing.

eight

---

southwards, to sindh

I took the bus back to Lahore the next morning. Sheila was packing her bags when I got to her house. She was off the next day to the quake-devastated town of Muzaffarabad in Pakistan-administered Kashmir, taking with her cash and boxes of medicines and bundles of clothes that she had collected from friends and relatives to distribute in a village near the town.

I wished I could accompany her, and she said that I possibly could. I had travelled widely in the Indian-administered part of Kashmir, and I wanted to see how things were on the other side of the blood-stained Line of Control. But, then, my visa did not permit me to do so. It was almost impossible for Indian citizens to get permission to visit the area even if they had the right contacts in the right places, which Sheila apparently did, because of what she said were her 'feudal' family connections, and which she unabashedly used on occasion. She could ask some top bureaucrat relative in Islamabad to do the needful, she offered, but I declined. An Indian applying for permission to visit Pakistan-administered Kashmir, or Azad ('Free') Kashmir as the Pakistanis called it, was bound to raise the suspicions of Pakistan's deadly and much-feared Inter-

Services Intelligence. And that was something that I could well do without.

It was decided, then, that Sheila would travel to Kashmir and that I would head in the other direction, southwards, to Hyderabad in Sindh, and from there to other places in that province. No sooner had that been settled a feverish debate broke out among Sheila's neighbours, who had come to her home to help her pack. Ziba decided that interior Sindh was much too dangerous for any outsider to travel around in. 'It's infested with dacoits and is completely lawless. And they hate us Punjabis,' she protested, wrinkling her nose in contempt. Husain, her husband, agreed. He had served for some years as an army officer in Sindh and, after his retirement, the government had offered him a sizeable chunk of land in northern Sindh at a ridiculous rate of fifty rupees an acre. That was not unusual. Most retired army officers—mainly Punjabis, Pakistan's dominant ethnic group—got such handsome benefits, he said. But, he had refused. 'The Sindhis resent our presence in their land. They think we Punjabis are a colonial power,' he frankly confessed.

'And why not?' interrupted Sheila angrily. 'Everything in this country is controlled by us Punjabis. We've used Pakistani nationalism and Islam as a tool to legitimize Punjabi hegemony over the other nationalities of this country. No wonder there are stirrings of revolt in Sindh, in Baluchistan, and now among the Pakhtuns.'

Ziba snorted in disgust. She refused to see any merit in what Sheila was saying. 'Hai hai!' she burst out. 'Don't listen to her. These Leftists keep jabbering like this, defaming our country. And what on earth are you going to Hyderabad for?' she turned to me and asked. 'There's nothing to see in that hellish place. Except probably for the one traffic light in that entire decaying city!'

But, since Sheila was leaving for Kashmir I had to leave

Lahore. The only other places for which I had visas—Hyderabad and Moenjo Daro—were both in Sindh, and so, finally, much to the disapproval of Sheila's neighbours, it was decided that I should leave for Hyderabad that evening. But just as that had been settled, another bout of bickering broke out. 'You must be either a masochist or quite out of your mind if you think you should go to Hyderabad by train,' Ziba protested when I mentioned that my tight budget did not allow me to fly.

'You have no idea how despicable the train system in Pakistan is,' she went on, convinced now that I harboured a perverse desire to torture myself.

'You could be drugged and robbed, who knows?' Husain interrupted, supporting his wife's case. 'Newspapers regularly report stories like that'.

'The length of tracks in the country has decreased by fifty kilometres since the British left,' Ziba helpfully added, 'and the trains are decades-old with cramped boxes for carriages, relics of the Raj.'

'What nonsense are you talking?' Husain butted in angrily. 'I've heard that the tracks have actually increased by fifty kilometres since the Partition, and now we have nice, new Chinese-made trains.'

Still, Husain remained adamant that there was no way that I was taking the train to Hyderabad.

Sheila brusquely countered her neighbours. 'Yogi must go by train,' she said. 'He must understand what the real Pakistan is.'

Finally, a compromise was reached. It was decided that I would indeed travel to Hyderabad by train, with the caveat that I should take the Karakoram Express, touted as Pakistan's finest train, that connected Lahore with Karachi, and which, Sheila assured me, was 'quite safe'.

Lahore railway station

We drove to the Lahore station, a grand colonial red-brickwork edifice. A serpentine queue stood before the ticket counter. Sheila waved out to an elderly man hauling a pile of files. He was a leader of a worker's union with which she was associated. She rushed up to the window, ignoring the angry protests of the people in the queue, and asked the man to come out.

I was introduced to Mr Khalid. Sheila explained to him that I was from India, and he broke out into a hearty grin.

'I am from India, too,' he said, giving me a warm handshake. 'I was born in Ambala in 1940 and our family came to Pakistan when I was seven. Both my parents were slaughtered while crossing the border but, thanks to Allah, my siblings and I managed to reach Lahore safely.'

I gulped in embarrassment and lowered my gaze. Although he probably did not mean it, I felt that I, as an Indian, had been somehow complicit in that orgy of violence that had erupted two decades before I was born and that had taken the lives of his parents.

There were no tickets available for a berth on the train, Mr Khalid said. But, he helpfully added, because I was from India and was also Sheila's friend, he could certainly manage something. He went back behind the counter, tapped away at his computer and printed out a ticket. 'It's for a seat, as there are no berths available, and so you won't be able to lie down. But that's all I could manage,' he explained.

The train was to depart in less than half an hour, and so we rushed into the station, pushing through knots of passengers idling in the sun in the porch outside, and shoving against droves of porters in red cloaks, bearing little mountains of luggage on their turbaned heads. The 42 Down Karakoram Express, painted in bold green and yellow stripes, was waiting at the platform and I scrambled in. Like most Pakistani trains, this one was made in China and, it seemed, made to suit smaller-built Chinese passengers, not burly Pakhtuns and Punjabis. Its roof was barely six feet high, and the corridors were so narrow as to allow just one passenger at a time to squeeze through and with considerable difficulty.

As I trudged down the compartment looking for my seat, the train pulled out of the station, and I saw Sheila reduced to a faint waving dot in the distance.

I nudged into my seat—a hard plank of wood, two feet broad and bereft of a back-rest. I stuck my face to the window, watching Lahore pass by. We sped past the squalid suburbs of the decaying city, past little townships with their ramshackle houses and makeshift tents fringed with massive towers of garbage. Then, an hour later, as the sky began to turn grey, we were out in the open countryside. The flat plains were dissected into little squares by rows of slim eucalyptus and giant banyan trees, marking individual plots. The land was cut through by canals, brimming with water that glimmered in the diffused evening light. These had been built by the British and had transformed the Punjab, the Land of the Five Rivers, into what had famously been called the breadbasket of the entire subcontinent.

I turned away from the window as darkness rapidly fell and a thick blanket of mist clouded out all vision save for the faint refracted light of electric bulbs in farmers' homes and the hearths burning in their fields. I glanced around the coach at the other passengers. Directly in front of me sat an overfed middle-aged man, with a beard of a few sparse hairs that grew out of his chin like stalks of straw, and a pair of dark, angry-looking eyes. The fierceness of his expression was amplified by the absence of a moustache, the dark rings of *kohl* that circled his eyes and the thick ring of blubber around his neck. He held a richly ornamented copy of the Quran in front of him, and he rocked forward and backward, reading out from it, muttering verses in a low drone. The four berths on the other side of the aisle were occupied by a pair of hefty, pink-skinned Pakhtuns, a young lad in a T-shirt and jeans, and a bald one-eyed man. Barring the Pakhtuns, who boisterously chattered away in guttural Pashtu, of which I could understand not a word, my fellow-passengers maintained a studied, stultifying silence.

I had left behind my reading material in Lahore, expecting that I would pass the twelve-hour journey gazing at the scenery outside, conversing with co-passengers and, hopefully, snatching a few hours of sleep. Nothing was now visible out of the window, and the latter two options had been ruled out. The men around me were definitely not the sort one could easily chat up, and sleeping on the stiff, backless seat was impossible. To keep myself awake and amused, I fiddled around with my cellphone, sending messages to various friends. When I had exhausted the list of people to whom I really wanted to write, I began to compose lengthy missives to remote acquaintances.

Just then, my cellphone rang. It was Ram Singh, a Hindu from Sindh whom I had befriended on a chat site on the Internet, although I had never met him. He had recently graduated from university and was working with an NGO in southern Sindh, where a sizeable number of Hindus, mainly Dalits, still lived.

'Namastey Ram-ji!' I greeted him excitedly.

He would be waiting for me the next morning at the railway station in Hyderabad, he said. He insisted that I stay with him, but I replied that Sheila had already arranged for my stay with a friend of hers.

'Namastey!' I said again when we finished talking.

No sooner had I placed my cellphone back in my pocket than the fierce-looking man opposite me interrupted his Quranic recitation and asked, 'Were you speaking to a Hindu?'

I looked up at him, stunned by his question and the tone in which he had asked it. In the darkness I could make out the deep furrows that creased his narrow forehead as he frowned angrily. His stony eyes, twisted under their hood-like lids, were fixed intently on me. He had not spoken to me before, and, indeed, had not even acknowledged my presence, so engrossed had he been in his rituals. Now, it seemed, I had become for him an object of some curiosity, a cause, perhaps, of considerable consternation.

'Yes, indeed I was,' I answered hesitatingly, shuddering at the thought of what might transpire next.

'Oh. I see. Hmm. And are you a Hindu, too?' he asked inquisitorially.

I could see the other passengers in the compartment turn towards us.

'I'm from India,' I answered.

'But that still does not answer my question. What are you? A Hindu or a Muslim?'

I had half a mind to tell the man to mind his business.

Of course, I could not, knowing that this would make him livid.

'I'm neither a Hindu nor a Muslim. I'm just a human being,' I replied as politely as was possible, faking a broken smile.

'But that's nothing special,' he shot back. 'Humans we all are,' he continued, turning to the other passengers, as if seeking their approval. 'You must follow some religion or the other.'

'Not really, I don't,' I replied, this time not making any effort to conceal my irritation, and went back to toying with my cellphone.

I did not sleep for even a moment that night. The unpleasant encounter with the man, the cramped, stiff seat, the bitter cold against which I had nothing to protect myself—having erred in assuming that Pakistan Railways provided for blankets and sheets for passengers in air-conditioned coaches—made sleep impossible. I skipped dinner, not because I was not hungry but because all that was available was chicken biryani with bits of cucumber, packed in a flimsy cardboard box and priced at a ridiculously high one hundred rupees. And, then, there was the accumulating, deafening din. The bald one-eyed man coughed and wheezed and spat incessantly; the young lad snored violently; the two Pakthuns, who stayed awake till early morning playing cards, roared alternately in anger and in jest; and my interrogator let off periodic, particularly pungent, masala-odoured farts.

So, I sat on my seat, playing verbal games in my mind and sketching cartoons of my co-passengers in my notebook. Just past midnight, the train stopped at Bahawalpur, and I got off to stretch my legs and hoping to get a bite. The platform was empty, save for an elderly turbaned man accompanied by three heavily veiled women who pushed past me and climbed into our compartment. Beyond the station, through the dense curtain of fog, I spied the contours of a minaret and the turrets of what looked like an ancient mosque. There were, I knew, numerous interesting historical monuments to see in this town in impoverished southern Punjab along the border with Rajasthan—the palace of the nawabs, scores of old madrasas and mosques, and the crumbling ramparts of forts, and then, in the surrounding sandy wastes of the Cholistan desert, a vast number of ancient Sufi shrines. I had half a mind to get off the train, to escape the tedium of the journey and to visit the town that I had read much about. But, I had no visa for Bahawalpur, and although I could have taken the risk of visiting the town without it, it was just too early in the morning to seriously consider that possibility.

Whiskers of pale orange light peeped out of the heavy curtain of darkness in the distant sky two hours later. We were now traversing through northern Sindh, and it was much warmer here than in Punjab. The countryside was harsh and unexciting—an endless, flat plain that stretched till the cloud-specked horizon, and was, for the most part, sandy and parched. Occasionally, small green patchwork-like fields and clumps of palm trees broke the drab brown monotony. Hidden behind long mud walls, the villages we passed seemed uniformly characterized by neglect and desperate poverty.

At eight in the morning, the train pulled into Hyderabad station. I heaved my bags from below my seat and bade farewell to the men with whom I had shared the compartment. The one-eyed man and the young lad grunted in reply, somewhat reluctantly. The man seated opposite me pretended not to notice my departure. But the garrulous Pakhtuns insisted on carrying my bags and depositing them on the platform. They pressed my hand against their chests and bowed their heads slightly before they lunged back into the train as it chugged off towards Karachi, its final destination.

Ram Singh was at the station to receive me. He hung a garland of roses round my neck and gave me a boisterous hug. Viewed on my computer through the web-camera, he had seemed somewhat stern, even sullen. But now, as he stood before me, he hardly matched the image that I had formed of him in my mind. A Hindu Rajput from the Thar, the desert that covered large parts of southern Sindh and western Rajasthan, he was stunningly good-looking. He was almost six feet tall, with a solid frame and finely chiselled features. His eagle-like nose suggested a certain authority and firmness, as did his large, coal-black eyes. These were set against a pair of ruby-red lips and an endearing smile that revealed two gold-capped teeth. A red and blue cotton *ajrak*, a lengthy sheet decorated with a block design, was thrown over his broad shoulders and around his sky-blue kameez.

Ram-ji, for that was how I addressed him, took me by the hand and we walked out of the station. He indicated a Hindu temple on the other side of the street, its white-washed cone-shaped *shikara* visible from behind a low wall. 'Many Hindus live here,' he explained, thinking that this might interest me.

We headed to a nearby tea-stall where Reza, Sheila's friend in Hyderabad with whom I was to stay, was waiting for us. I recognized him from the photographs that Sheila had shown me: tall, lean and slightly bent, with a small, dark face and teeth stained grey from chewing tobacco. He had come along with half a dozen friends, including, I noted from their names, two Hindus.

Hugs and pleasantries were exchanged, and I was bundled

into a jeep that hurtled down a road lined with crater-sized potholes towards Qasimabad which, Reza explained, was the largely ethnic Sindhi part of town. We passed by what seemed the empty basin of what had once been a vast lake, surrounded by a range of hills of rotting garbage. On either side of the road stood unpainted, half-built brick houses, fringed with stagnant, fly-infested sewers. Their walls were occupied by political graffiti, in the distinctive Sindhi script, that is closer to Arabic than the Persianized Urdu, hailing particular political parties and heroes. Some denounced Punjabi domination and called for Sindhi independence. 'Long Live Sindh!' they boldly cried out. Narrow unpaved lanes led off the main road into residential localities that, it was clearly evident, lacked many of the most basic civic amenities. The traffic followed no rules at all, and I spotted no policemen. We passed the city's monumental single traffic light that Ziba, Sheila's friend in Lahore, had mockingly mentioned. It had long since been rendered dysfunctional. A sea of filth and squalor seemed to envelop the entire city. If some parts of Lahore that I had visited were simply unbearable, this city must be, I had already concluded, a little piece of Hell.

I spent much of my time in Hyderabad with Ram-ji. He was from the Hindu Sodha caste, a branch of the Rajput Parmars who, along with the Soomras and the Sammas, two Rajput clans that had converted to Islam, had ruled Thar Parkar, a largely desert tract in southern Sindh bordering Gujarat, till the sixteenth century, when it was conquered by the Baluchi Kalhoros. A sizeable proportion of Thar Parkar's inhabitants had converted to Islam over the centuries, but they still retained much of their pre-Islamic culture. Thar Parkar had

remained Pakistan's only Hindu-majority district till long after
the Partition, but in the course of wars with India in 1965 and
then in 1971, several thousand Hindus from the area had
migrated to India, and a smaller number of Muslims from
adjoining Kutch and Barmer in India had shifted to Pakistan.
This had changed the demographic balance of the district, but
Hindus still remained more than 40 per cent of its population
of around a million. The vast majority of them belonged to
various Dalit castes, though the main landowners were Hindu
Sodhas, Arbab Muslims—converts from the Sodhas—and
Baluchis.

One morning, Ram-ji decided to take me on what he called
a tour of 'Hindu Hyderabad'. We stepped out of his one-room
house and into the narrow lane outside. A line of women,
chiffon dupattas carelessly thrown around their heads, stood at
the communal hand-pump, with plastic buckets and mud pots
at their feet, waiting for their turn to fill water. On the
threshold of a hovel sat a dark woman, her legs stretched over
the open drain that ran along her house, intently at work,
slicing a bamboo pole with a scythe that she wielded with
practised dexterity. She was dressed differently from the other
women in the area. She wore a mustard-yellow blouse that
reached till her elbow. Instead of the pantaloon-like shalwar
worn by Sindhi Muslim women, she wore a long, heavily
pleated crimson skirt, decorated with leaves, flowers and buds.
Her ear lobes drooped under the weight of chunky silver
earrings crafted in the shape of parrots, which reached almost
to her neck. Encircling her nose and covering half of her right
cheek was a golden bangle-sized *nathni*, speckled with little
green and red stones. This was balanced with the help of a
thick black chain that connected it to a pin tucked into her hair
above her ear. Tied around her ankles were thick silver *payals*
with little bells that danced and jingled as she went about her
work vigorously. In the darkness of the room behind her, I

could see neat stacks of cane plates, brooms and baskets.

'She's a Hindu,' pointed out Ram-ji. 'Sita behen, meet this guest of ours from Hindustan.'

Sita behen abruptly halted her work and hurriedly draped her dupatta over her head, adjusting it so that it fell over her nose and revealed of her face only her grey-brown lips and her heavily tattooed chin.

'Arey, don't be embarrassed, sister. He's our brother, after all, from India,' Ram-ji admonished her playfully. 'At least say *Ram-Ram* to him.'

Sita behen let out a barely audible giggle from under her veil.

'Oh ho, now stop all this drama,' Ram-ji scolded her. 'In front of me you don't hesitate to behave like a witch sometimes!'

Sita behen let the scythe fall at her feet and buried her face in her hands. '*Ram-Ram sa*,' she whispered and broke out into a muffled laughter.

'Arey Sita-ji,' I said in a low voice as I squatted on my haunches near her feet, 'nothing to be shy of at all. I'm from India and I'm writing a book about the people of Pakistan. Many Indians don't know anything about the Hindus of Pakistan—that they even exist—and so, whatever you tell me would be very useful.'

Sita behen slid back the dupatta from her head. 'What about the Hindus?' she asked with an unexpected boldness. 'The Banias, the Brahmins and the Rajputs treat us like *achhoot*s, Untouchables. To them we are Hindus only when it comes to voting for their candidates. Otherwise, we mean nothing to them.' Turning her head to Ram-ji, she said, 'Is it not true, babu-ji? You are a Sodha Rajput, from a high caste, but although you treat us like equals, your people think we Gurgulas are low and despicable, is it not?'

Ram-ji nodded hesitantly. 'That is true, sister, sadly.'

'We Gurgulas,' Sita behen went on, her temper rising, 'have been doing bamboo work since time immemorial. That's the work of our caste. We make baskets and plates for others. If we did not make their brooms, how would they keep their homes and streets clean? And, although they sometimes call us fellow Hindus, especially just before elections, the Banias, the Brahmins and the Rajputs think we are no better than animals.'

A small crowd had gathered around us, attracted by Sita behen's loud harangue. Pointing to a bearded vegetable-vendor silently observing us, she mocked, 'See, those people are Muslims. But they also treat us as Untouchables, although their religion teaches just the opposite. They refuse to allow us to enter their eateries, and, if we do, they keep a separate set of glasses and plates for us, which we have to wash ourselves after use. Muhammad Sahib made Bilal, a freed black slave, his close companion. He treated the rich and the poor as one, but these Muslims here are not real Muslims. They are children of the Hindus, and continue to follow Hindu customs.'

The vegetable-vendor glanced at me fleetingly and bent his head low in embarrassment, shuffling his hands about him.

'Why, Husain bhai, am I not speaking the truth? Am I lying or what?' Sita behen chided him, but in a friendly way.

'What you say is right, Sita apa,' interrupted a man in the crowd, who looked like a maulvi with a skull-cap on his head.

'See,' she said triumphantly, 'I always speak the truth.'

We trudged down a series of lanes till we got to a bustling market, where vendors were selling fresh vegetables and fruits and hunks of meat, on which armies of flies hungrily feasted. Pushing through the milling crowd and swerving to save ourselves from the onward rush of donkey-carts, cycles and autorickshaws, we entered a broad road. This, Ram-ji explained, was Hirabad, the main commercial centre of Hyderabad before the Partition. On both sides of the road stood the crumbling ruins of colonial-style mansions, only a hint of their former glory evident from their cracked stained glass windows, their badly chipped carved pillars, their latticed window screens and their wrought iron staircases that led up to their terraces.

'This is where the rich Hindu Banias once stayed. The entire economy was in their control,' Ram-ji went on. 'See, you can see the faint traces of an *Om* and two *swastik*s on that building. And there,' he pointed to a badly scarred mansion that was now used as a laundry, 'you can see, in Urdu, Hindi and English, the words *Hingorani Nivas*. Lala Surender Hingorani, who lived there, was one of the richest merchants of Hyderabad. He had three cotton factories in Sukkur and a vast estate of over five hundred acres near Dadu.'

In 1947, almost a third of Hyderabad's population was Hindu. For centuries, their relations with the Muslim majority had been fairly harmonious. Many of the town's hospitals, schools and other charitable institutions, which still existed, had been set up by Hindu traders. Following the Partition, most of the wealthy Hindus of Hyderabad fled to India. Only some of them, mainly the Amils and the Lohanas, remained in the town after Pakistan came into being, Ram-ji said. A few had flourished in the new country but, particularly in the aftermath of the destruction of the Babri Masjid in India in 1992 and the ensuing mass violence against Muslims across the border, what had been a trickle of Sindhi Hindu migrants to India had threatened to turn into a flood. Hundreds of Hindu temples, many of them small roadside shrines, others large, unused structures, had been destroyed all across Pakistan, including in Sindh, where most of the country's Hindus lived. Mercifully, Ram-ji said, less than a score of Hindus was killed in the violence, nothing compared to the thousands of Muslims who were slaughtered by Hindu mobs in India. Yet, these attacks and, to add to them, the growing presence of radical

Islamist outfits in parts of Sindh that had hitherto remained largely immune to their appeal, were increasing Hindu insecurities. Cases of kidnapping of rich Hindu businessmen for hefty ransoms were not infrequent. There had been several incidents of kidnapped Hindu men being shot dead because their families could not cough up the money demanded for their release. In many parts of interior Sindh, Hindu traders could survive only if they paid regular 'protection money' to armed gangs, who were in the service of local landlords. It was, thus, hardly surprising that many Sindhi Hindus wanted to flee to India. Many had already done so, in fact.

'Some Islamist extremists think that kidnapping or even killing Hindus and driving them out of Pakistan is not just allowed in their religion, but even demanded by it,' Ram-ji went on. Increasing numbers of Sindhi Hindu merchants had begun to send at least one of their sons to settle in India and set up business there, so that in the event of conditions for the Hindus in Sindh worsening they could, if they felt compelled to, migrate *en masse* across the border. But this was not an option for the vast majority of Sindh's Hindus. Eighty per cent or more of the Hindus in the province were desperately impoverished Dalits, like Sita behen, the Gurgula bamboo-worker. Procuring a passport, travelling more than a thousand miles to Islamabad to apply for a visa at the Indian High Commission, and then taking the train from Lahore to Amritsar was much beyond their meagre means. But, even if they managed to get to India, where would they go? Who would employ them? 'And,' Ram-ji added matter-of-factly, 'in India, too, they would still be treated as Untouchables.'

nine

among 'untouchables' in the 'land of the pure'

Ram-ji offered to take me on a tour of several historical monuments scattered around Hyderabad and on a boat ride down the Indus, but time was short—I had given myself just two more days for the town and I wanted to use them to learn more about the Hindus of Sindh instead.

I asked Ram-ji where I could buy books on the subject. He shrugged. As far as he knew, barring some scattered news reports, there was no written matter available on the Pakistani Hindus. But it was not just the country's Hindus about whom nothing had been written, he explained. 'You won't find any books dealing with a whole host of poor Muslim castes in Pakistan either—the Mohana boat-men of the Indus, the Mallah fishermen, the Siddis, descendants of African slaves, the Raima and Hingorja cattle-grazers, the Balashahi sweepers, the Shaikh weavers, and who knows how many hundreds more? Our historiography continues to be extremely élitist, besides being fixated with what is called the ideology of Pakistan, the theory of Hindus and Muslims being allegedly two separate and antagonistic nations.' The state of social science research in

the country, he said, was pathetic. Moreover, most Pakistani
Hindus were illiterate Dalits, and there were few well-educated
people among them who could write their stories or voice their
sorrows.

We spent that day strolling through the streets of the town.
Walking past the enormous Ghanta Ghar, we entered a clock
tower with a quaint Victorian-style steeple, the pretentiously
named Shahi Bazaar, the 'Royal Market'. We stopped at a
small Shiva temple located in a lane that led off the main street,
and descended a short flight of marble-topped stairs. 'Even
now, sixty years after Independence, and despite the fact that
the Hindus of Pakistan are a vulnerable minority, Dalits are
forbidden by the Brahmin priest to enter this temple,' Ram-ji
explained as we passed through the entrance door.

The open courtyard of the temple led into a dark inner
chamber, where a little clay lamp burnt at the foot of a phallic-
shaped stone, shedding a pale ochre glow that hesitatingly
pierced the darkness of the tomb-like room. From a plank of
wood above hung a steel pot, from which water dripped through
an invisible hole at its base on to the stone, and then trickled
through a channel coiled around the base of the stone, symbolizing
the *yoni*, the female reproductive organ. A thick spiral of smoke
silently swirled out from a bunch of incense-sticks stuffed in a
brass container. As my eyes grew used to the darkness, I
noticed, sitting at the far end of the chamber, a mendicant
deep in meditation. A saffron sheet covered his loins, and his
chest was bare. In his ears he sported a pair of wooden earrings
the size of bangles. His hair, which reached down to his
shoulders, was a tangled, unkempt, unwashed mess, and his
beard, largely black, seemed to occupy most of his face. He was
seated in the lotus-pose, with his eyes tightly shut and his
palms placed on his knees, like a stone Buddha, supremely
oblivious to the maddening chaos of the city around him.

Some blocks away from the Shiva temple was the sweepers' locality, where three dozen families belonging to the Valmiki caste lived. The traditional occupation of the Valmikis was sweeping and clearing away dead animals. Because of their association with dirt and death, they were regarded as the lowest of the low, and were placed by Hindus at the bottom of the caste hierarchy. The Valmikis of Hyderabad continued in the profession of their forefathers, but since most of them, men and women, were now government-paid employees of the Hyderabad Municipality, they were economically somewhat better off than before. The covered drains, lined with bleaching powder, that ran along the sides of the well-swept lane that led into their locality, the whitewashed walls of their homes and the modestly sized, yet neatly kept, Valmiki temple located in the centre of their settlement, provided a refreshing contrast to the nauseating squalor that spread like some deadly vermin throughout the parts of Hyderabad that I had hitherto visited.

We shook off our sandals and climbed into the temple, a one-roomed structure with a Hindu-style shikara on top, shaped like a multi-layered pyramid. At the centre was placed a life-sized painted clay statue of a man dressed like a *sadhu*. His long shock of wiry hair was bunched up in a knot, and a saffron robe covered his body, revealing half of his hairless chest. His body was painted a cheery strawberry pink. In his hands he held a book, on which were inscribed the words *Shree Ramayan* in the Sindhi script. Slabs of marble were built into the inner walls around the statue, bearing the names of devotees who had donated money for its construction.

'This is Valmiki Maharaj, author of the Ramayana, from whom we are descended and from whom we derive our name,' explained Diler, a toothless Valmiki elder who had followed us inside. He bent low before the statue and folded his hands in salutation. The contrast between Valmiki's pale pink, almost European, pigmentation and that of the old man who claimed to be his descendant was stark. Diler's leathery, wrinkled skin was cocoa-brown, approaching black, like the other Valmikis I had seen as I had wandered through the settlement outside. The 'Aryan'-featured representation of the putative ancestor of the Valmikis that sat before me represented, it seemed to me, the subtle transformation of an ancient pre-Aryan tradition and its gradual absorption into Brahminical Hinduism, that was based on the myth of Aryan supremacy and the cult of the fair-skinned Aryan race.

The temple was, quite evidently, new, and so was, as Ramji later explained, the cult of Valmiki among the sweepers of Hyderabad. For centuries, he said, the sweepers, derisively termed variously as Bhangis, Mehtars, Halalkhors, Lal Begis, Balashahis and Chuhras, had been shut out of the Hindu caste system, considered by caste Hindus to be polluted and polluting. Over time, they had evolved their own forms of worship that combined the pre-Aryan customs of their ancestors and some Hindu beliefs and customs, to which was added a host of Muslim practices. They buried their dead in Muslim fashion and took out *tazia*s in the Islamic month of Muharram, marking the martyrdom of Imam Husain, the grandson of the Prophet Muhammad. At the same time, they revered, to the point of deification, their patron-saint, originally known as Bala Shah, in little shrines that they built in their own segregated localities, being forbidden, on pain of death, from entering Hindu temples.

Bala Shah was known by various other names as well: Lal Beg, Salal Beg, Samali Beg, Bala Pir, Bal Rikh, Lal Guru, Lal Khan, Miran Shah, and, recently, Bal Miki or Valmiki. About this person, as about his real name, confusion abounded. Some claimed that he had actually been a Buddhist monk by the name of Lal Bhikkhu, while others believed that he had been a Muslim saint, perhaps an Ismaili Shia missionary who operated in a Hindu guise.

Contrary to what the 'upper' castes expected and made every effort to ensure, the sweepers did not simply passively accept their oppression. Legends associated with Bala Shah clearly suggested that many sweepers stubbornly resisted 'upper' caste hegemony. In his entry on the religion of the sweepers of north-west India in the *Encyclopaedia of Religion and Ethics*, published in 1913, W. Youngson analysed the sweepers' oral narratives, the *kursi namah*s associated with Bala Shah, bringing out two striking aspects. First, the insistence of many sweepers that they were neither Hindus nor Muslims but a separate community. And, second, that, contrary to what others thought of them, they were, in fact, superior to both Hindus and Muslims in the eyes of God.

Youngson rendered a certain kursi namah thus:

> *God said: 'O Bala, be wise: understand and know*
> *That on the resurrection day their deeds*
> *Will bring these to despairing grief.*
> *I'll make of Hindu and Muslim faiths a sea.*
> *Beyond it I will make a heaven that they*
> *Shall see but enter not.*
> *The burning sun will come within a spear and a quarter's*
> *length.*
> *The dread alarms of Hell will compass them.*
> *The worshippers of Ram and of Rahim*
> *Will hide themselves in dark despair.*
> *But thine will cross themselves secure, in safety.*
> *They will enter Heaven at last.'*

While this kursi namah articulated the claim of the sweepers as being superior to the Hindus and the Muslims, it subtly accepted the logic of the caste system and the Brahminical ideology, at the same time mocking the Brahmins for their duplicity. This would facilitate twentieth-century Hindu revivalists in their attempts to incorporate the sweepers of northern India into the wider Hindu fold without, however, changing their social status.

It was only around the 1920s that Bala Shah began to be identified with the author of the Hindu epic *Ramayana*, the Brahmin Valmiki (or Balmiki, as he was called in Hindi, Urdu and Sindhi) as a result of a subtle linguistic transformation. This was the time when Hindu and Muslim leaders were engaged in a frantic race for numbers, and when the revivalist Hindu Arya Samaj movement began targeting Dalit communities, such as the sweepers of Punjab and Sindh, who were outside the pale of Brahminical Hinduism, in order to draw them into the Hindu fold. The Arya Samajists twisted the name 'Bala Shah' into 'Balmiki' or 'Valimki' and invented the story that the sweepers were actually his descendants. On their part, the sweepers readily accepted this new theory for, through it, they could try to claim a higher status within the Hindu caste hierarchy.

But, of course, the myth had not worked out in quite that way, for the Valmikis of Hyderabad were still treated with utter contempt, as Untouchables, by not just caste Hindus and Muslims but also by the other various Dalit castes. Only Valmikis worshipped at the temple in the Valmiki mohalla, admitted Diler. 'Our caste follows us like a dark shadow wherever we go, until we meet our death,' he mumbled through his toothless gums. 'I thought things would be different in India, but a nephew of mine went there and found that in India, the holy land of the Hindus, we are treated in just the same way,' he added. It was little wonder, he said, that almost all the sweepers in Pakistani Punjab had converted to Christianity, as had a large section of the community in Sindh. 'In contrast to others, the *padris* treat us as fellow human beings. They educate our children and provide us with health facilities, so why should we not accept their religion?' Diler asked. I grunted in agreement.

If he felt Christianity was the best available option for his people, I asked Diler, why had he not converted too? He tugged at his cigarette, shut his eyes as he curled the smoke around in his toothless mouth, and thought for a while. 'I'm an old man now, and for the last seventy-five years I have been worshipping Valmiki Maharaj every day,' he replied. 'It's too late for me to learn about another religion. If our children want to become Christians, to be educated, to get better jobs, to abandon this accursed ancestral profession of our caste, I don't mind at all. Let them.' He picked up an insect crawling up his shalwar and gently blew it away. 'My philosophy is simple', he carried on. 'God is one, no matter what name you call Him by. If one religion treats you badly, then what is the harm in adopting another that treats you with respect?' After all, he explained, that was how most of what was Pakistan had become Muslim over the centuries. Many Pakistanis were descendants of Hindus from oppressed castes, who had accepted Islam to gain equality and self-respect, which the Brahmins had denied them.

In a middle-class locality in Hyderabad, carefully sequestered from the din and squalor of the city, lived M. Prakash, a leading Hindu advocate and member of the Pakistan Government's Evacuee Trust Property Board that controlled the vast properties left behind in Sindh by Hindu merchants who had migrated to India in the wake of the Partition. As we drove to his house, Ram-ji warned, 'The Board is rife with corruption. But don't talk about it.'

Mr Prakash was getting ready to attend a meeting, but he welcomed us in. We settled down on lacquered chairs set around a cane table in the garden. The conversation veered round to the issue of Hindus in Pakistan. Mr Prakash reconfirmed what Sita behen had said earlier that day. 'There is really no overall Hindu identity or feeling of unity among the different Hindu castes in Pakistan. The upper castes have little or no concern for the Dalits, most of whom are desperately poor haris, landless labourers,' he rued. In some parts of Sindh where Hindus lived in significant numbers, Dalits had separate wells and were banned from Hindu temples. There was, he said, not a single Hindu organization in the entire country that worked for all the different Hindu castes.

The problems of the Hindus of Pakistan, Mr Prakash explained, were intricately linked to the fate of the vast Muslim

Haris working in the field

minority across the border in India. 'Minorities everywhere face problems, and the fates of the different minority communities in South Asia are critically interdependent. Each time there is an attack on Muslims in India, there is a reaction in Pakistan. When Muslims were slaughtered in India in the wake of the destruction of the Babri Masjid, there were reprisal attacks on Hindus in Pakistan. And now, with the rising tide of Hindutva fascism in India, brutally targeting India's Muslims, the implications for Pakistan's Hindus are ominous. If you Indians really want Hindus to prosper in Pakistan,' he said, 'you will have to counter Hindu fascists in your own country.'

The next morning, I met up with Aslam Khwaja, a friend of Sheila's. Along with some friends, he was in the process of establishing a separate hamlet outside Hyderabad for Dalit landless labourers or haris who had been rescued from the clutches of powerful *wadera*s, Sindh's dreaded landlords.

We met opposite the Hyderabad Press Club where, squatting on the pavement, was a crowd of men and a single woman under a makeshift canopy. A cloth banner, nailed to the wall against which they rested, announced, in big, bold Urdu letters, 'Justice for Manu Bhil: An Appeal to the Conscience of Pakistan'.

Aslam led me to a tough-looking, dark-skinned, middle-aged man. Manu Bhil gave me a firm handshake and, when Aslam told him I was from India, he folded his hands in a namastey. He proceeded to tell me his story, which numerous liberal Pakistani newspapers as well as human rights activists had taken up, despite which, justice still eluded him.

'I am a poor man, a Hindu of the Bhil caste,' Manu Bhil

began. 'Life has always been tough for us. Rarely did we experience any joy. Our men earned a measly sixty rupees a day for backbreaking work in the scorching sun, and our women got only half of that. But, still, with God's grace, we managed to survive, as our people have done for centuries.'

But then tragedy struck. Sometime in the mid-1980s, a severe drought in his native Thar Parkar drove Manu Bhil and his entire family to seek employment with a Muslim landlord named Hayat Rind. After working with him for some years, Rind and Manu fell out with each other. Rind claimed that Manu had taken an advance from him. Refusing to give Manu his wages, he sold him—along with twenty members of Manu's family—to another landlord, Abdur Rahman Marri.

Living conditions for Manu and his family on Marri's estate were brutal. Somehow, a group of social activists got wind of the vast number of Marri's haris. Under pressure from them, the police raided the estate and liberated seventy-one bonded labourers, including Manu's relatives. As ill-luck would have it, at the time of the raid Manu was away, working in another field belonging to Marri, and so he remained in his custody. As the landlord's only remaining captive, he was subjected to severe torture. Somehow, however, he was released, in 1996.

But this was only a brief respite for the hapless man. Manu and his family were transferred to a camp for freed bonded slaves, but not even two years had passed after their release when Marri and his henchmen raided the camp and kidnapped nine members of Manu's family, including his aged parents, his wife, his brother and his four children, the youngest of whom was just a year old. Although the governor of Sindh and the high court of the province had issued directives to the police to apprehend Marri, nothing had come of that. Manu had been on token hunger strike outside the Hyderabad Press Club since January 2003 to draw attention to his plight. Since then, he had been detained by the police several times, and they had tortured him in a bid to force him to issue a statement to the effect that his family had not been kidnapped. The defiant man, however, had refused to budge.

Tears welled in Manu's dark, tired eyes. 'I have had no news of my family since they were kidnapped,' he whispered. 'God alone knows where they are. They might even have been killed.'

'Such is the awesome power of the waderas of Sindh,' Aslam sighed. Manu Bhil's case was not an isolated one, he explained. It was common for landlords in Sindh to keep dozens of Dalit labourers as hereditary slaves. Some shackled them in chains to prevent them from escaping, and, often in league with the local police, even ran private torture chambers and prisons.

Sindhi camel-herders

Later that afternoon, we drove out of Hyderabad, past empty fields and hillocks of bare sand, and swerved off the road on to a sandy track that ran along a narrow canal lined with towering cacti. A couple of miles ahead, we stopped at a clearing encircled by diminutive huts made of plastic sheets stretched over wooden poles. Christened by Aslam and his colleague Kaleem Sheikh as 'Himmatabad' or 'The Abode of Courage', this fourteen-acre campus was a rehabilitation centre for some twenty-five Dalit families from the Koli and the Bhil castes who had recently been rescued by human rights activists from the private prisons of local landlords.

Aslam took me to the far end of the settlement, where feverish construction activity was going on. He and his group had collected money from well-wishers and were building proper houses for these landless Dalit families, each with two rooms, a toilet and a kitchen. Half a dozen houses, painted a pearly pink, had already been completed, and the rest were in various stages of construction.

'All our lives we've lived in one-room mud hovels, like cows and goats,' beamed Dali Bai, a crumpled, toothless Koli woman who joined us. Indicating Aslam with a nod of her chin, she said, 'Thanks to God and the help of these brothers, we might now be able to live like human beings.'

Soon, we were joined by Lali Koli, hailed as Himmatabad's voice to the outside world. Born in a desperately poor family, she had spent almost six years virtually as a slave in the private prison of a local landlord. She and her family, including her six children, had been recently rescued and set free. She now worked as a daily wage labourer in a neighbouring village. 'I am still poor, but at least I am free,' she said firmly as she bent over a clay oven in her hut made of reeds bound together with rope, blowing into the fire through a metal pipe to keep the sagging flames going.

'Lali comes with us to our meetings, to interact with journalists

and human rights activists, to speak at various venues about the
plight of Sindh's haris,' Aslam said.

'I've even been to your India,' Lali interrupted. She laughed
as she threw her head back and reminisced about the places she
had visited across the border. 'I liked Delhi the best. So
organized! So many big buildings! And the train that runs
under the ground! And the many nice people I met at the
convention of the Pakistan–India People's Forum for Peace
and Democracy.'

Lali dragged a charpai into the sunlight, on which we sat
while she plied us with thick, syrupy tea and little bits of *gur*.
Soon, word of our arrival spread throughout Himmatabad and
we were encircled by a knot of curious villagers, mainly women
and children. The women wore short-sleeved blouses and long,
heavily pleated skirts in a range of brilliant colours. Chunky
silver jewellery adorned their ears, noses, hands, ankles and
toes. They hid their faces under their tie-and-dye dupattas that
trailed from their heads and reached almost till their ankles,
allowing just enough space for a single eye to peep through.
The children, without exception, appeared pathetically
malnutritioned. Dressed in tattered rags, their dark faces were
stained and unwashed, their hair dry and wiry and turning a
pale orange—clear signs of extreme kwashiorkor.

Lali began to speak about her people. 'We Kolis are originally
from Gujarat, in India. Our caste occupation was fishing in the
deep seas, but desperate poverty drove us to do manual labour
in the fields of landlords. That is how we migrated to Sindh,
before the Partition.' As in India, she said, the Kolis in Sindh
were treated as Untouchables. So, too, were the Bhils, who
shared Himmatabad with the Kolis but whose ancestors had
migrated to Sindh from Rajasthan. Even after the Partition,
Lali explained, the Kolis, the Bhils and several other Dalit
castes would freely cross the Indo-Pakistani border, moving to
Sindh in the harvest season, where daily wages were higher

than in India. This was suddenly stopped in the wake of the 1965 war between India and Pakistan, after which India set up a fence all along the frontier. Consequently, tens of thousands of Dalits, like Himmatabad's Kolis and Bhils, found themselves stranded in Pakistan, unable to return to their ancestral homes, where they still had close relatives. They now lived in scattered settlements all over Sindh, but mainly in the central part of the province, where they formed up to 80 per cent of the landless agricultural workforce.

'The state has done nothing for these people. They are triply discriminated against: for being Hindu, Dalit and poor,' said Aslam. 'The state knows which landlords have how many debt-slaves and also the location of their private prisons, where they keep these slaves in chains and force them to work. But, it does nothing.'

Lali and the other women who had gathered around us stood motionless as Aslam elaborated on the plight of Pakistan's Dalits. Because the Dalits were a small, scattered, insecure and desperately poor minority, he went on, waderas preferred to employ them as labourers instead of Muslim haris. They found the Dalits easier to control and exploit, for the Dalits were too scared to protest or demand their rights.

We returned to Hyderabad later that evening, stopping by two other miserable settlements that had been set up for recently released landless haris. One of them was inhabited entirely by Dalits, and the other had a mixed Dalit and Muslim population. The Muslim haris, Aslam explained, were as desperately poor as the Dalits, and were mainly descendants of 'low' caste Hindus who had converted to Islam over the centuries.

That night, at a tea-shop near Aslam's home, I met Zahid.

He was a short, dark, emaciated man, and was dressed in a crumpled, heavily stained shalwar-kameez that hung about him loosely like a sack. From the distinctive Sindhi cap on his head I presumed him to be a Muslim, but I also noticed the Hindu sacred syllable 'Om' tattooed on his right hand. Curious to know about him, I asked his name and from where he was. He mentioned his Muslim-sounding name, but then I asked him about the tattoo.

His face suddenly contorted with fear. He hesitated for a while, looking around to see if anyone could overhear us.

'Are you a Hindu or a Muslim?' I asked.

'First you tell me what you are,' he shot back.

It was clear that my question was an unwanted embarrassment. I told him my name and said that I was a visitor from India. My answer seemed to calm him somewhat. He nodded his head in the direction of the street, indicating that it was not advisable to talk inside the tea-shop. I paid for our tea and we walked out into a dark, lonely lane.

Zahid began to tell me his story. 'Brother, I am actually a Hindu, from the Bhil caste,' he said. 'Three years ago, I converted to Islam because a maulvi of a mosque in Karachi told me he would give me one lakh rupees and a good job if I did so.' The maulvi had taught Zahid to pray in the Muslim fashion. 'I can recite the *namaz,* which took me two months to learn, but I don't know what it means,' he stuttered. 'It's in Arabic and I, an illiterate hari, don't know the language.'

After he converted to Islam, Zahid continued, the maulvi refused to live up to his promise. 'I got nothing from him,' he shrugged. 'He cheated me.' Zahid then returned to his wife, but she refused to let him into their home. His family cut off all relations with him for having changed his religion, and the Bhils cast him out. 'No one in my clan now accepts me,' he went on. He could not officially renounce Islam as he feared he might be killed because most Muslims believed that the punishment for apostasy was death. Several times he had contemplated suicide. 'I've absolutely no hope in life,' he cried. 'I'm not a Muslim in my heart. I long to rejoin my wife and the people of my caste, but they will never take me back. These Hindus are as heartless and unforgiving as the Muslims. There's no difference between the two.'

Zahid clutched my hand in his. His dark, heavily lined face was stained with tears. 'Sir, you are from our country. I wish I could go back with you,' he sobbed. Like many other Bhils in Pakistan, his parents had migrated to Sindh from Jaisalmer, now in India, years before the Partition, in the wake of a severe famine. India was his 'real home', he said, where many of his relatives still lived, although he had never met any of them. If he had the money, he said, he would have willingly gone back 'home'. 'Living in Pakistan is sheer hell for us Hindus,' he stuttered.

I kept silent for a while. I knew I could give no words of comfort to this hapless man, trapped in a religion and a land that he did not consider his own.

'But in India, like here, you might still be considered an Untouchable Bhil,' I said, after a while.

'That is true, sir,' Zahid replied, 'but at least there I would be among my own people.'

ten

among sindhis and muhajirs and a hindu

Ｏne morning, I decided to explore Hyderabad on my own, taking an autorickshaw across the city to Latifabad, Hyderabad's predominantly Muhajir quarter. Named after the acclaimed Sindhi Sufi poet Shah Abdul Latif, it was formed immediately after the Partition to accommodate the flood of migrants from India, who had quickly turned the ethnic Sindhis into a minority in their own town. Most of Latifabad's Muhajirs were migrants and their descendants from the Indian states of Gujarat, Maharashtra and Rajasthan. Muhajirs from Uttar Pradesh and Bihar had preferred to settle in the more cosmopolitan Karachi. Till the late 1970s, Latifabad had a mixed Sindhi–Muhajir population but, following the deadly ethnic riots that had broken out between the two communities, Latifabad had been virtually emptied of its Sindhi inhabitants, most of whom had shifted to the Sindhi-dominated Qasimabad locality on the other side of the city.

Touted in government publicity brochures as 'Pakistan's first planned urban settlement', Latifabad was a giant mess of crumbling and half-built houses, some of them heavily bullet-

190BEYONDTHEBORDER

riddled, hillocks of rotting garbage, overflowing sewers, rutted roads scarred beyond recognition and rendered virtually impassable, and snarled traffic that obstinately refused to follow any rules whatsoever. Enormous cardboard cutouts of a gangster-like figure occupied virtually every street corner. His eyes were hidden behind a pair of thick dark glasses, his greying hair, neatly oiled, was pushed back, revealing a glistening broad forehead, and his puffy cheeks sagged down to his chin. His thin lips were pressed together, as if deliberately, in order to lend him an air of authority. He was depicted in a range of poses: leading a massive march of wonder-struck, fist-raising followers; seated at the head of a conference table, surrounded by a posse of dignitaries; accepting bouquets of roses from a bunch of smiling schoolchildren; addressing a mammoth public rally from a podium, his hands angrily flaying about in the air. This was the enigmatic, London-based Muhajir leader, Altaf Husain, head of the Muhajir Qaumi Movement (MQM). To many Muhajirs, he was a hero, the saviour of what he termed the 'Muhajir nation'. But to many others, he was a mafia don, a firebrand despot, a power-hungry terrorist, a brutal megalomaniac, a demonic dictator, a blood-thirsty, Hitler-like fascist. To most ethnic Sindhis, he was the symbol of Muhajir domination that they deeply resented.

Altaf Husain's past was as shadowy as his politics. Born in 1953 in Karachi, his lower-middle-class parents were migrants from Agra in India. It was alleged that when he worked as a taxi-driver in Chicago he was recruited by Pakistan's deadly secret service agency, the Inter-Services Intelligence, to form a new Muhajir party in order to counter the influence of opposition parties such as the Islamist Jamaat-e Islami, which had a strong presence among Muhajirs in urban Sindh, and the ethnic Sindhi-backed Pakistan People's Party. The MQM was established in 1984, and soon became the voice of the majority of Sindh's Muhajirs, who felt increasingly marginalized by the

Punjabi-dominated Pakistani state and the growing assertiveness of ethnic Sindhis. Altaf Husain went so far as to declare publicly that the Partition of British India and the creation of Pakistan had been a monumental blunder, which had hit the Muhajirs the worst. He even denounced the 'two-nation' theory, the official ideology of Pakistan. This represented a major turnaround in Muhajir politics, for the Muhajirs had once been the most ardent backers of the creation of the separate state of Pakistan. Not unexpectedly, his opponents— and they were many—branded Altaf Husain as an 'Indian agent'. His seemingly unquenchable thirst for power drove him to organized crime and even terror. He and his shadowy outfit were implicated in scores of cases of murder, kidnapping, extortion and sectarian killings, which had forced him to flee to England in 1992, where he now lived in self-imposed exile.

Jiye Altaf Husain! ('Long Live Altaf Husain!'), *Hum Altafi Hain*! ('We are Altafis!') screeched the slogans splattered on almost every crumbling, urine-stained wall of Latifabad. These shared space with posters of the latest Urdu movie, depicting a woman cringing in abject surrender before the outstretched feet of a burly, moustached man. Her tongue lolled out between her thick painted lips, just above the man's unlaced shoes. All around I could hear men (hardly any women were visible) talking in Urdu in distinctly north Indian accents. It reminded me of home. It had been over two weeks now since I had heard Hindustani spoken in that fashion.

I made a hurried exit out of Latifabad. The abject misery that trapped the entire squalid locality in its powerful grip, like the angry raised fist of Altaf Husain that I saw all around me, was simply too much to bear.

It was by mere chance, and a bit of trickery, too, that I met Ajay that afternoon. Fleeing from the deadening gloom of Latifabad, I entered a well-furnished, air-conditioned restaurant near the railway station. Waiters in crisp white coats and trousers flitted about, bearing trays gingerly placed on the palms of their hands. The manager, nattily dressed in a black suit, chatted with a group of men who, from their manner, seemed to be regular customers. Lithographic reproductions of paintings of Hyderabad by colonial-period British artists decorated the walls. They showed wide, open roads, graceful mansions, flowing fountains, a robust fort guarded by handsome Baluch warriors, Hindu merchants dressed in flowing robes and an assortment of ancient, domed, tomb-like structures—a picture of Hyderabad that bore no resemblance whatsoever to what I had seen of the city.

I ordered a fresh lime soda, and twisted about in the sofa I had sunk into till I arrived at a comfortable position. I glanced around the room, hoping to catch someone's attention and then possibly converse. It would add to my repertoire of stories and perspectives for the travelogue I hoped to write. But, and this was the hitch, how was I to chat up anyone sitting there? If it were some other country it might have been easier, because I would appear distinctive, which might attract people's curiosity, but here in Pakistan I looked just about like anyone else, and, therefore, not worthy of the special attention that foreigners often get.

I thought of a trick. I took out a Hindi book from my bag and busied myself pretending to be immersed in it, pressing it almost against my face so that its cover, with its title written in big, bold Devanagari letters, would be easily seen even from a distance. That way, I thought, I would be immediately identified as a foreigner reading a strange script, or, as I hoped, as an Indian by someone who was familiar with the Hindi script from watching Bollywood movies, which were such a rage all across Pakistan.

Half an hour passed but I still drew no attention. The men at the table next to mine loudly guffawed at lewd jokes and downed their sodas, mixed with whiskey from a bottle that one of them kept carefully hidden under his encompassing shawl. The young couple seated in front of me were too preoccupied whispering sweet nothings to each other to notice me. Just then, a man strode up to me. He seemed to be in his mid-thirties, and was dressed in tight-fitting jeans, over which he wore a loose cotton kurta that trailed to his knees. He had a rectangular face, shaped like a box, and his head was disproportionately large for his body. This, however, was offset by a pair of large, liquid eyes, deeply set against protruding cheekbones that at once suggested intelligence as well as amiability.

'Excuse me, but are you from India?' he asked hesitatingly.

I nodded in reply.

My trick had worked!

'I'm a Hindu. I'm Ajay,' he introduced himself in impeccable English. 'Mind if I join you?'

I was the first Indian that Ajay had ever met. We talked for a while, mainly about my impressions of Pakistan, and then turned to the issue of the country's Hindus. Ajay looked carefully around us, and then lowered his tone to a whisper. 'It's better to go outside.'

We strode down the street to a park, a patch of mangy grass littered with discarded bottles and plastic bags and a swing that no longer worked. Ajay began to speak about himself. He was, he told me, a Brahmin from interior Sindh, and worked in a mid-level post in a garment factory in Karachi that exported clothes to the West and the Gulf. 'To be honest,' he said, 'many Pakistani Hindus do not consider Pakistan their country. Many of us secretly wish to migrate to India if we could. India is our motherland, our holy land, the land of the Hindus, although we would never dare say this publicly.'

I could understand Ajay's sorry predicament, for the Hindus of Pakistan lived in a self-proclaimed 'Islamic' state. They were a silenced and increasingly vulnerable minority in a country whose very founding myth was based on the untenable notion of Hindus and Muslims being two distinct—indeed antagonistic—'nations', perpetually at war with each other. They were thus easily branded as 'enemies' of Pakistan, as dangerous fifth-columnists and 'Indian agents', mirroring, in much the same way, the pernicious logic of Hindu fascist groups in India that saw India's Muslims as 'treacherous', 'anti-national' and 'pro-Pakistan'. It was then quite natural, I felt, that many Pakistani Hindus should have mixed feelings about the land of their birth. Their unenviable dilemma was only getting worse with the alarming rise of radical, anti-Indian and anti-Hindu Islamist forces in the country.

In Punjab, where there were hardly any Hindus left, most people did not even know that parts of the country still had a sizeable Hindu community, Ajay explained. In Sindh, Hindus formed around 8 per cent of the population. The Muhajirs tended to despise them, mainly because of the bitterness caused by the Partition, which had forced the Muhajirs to flee 'Hindu' India. Sindhi-speaking Hindus had better relations with ethnic Sindhi Muslims, however, because they spoke the same language and shared a common culture. Sometimes, Ajay said, he was treated with additional respect, indeed admiration, by avid Pakistani Bollywood buffs, who linked him with the flamboyant Indian Hindu actors and seductive actresses who pranced around on their television screens.

'But I've had more than my share of unpleasant experiences,' added Ajay in the same breath. It was not always wise to publicly admit his Hindu identity, he said, especially outside Sindh. He had worked in Lahore for almost a year a decade ago, and initially found it impossible to get a flat on rent. Landlords would slam their doors in his face when they learnt he was a Hindu. Finally, he gave up, faked a Muslim name and managed to get a place almost immediately.

Such discrimination, deeply rooted in Pakistani society, was also heavily reinforced by the state, Ajay went on. Textbooks prescribed by the government for school students for the compulsory Pakistan Studies subject were filled with virulent anti-Hindu (and anti-Indian) propaganda. They depicted Hindus as 'mean and despicable' and as 'inveterate enemies' of Islam and Muslims. They insisted that Hindus and Muslims were enemy 'nations' that could never live at peace with each other—the pernicious logic of the 'two-nation' theory that was Pakistan's official ideology. They even called for an armed jihad against Hindus and India. Pakistani Hindu children, who had to study these texts, were thus branded as permanent enemies of their own country and were taught to hate themselves and their religion. Even books for such subjects as Urdu literature, civics and geography contained a heavy dose of 'Islamic' teachings that reflected a sternly literalist, authoritarian and exclusivist version of the faith. Hindu and other non-Muslim students could not escape studying these texts, with disastrous consequences for their self-esteem. Some Hindu parents chose to keep their children away from school rather than subject them to this venomous propaganda. His own children, Ajay rued, could recite Islamic prayers that they learnt at school but knew next to nothing about Hinduism.

Ajay had travelled extensively in Sindh and beyond, and had visited Hindu groups scattered widely across Pakistan. Just under 2,000 Hindus remained in Lahore, he said, a city with a Hindu majority at the time of the Partition. Almost all of these were Valmikis, who worked as sweepers in the city's municipality. The rest, some twenty families, were Khatri and Arora merchants. Some of Lahore's Hindus had adopted Muslim-style names in order to conceal their identities. Smaller groups of Hindus, mainly Khatris, Aroras and Jat peasants, lived in pockets in other parts of north and central Punjab, as did a large number of Hindu families that had turned Muslim at the time of the Partition in order to save their lives and property. More sizeable clusters of Hindus, mostly landless Dalits, inhabited the dry, impoverished districts of Bahawalpur, Bahawalnagar, Multan and Rahim Yar Khan, in the Cholistan desert in southern Punjab. Scattered groups of Hindus also lived in small towns in the North-West Frontier Province and Baluchistan, mainly traders as well as Valmikis, who worked as sweepers.

Some nine-tenths of Pakistan's three million Hindus lived in Sindh, Ajay went on. Some districts in Sindh had a significant Hindu population. The proportion of Hindus in four districts—Thar Parkar, Umerkot, Mirpur Khas and Sanghar—was more than 35 per cent, and they belonged to various caste groups. Some of them were Sindhi-speaking and native to Sindh. Many others had migrated from Gujarat and Rajasthan before the Partition in search of work. A fairly significant number of Lohana traders, who claimed Rajput descent, lived in upper Sindh, abutting southern Punjab, where they exercised a stronghold on the wholesale trade in grains, pulses, cotton and alcohol. Some thirty thousand Hindus, mainly Dalits of the Meghwal caste, were employed in textile mills in Karachi, where there was also a sprinkling of 'upper' caste Hindu and Jain professionals and wealthy industrialists. A few Sindhi 'upper' caste Hindus had attained high positions in public life. Ajay mentioned a Sodha Rajput landlord from Thar Parkar who had served for several years as a Federal Minister, a well-known Karachi-based fashion designer, and Rana Bhagwandas, acting Chief Justice of the Pakistan Supreme Court. But these, he hurriedly added, were exceptions.

There were scores of small Hindu shrines across the Sindh province, Ajay went on. Karachi alone had seven functioning Hindu temples. In addition to these, there were some large ashrams, such as at Mirpur Mathelo, Thana Bula Khan and Sadhu Bela, on the Indus in upper Sindh, Uderolal, in lower Sindh, and also in the Thar. It was not easy to get permission for establishing new temples or expanding existing ones, though. 'It isn't just the officials who generally oppose this, but local Muslims as well, especially the maulvis,' Ajay explained. Several cases had been reported of Hindu temples and crematoriums, some of which occupied prime property in urban areas, being forcibly taken over by Muslim real-estate sharks in league with the police.

There were only a few Hindu organizations in the country, such as the Pakistan Hindu Panchayat, the Pakistan Hindu Welfare Association and the Karachi Hindu Gymkhana. But these were all controlled by the 'upper' castes. They did nothing for the Dalits, though, who formed the overwhelming majority of Pakistan's Hindu population, limiting themselves mainly to organizing festivals, conducting religious classes and printing Hindu literature. Their indifference to the Dalits was not just because of deep-rooted caste prejudices, Ajay explained. Their class interests coincided with those of the Muslim élite, and there was also the fear of antagonizing powerful Muslim landlords, for whom most Dalits worked as landless labourers. While in pre-Partition Sindh, wealthy Hindus had set up a number of philanthropic institutions, this had largely ceased now. Most of the rich Hindus had migrated to India, and now, even those Hindus who had the money to set up schools, colleges and other institutions for the community, hesitated to do so. They preferred to maintain a low profile, for fear of being branded as 'Indian agents'.

A cold wind rushed relentlessly through the park, stirring up dust and sand into a giant curtain that flapped about us violently, blocking out everything from view. Shopkeepers hurriedly downed their awnings. Passers-by scurried for safety under empty tin sheds that littered the road. Beggars hurriedly covered their heads with their patched shawls. The dust swirled through our noses and into our throats. Ajay grabbed me by the hand and we scampered out of the park and across the road, our eyes tightly shut against the brewing dust-storm and oblivious to the oncoming traffic.

Ajay's friend Husain lived just a block away from the park, and we scuttled down the road to his house with our heads buried deep inside our shawls, the wind howling against our shrouded faces. Husain drew us inside his handsome mansion, indicating commodious leather cushions placed on a pale red Persian carpet that occupied the entire floor of the spacious drawing room. I slumped into a cushion and shook off my shawl.

Husain entered the room clutching a feather-duster, which he wielded as a club on my back, beating out the dust. He broke out into a full-throated laugh, his eyes crinkling like a schoolboy's. 'What a fine way to welcome you! Beating up my Indian guest!'

We roared in delight.

The room was tastefully decorated, befitting Husain's status as an art critic of sorts, a noted intellectual and scion of a politically powerful, feudal family of waderas. Translucent camel-leather lamps, shaped like minarets and half-moons and painted in soft, earthy colours, stood atop lacquered book-racks. A life-sized eagle, crafted from a single slab of pale green onyx, perched on a mantelpiece. Dark, and evidently antique, Afghan rugs hung from the walls. Scattered about on an enormous mahogany chest of drawers, whose legs were shaped like roaring lions, was an assortment of curios: hand-painted pottery plates from Hala, a ponderous silver hukkah with a carved ivory handle, a broad-rimmed water jug made of rhino horn, a framed photograph of a man in an enormous turban and a long robe that swirled around his feet, standing before a slain tiger and surrounded by a bevy of retainers. 'My great-grandfather. An intrepid *shikari*, and one of the biggest waderas in this part of Sindh,' Husain explained.

Like many other ethnic Sindhis, Husain was an ardent Sindhi nationalist, a fervent supporter of Sindhi self-determination. 'Sindh has been reduced to being a veritable colony of Punjab,' he complained. Pakistan's Punjabi rulers, he said, had actively encouraged the settlement of Muhajirs in Sindh, as a result of which ethnic Sindhis now accounted for less than four-tenths of the population of their own homeland. The Muhajirs, being better educated and more urbane, tended to look down on the Sindhis as rustic bumpkins, and had gobbled the lion's share of jobs in the province. Despite having lived in Sindh for more than half a century, many Muhajirs still refused to learn the Sindhi language, which they disdainfully regarded as the language of peasants. Vast tracts of lands in northern Sindh had been parcelled out by the Pakistani Government to retired Army officers, mostly Punjabis and Pakhtuns, to further 'colonize' the Sindhis, as Husain put it. 'And now,' he angrily spat out, 'the Punjabis are setting about constructing the Kalabagh Dam on the Indus, one of the largest such projects in the world, to divert the waters of our river to their fields and to turn the whole of Sindh into a barren desert. That's just the latest of their tricks to enslave us. We can't trust the Pakistani government anymore.' Massive demonstrations against the controversial dam had been taking place in all the provinces of Pakistan except Punjab. I had witnessed a huge band of anti-Kalabagh Dam processionists that morning, winding down the city's main road near the railway station, raising placards, banners and angry slogans.

Sindhi man wearing ajrak shawl and mirror-work cap

Vigorous thumping on the door abruptly interrupted Husain's harangue. A dark man, wearing a black Sindhi-style cap on his head and an indigo-blue *ajrak* wrapped across his shoulders, slipped in and joined us. Husain introduced him as Waris, a social activist and a budding writer. 'Waris is a communist, fiercely anti-feudal, and even though we obviously disagree on many things, we are great friends,' Husain said smilingly. Waris slipped off his ajrak and nodded vigorously. 'Husain is the only wadera in Sindh I can dare fool around with,' he winked.

We picked up where we had left off, discussing various dimensions of the Sindhi nationalist movement. Husain remained silent, letting Waris speak his mind. 'I'm all for Sindhu Desh, an independent Sindh, if we can get it, a secular, socialist, democratic, sovereign country of our own. Failing that, we could settle for a genuinely autonomous Sindh perhaps, with Pakistan controlling only our foreign relations, defence and currency.'

But was that at all possible, I asked? After all, I reminded Waris, similar movements for self-determination in many other countries, including India, had only provoked state repression on a brutal scale. He twisted his eyebrows in a sign of disagreement. 'Just because it sounds impossible it doesn't mean that it is not desirable and legitimate,' he shot back.

'But we have a major internal problem,' Waris continued. 'It's these treacherous waderas.' He looked pointedly at Husain and kept silent for a while. Husain's shook his head in mock anger. Cracks of a faint, controlled smile rose from the corners of his mouth, suggesting that he knew what Waris was about to say. 'Most of these so-called nationalist Sindhi groups are led and controlled by powerful wadera mafia-bosses, who are as oppressive as the Punjabi masters against whom they claim to be struggling. By mobilizing the Sindhi peasantry and the landless haris behind them in the name of the Sindhi nation, they want to deny the very sharp class contradictions in our own society. They care two hoots for the haris, whom they treat as virtual slaves.'

A sudden hush fell upon the room. Ajay shuffled his feet and trained his eyes on the curios placed on the chest of drawers. Waris cleared his throat and adjusted his cap. Husain let out a short, snort-like snigger.

I tried to break the ice. 'But I guess that's true for almost all ethnic and nationalist movements, isn't it? The same thing happened in India, Pakistan and Bangladesh. Freedom essentially meant a change of masters. I mean, black sahibs replacing white sahibs and still being beholden to the latter. No?'

'Yes, that's true,' chimed Ajay, who had all this while maintained a studied silence.

Husain slipped out of the room. I heard him instruct a servant to prepare mutton samosas and onion pakoras for us. Waris noticed my embarrassment. 'Yogi-ji! Don't worry! We keep having these squabbles, and we make up immediately after. Husain is my *jaan*, my love. Even though he is a wadera, I know he is a crypto-communist, a comrade at heart!'

'Husain is a Syed, but I am a Samat,' he went on. In other words, Waris was an indigenous Sindhi, in contrast to the Syeds, who claimed to be descended from the Prophet Muhammad and to have come to Sindh from Arabia centuries ago. 'See,' he said stretching his hands about him, 'I'm dark brown, almost black, while Husain is almost white. Two very different people we are, although we follow the same religion.' Most Sindhi Muslim élite, including the waderas, he said, were descendants of outsiders, such as the Iranians, the Baluchis and the Arabs, who had settled in Sindh as conquerors. It was, he went on, like the Europeans who had come to Africa, with the Bible in one hand and a gun in the other. 'First, the Aryans conquered our lands, and reduced us to the status of outcastes, using the Hindu religion to justify the caste system. Two thousand years later, we Samats converted to Buddhism en masse in protest against Hindu imperialism. Another two thousand years later, came the Arabs, led by Muhammad bin Qasim. The Samat Buddhists welcomed the Arabs with open arms, seeing them as liberators from the tyrannical Brahmin rule, and converted to Islam in droves. Islam preached the doctrine of social and economic equality, but the foreign Muslims—the Syeds and the Baluchis—forgot all that and turned us into miserable serfs. They stole our land and reduced most of the Samats to utter poverty.' Numerous Sufis, he went on, had appeared over the centuries in Sindh, they had protested against exploitation and preached the oneness of humanity, irrespective of religion, caste and class. But even their message and legacy had been cleverly subverted. Ironically, Waris said, some of their descendants, whom he called 'fake Pirs and pseudo-holy men', were now among the largest and cruellest landlords in all Sindh.

Waris's face flushed angrily, turning even darker. 'Pakistan's rulers don't want us to know anything about our past. They want us to forget it, so that we can be their willing servants,' he thundered. 'We must revive the legacy of our glorious pre-Islamic and pre-Hindu traditions, which we have been taught, through the media, the education system and religious propaganda, to despise,' he asserted with a burning sense of mission. 'We have to cultivate in our people pride in being descendants of the inhabitants of the Indus Valley Civilization, one of the leading civilizations of its times, perhaps the oldest civilization in the world.'

eleven

a week in interior sindh

I first met Khurshid Khan Kaim Khani at a Dalit conference in Delhi some twenty years ago, after which we had kept in regular touch by mail. Now in his mid-seventies, Khurshid had resigned from a senior post in the Pakistan Army in 1971, just before war broke out between India and Pakistan, in protest against gruesome human rights abuses by Pakistani troops in erstwhile East Pakistan. Thereafter, he got involved with various social causes, including the communist and nascent Dalit movement in Sindh. He was a well-known writer, mainly in Sindhi and Urdu. Among his several books was a collection of essays on the Pakistani Dalits, the first of its kind, as well as a novel based on the Partition of India.

Khurshid lived in interior Sindh, in the town of Tando Allah Yar, an hour's journey by train from Hyderabad. We arranged to meet at a restaurant in Hyderabad, from where he was to take me to his home. He appeared to have aged considerably, but was still as energetic and irrepressibly garrulous as he had been when I met him two decades ago. He insisted that we walk all the way to the railway station, more than two kilometres away, through traffic that wound through interminable knots and accumulating hillocks of rotting garbage. 'I know you must find Hyderabad sheer hell,' he joked, 'but I insist I must test your tenacity.'

When we got to the station, we were informed that the train to Tando Allah Yar was five hours late. 'That's usual here,' Khurshid shrugged. Two men stood nearby and I overheard them speaking. One of them, who seemed to have recently returned from a visit to India, bragged, 'I travelled all over India in trains that are as clean as hospitals and are inevitably right on time.'

I could not help interrupt him.

'Brother,' I turned to him and said, 'I'm from India, and I can assure you that your experiences with the Indian Railways were an exception, not the rule.'

The man's friend burst out in childlike laughter and slapped him on the back. 'See, I knew you were lying!' he cried out. 'How can anything at all be better in India than in Pakistan?'

But as far as the toilets in Hyderabad railway station were concerned, the man's friend was most definitely wrong, as I soon discovered to my horror. I desperately needed to relieve myself, but Khurshid cautioned me against using the men's toilet. 'I assure you it is absolutely, completely, wholly unusable,' he warned. But, unable to control myself any longer, I rushed to the toilet, which I located from the powerful stench of fetid urine that led like a trail to a dark room near the entrance to the station. I looked about for a cubicle, but there was none. Instead, a long, open drain, clogged with urine and bits of excreta, stretched below a wall, before which a row of men squatted, the tails of their shalwars lifted to reveal their hairy buttocks. I selected a vacant corner, and urinated while standing. Hardly had I started than the man sitting next to me angrily growled, 'Hey, you bloody animal! What do you think you are doing? Don't you know it's against the *shariah* to stand and piss! Bloody dog!'

I turned around to see half a dozen angry men sitting on

their haunches, their stony eyes fixed on me. I ducked down, stripped my jeans to my knees and tried urinating Muslim-style. It was simply impossible to manoeuvre in that awkward position. I wet my jeans, but at least I saved myself from being lynched.

The train drew into the platform a little after sunset, when the sky had turned a deep purple and was littered with crows heading to their nests. Amidst aggressive pushing and shoving, we managed to enter an overcrowded compartment. We found vacant seats, dusting off the thick sheet of sand that had entered through the broken window. A ticket collector trundled along the corridor, collecting money from ticketless passengers without giving them receipts. 'He's probably charging them half the fare and letting them off and pocketing the money himself,' said Khurshid.

Half an hour after we had boarded the train, it suddenly ground to a halt—mechanical failure of some sort, which took almost three hours to repair. We were not far from Tando Allah Yar, and I suggested to Khurshid that we could probably walk to his home. 'You must be out of your mind!' he laughed. 'This place is infested with dacoits. They'd even steal the skin off our backs if they could.' And so we sat, resigned to our fate, shooing away the army of flies that buzzed around us, and chatting with fellow-passengers till at last an engineer arrived from Hyderabad to repair the train.

It was almost midnight when the train pulled in at Tando Allah Yar station. We wound our way through a maze of dark, narrow lanes ribboned with heaps of garbage and wedges of human excreta. 'This is the town councillor's new clean-up drive,' Khurshid chortled as I struggled to avoid the filth piled up along the drains. 'He's been instructed by his boss to have the drains cleaned, and that he has done by ordering the sweepers to dredge out the filth from the drains and spread it out along the road.'

Khurshid's house was a modest two-storey structure sheltered behind a high wall. We slipped through the gate and climbed up a flight of stairs to a single-room tenement. His son and wife lived below, but, he said, he rarely spoke to them. 'This is my own little nest, my own little world, far from that horrendous hell that is Pakistan.' This was where, he said, he stayed almost all day by himself with his books, rarely venturing out save to meet his friends in the Dalit locality at the other end of the town. 'As you'll realize tomorrow, when we go around,' he assured me as we slipped under our blankets and readied to sleep, 'Tando Allah Yar is a dreary town, stifling, stultifying and utterly depressing.'

Khurshid's description of his town was not quite accurate, but wasn't he wide off the mark, as I was to discover over the next few days that I stayed with him. It was true that Tando Allah Yar boasted little by way of monuments of historical interest, but for the crumbling ramparts of what had once been a fort, a couple of public fountains built by Hindu traders before the Partition that had long since fallen into disuse, and a century-old temple dedicated to the Dalit hero, Rama Pir. It was also unbelievably filthy, even more so than Hyderabad. Most of its denizens seemed to be pathetically poor and lived in crammed, broken-down hovels. But, being with Khurshid more than made up for all this. One of Sindh's leading intellectuals and social activists, he possessed a remarkable knowledge of the history and culture of the peoples of his land, an understanding that had grown from years of involvement with the struggle for democracy and social justice, and from the personal sufferings and traumas that he himself had undergone. His was a critical understanding of his country that might, on the face of it, have been interpreted as cynical, or even as 'anti-national', but which reflected a deep sense of commitment to Pakistan's suffering millions who, he believed, had been cruelly cheated by their rulers, who had consistently manipulated religion to stay in power.

Khurshid was born shortly before the Partition, in a village in Sikar, in what is now the Indian state of Rajasthan. His father, a middle-ranking officer in the British Army, was posted in Peshawar, and when the Partition was announced, his part of the family found themselves in what had, literally overnight, become Pakistan. Many of their relatives remained behind in India.

Khurshid was a Kaim Khani, a descendant of Chauhan Rajputs who had converted to Islam some six centuries ago. Their conversion was, in many senses, superficial, and they continued to follow many Hindu customs. The Kaim Khanis who had remained behind in India after the Partition, and who lived mainly in north-western Rajasthan, still retained many of their pre-Islamic traditions. Those who migrated to Pakistan had abandoned most of them but, like several other Muslim castes in Pakistan, they continued to strictly practise caste endogamy.

The Kaim Khanis derived their name from their first Muslim ancestor, the fourteenth-century Nawab Kaim Khan who, before his conversion to Islam, had been known as Karam Chand. He was the son of Raja Motey Rai Chauhan of Dadrewa, a small town in the Bikaner district of Rajasthan. Upon his conversion to Islam, Kaim Khan was appointed by Firoze Shah Tughlaq, sultan of Delhi, as governor of Hissar, a town in the present-day Indian state of Haryana. His descendants had subsequently established several small principalities in Punjab and Rajasthan, including Hissar, Hansi, Narhar, Barwasi, Kayad, Fatehpur and Jhunjhunu.

Inevitably, as I had experienced with people I had met in Lahore, much of our conversation centred on the Partition. For Khurshid, the Partition had been a personal tragedy of monumental proportions. It had torn him away from his ancestral home in Rajasthan, forcing him and his family to live, much against their will, in a country where they would be perpetually marked as aliens. The Partition, which he ascribed to the sinister politics of 'upper' caste Hindu chauvinists and Muslim communalists, had forced him to confront and contend with multiple and conflicting identities, each of which made its own claims on him. What was he really as a Kaim Khani? A Rajput? A member of a caste that, for centuries, had been considered as being neither fully Hindu nor properly Muslim, but a bit of both? A caste that followed the cult of the hero Goga Pir, which Muslim maulvis derided as un-Islamic? And what was he now, after the Partition? A Muhajir, a refugee in a land with which his people had no link, save for a common, although deeply contested, religious identity? A Pakistani Muslim, who, by definition, must be fiercely anti-Indian and anti-Hindu? But, was that possible, given that he still considered as his true home the village that he had left behind in India, where generations of his ancestors had been born, had lived and died? It was not the squalid slums of Tando Allah Yar but that village, now located on the other side of an impermeable border, with its sand-dunes and mud-huts and neem trees, of which he thought as his motherland.

It was almost half a century after the Partition that Khurshid was finally able to return to visit his ancestral village. 'The memory of home constantly haunted me all those years, beckoning me to come back. But I never gave up hope,' he said wistfully. 'Something within me kept telling me that the

combined machinations of the rulers of India and Pakistan and
Muslim and Hindu chauvinists could never stop me from
returning to the land of my birth.'

At first, when he entered the village, nobody recognized him.
Dressed in jeans and a T-shirt, he was mistaken for a city
Bania. He stopped at a house in the Bishnoi locality and asked
if he could meet the oldest man present. He was guided to a
hut, outside which, in the shade of a mango tree, an elderly
man rested on a cot. The moment he set his eyes on him, he
knew it was Sohan Lal Mamu, the *rakhi* brother of his
grandmother, Bhuri.

Sohan Lal wept like a child as he held Khurshid in his frail
arms. 'Bhuri! Bhuri! Yes, Bhuri was my sister, and I was her
dharam bhai,' he kept saying. 'She unfailingly tied a rakhi on
me every year till she died. Not once did she miss it,' he
repeatedly mumbled. 'Why, my child, did your father and his
brothers flee this village?' he asked Khurshid. 'We wanted to
save our Muslims, but we could not. Those were bad times.
May God never let that happen again. Our village is not the
same without your people.' He pleaded with Khurshid to
return. 'It is your village, son,' he said. 'After all, it was settled
by the Kaim Khanis, your ancestors.'

'Mamu, if only that could happen,' Khurshid replied, 'but,
sadly, it cannot. The governments of India and Pakistan would
never let it.'

Sohan Mamu had lovingly preserved the village mosque and
Bhuri's house, decades after the Partition. He had collected
money from his fellow Bishnois and had recently had it
whitewashed, although it was no longer used after all the village
Muslims had fled to Pakistan. 'I thought, who knows, your
family might come back to India one day, and then what face
would I show them if I allowed your home and the mosque to
be occupied by someone else?' Sohan Mamu said. Khurshid
had replied that it was now impossible for them to return, and

so he could convert his grandmother's house into a school for the benefit of the children of the village.

I struggled, but unsuccessfully, to hold back my tears as Khurshid continued. His story was one with which everyone affected by the Partition could readily identify. I thought of Nani and Nana and the tragedy that the Partition had meant for their families. I thought of their villages, now in Pakistan, which I would probably never get to visit. I thought of their forefathers, whose ashes had been mixed with the soil of that land from which they would never be separated, the very same land that most Indians now thought of as 'enemy' territory. Who knows, I thought, if the Partition had not happened, I might have been living in the village of my ancestors in Gujranwala, while Khurshid might never have left the hamlet in the desert, now in India, of which he still thought as home.

It was perhaps now no longer possible to undo the Partition, Khurshid opined. But that did not mean, he said, that the deadly wounds that it had inflicted could not be healed. Khurshid's way of seeking to do that was through his literary activities. Some years ago, he had set up the Pakistan Hindi Sabha to promote the study of the Hindi language in Sindh. Like Khurshid, a fairly large number of Muhajirs in Sindh, who had been born and brought up in what was now India, had studied Hindi in school. But the language was virtually dead in Pakistan, where it was no longer taught, except in a few Hindu-run religious *pathshala*s in Sindh. It was considered 'Indian' and 'Hindu' and thus, the antithesis of Pakistani nationalism and of Islam, just as Hindu chauvinists in India treated Urdu as 'Islamic' and 'Pakistani', and as an affront to their version of Indian nationalism and Hinduism. The Pakistan Hindi Sabha had existed for a few years but, for want of public support, had been forced to wind up.

A year ago, Khurshid had published a collection of short stories in Urdu, titled *The Land of Dreams*. It was about the

village in Sikar which he still considered home, and which, as
its title suggested, he never ceased dreaming about. Recently,
with the help of a Sindhi Dalit friend, he had launched
Pakistan's first Dalit tabloid. The bi-monthly *Dalit Adab*,
published in Sindhi, sought to create a sense of a common
Dalit identity, embracing more than forty Dalit castes in
Pakistan. This was an uphill task, he explained, for these castes
had themselves internalized the pernicious logic of the caste
system, seeking to compensate for the inferior status that had
been thrust on them by claiming superiority over other Dalit
groups considered to be lower than them. This new Dalit
identity that the magazine sought to fashion in a society where
even the word 'Dalit' was still alien and unheard of was crucial
for the political empowerment of these communities, who
continued to suffer neglect and discrimination at the hands of
the Muslims, the Hindus and the Pakistani state. By highlighting
the little-known or completely forgotten stories about Dalit
heroes, going back all the way to the days of the Indus Valley
Civilization in Sindh which, Khurshid believed, was the legacy
of the ancestors of today's Dalits before they were forced into
religiously sanctioned slavery by the invading Aryans, *Dalit
Adab* wanted to help the Dalits of Pakistan transform their
own image of themselves, to take pride in, rather than deny,
their own heritage. It also sought to build bridges between
Pakistani and Indian Dalits by translating key writings of
Babasaheb Bhimrao Ambedkar, the unchallenged Indian Dalit
hero, into Sindhi, and by publishing news about Dalit activism
across the border.

'The ruling castes of India and Pakistan thrive on fomenting
hatred between the Hindus and the Muslims, and between our
two countries. That's their principal weapon to keep themselves
in power over their peoples, most of whom are from various
Dalit castes,' opined Khurshid. 'If the Dalits of the entire
subcontinent, including those now considered to be Hindus or

Muslims, could unite and become a solid block, they could prove to be a powerful force for South Asian unity.' He saw *Dalit Adab* as a step in that direction. 'I know it won't happen in my lifetime,' he admitted. 'It may not happen in a hundred years. But I know it will one day, and that is why we must continue the struggle, even though it might now sound completely far-fetched.'

Tando Allah Yar had once been a Hindu-majority town, as were most other towns in Sindh. However, following the Partition, most of its Hindu denizens had migrated to India. Their homes were taken over, almost overnight, by Muhajir refugees from India, mainly small traders and artisans from Gujarat and Rajasthan. The town no longer had a Sindhi majority. In the years following the creation of Pakistan, richer Muhajirs gradually began to leave for bigger cities in Sindh, such as Hyderabad and Karachi, where opportunities were better, and soon Tando Allah Yar fell into what appeared to be irretrievable decay. There were hardly any proper schools in the town, Khurshid said, and its municipality was as good as nonexistent. Garbage collected in towering heaps; the roads were riddled with potholes far beyond repair; and the town's few public parks were now dumping grounds for construction waste. While schools declined—many of them existed only on paper—conservative madrasas flourished. Armed dacoits spread terror in the countryside beyond. If Khurshid were to be believed, Tando Allah Yar epitomized all that he felt had gone wrong with Pakistan.

Many of Khurshid's close relatives also lived in Tando Allah Yar, in a locality almost entirely inhabited by fellow Kaim Khani refugees from India. The town appeared to be a patchwork of localities identified on the basis of caste, an indication of how deeply rooted caste and tribal identities continued to remain in Pakistan despite Islam's stress on the absolute equality of all Muslims. The majority of the inhabitants of Syed Paro were Syeds, who claimed to be descendants of the Prophet Muhammad. Chhippa Paro was home to dozens of families of the Chhippa caste, whose caste profession was printing designs on cloth. The Silavat inhabitants of the locality named after their caste were stone-workers. The Sheedhis or Siddis, descendants of African slaves brought to Sindh by Arab traders and who were easily identifiable by their dark complexions, frizzy hair and stubby noses, lived in their own separate enclave. Meghwal Paro was inhabited by almost a hundred families of Dalit Meghwals, only some of whom still carried on with their ancestral craft of weaving. The miserable huts of the Bala Shahis, Muslim sweepers, were located at the edge of the town, not far from where the Bhangis, their Hindu counterparts, lived. And just outside the limits of Tando Allah Yar, on a vast, arid plot of sand-blown land owned by the government, was the sprawling slum that was home to several dozen families belonging to various Dalit communities. That was also where many of Khurshid's friends lived.

Khurshid spent little time with his family and relatives in Tando Allah Yar. 'After we shifted to Pakistan, most of our Kaim Khanis drastically changed themselves. They gave up their practices which the mullahs consider to be Hindu or un-Islamic. Many joined various Muslim revivalist outfits, and now have no interest whatsoever in the history and traditions of our ancestors. Some of them even consider these to be an embarrassment which they want to forget,' he bemoaned. Several Kaim Khanis were now ardent activists of the Tablighi Jamaat, the conservative Muslim revivalist movement that I had spent years studying for my PhD. In line with the diktats of the movement, the men sported long, unkempt beards ('the longer down it travels towards the belly, the more religious merit it brings', a Muslim critic of the Tablighi Jamaat had once joked to me), and their womenfolk were enjoined to observe strict seclusion ('Women's voices must also be veiled because they can sexually entice others,' a Tablighi maulvi had once told me). Khurshid characterized what he contemptuously called this 'pseudo-religiosity' as driven by unrelenting hatred, fear and anger, a complete antithesis of popular Sindhi Islam. It had no space for tolerance, love and compassion, particularly for women and non-Muslims, and was the principle factor behind the rapidly mounting authoritarian tendencies in Pakistani culture which, he argued, were also reflected in the behaviour of the Pakistani state towards its own citizens. It was dull, dour and humourless, a version of Islam that, he said, was becoming increasingly popular among significant sections of the Pakistani middle classes. Quite naturally then, as I could gather, many of his fellow-Kaim Khanis found Khurshid's views on religion wholly heretical. It was only in the squalid Dalit slum on the fringes of Tando Allah Yar that Khurshid could find what he still pined for—something that reminded him of 'home' in distant Sikar.

The slum, separated from the rest of Tando Allah Yar by a sprawling swamp, consisted of several rows of miniscule one-room hutments made of bundles of straw, plastic packets and sticks strung together. It lacked every basic amenity—even a communal hand-pump. It was obvious that its inhabitants were of no concern at all to the authorities.

We walked through the slum till we came on to a clearing, at the entrance of which was a board nailed on a pole driven into the ground. *Welcome to Goga Pir Jogi Colony*, it announced in fading Urdu letters. The board had been Khurshid's idea so that the Jogis who lived there—on what was still government-owned land, despite the fact that they had been there for decades—could have some sort of claim to the plot. It would possibly make it somewhat more difficult for them to be evicted, Khurshid hoped. Few non-Jogis ever entered the Jogi settlement—no one was bothered about them. And because the Jogis kept poisonous snakes in their homes, nobody, Khurshid said, dared trespass into their 'colony'.

The colony had been named after Goga Pir—this, again, had been Khurshid's idea. This folk hero, whose shrine in Ganganagar in India I had visited several years ago, was considered the patron saint of both the Kaim Khanis and the Jogis. As was common with many such figures, his religious identity was blurred and ambiguous. Hindus and Muslims both laid claim to him. No one knew for sure what his religion had been, and that, Khurshid joked, was what he liked best about him.

Half a dozen black, bare-bottomed children, their scraggly hair turned orange with malnutrition, raced towards Khurshid as we stepped into the Jogi colony. 'Uncle! Ustad! Chacha!' they shrieked and raced into his drawn-out arms. They and their parents were, Khurshid said, his only friends in Tando Allah Yar. Years ago, he had started a make-shift school in the colony, with himself as the only teacher. He had also set up a small shrine in the colony, dedicated to Goga Pir and to Mahadev or Shiva who, he believed, had been an ancient tribal deity of the Dravidians of the Indus Valley Civilization. The brass bell, the harmonium and the *dholak* that were carefully kept in the shrine had been bought by him while on a recent trip to India.

Kalia Jogi, the oldest man in the colony, embraced us warmly. He led us to a cot that stood in the sparse shade of a *khejdi* tree. His wife and daughter-in law, both dressed in

Rajasthani-style cholis and ghagras that swirled around their ankles, came out to greet us. Kalia Jogi explained that the Jogis never allowed their womenfolk to appear before unrelated men with their faces uncovered. 'But Khurshid bhai is part of our family, and since you are his friend, you, too, are one of us,' he said.

Kalia Jogi was around twenty years old when India was partitioned. That made him almost eighty now, although he did not seem a year older than fifty. His face was a pale, coppery brown. In his ears, the lobes of which reached halfway down to his chin, he wore rings made of buffalo bone. He sported a saffron turban on his head, wound up in several layers like a cone.

Kalia Jogi was the head of the Jogis of Tando Allah Yar. There were several thousand Jogis in Sindh, and a sprinkling in Punjab and Baluchistan, he said, but no one knew quite how many. Almost all of them were Marwari-speaking, having migrated to Sindh years before the Partition from Rajasthan. Unlike other more powerful and influential castes, the Jogis lived in scattered groups and had no organization of their own to work for their collective welfare. Most Jogis continued, like their ancestors before them, to be nomadic. They moved from place to place, searching for snakes, curing snakebites, selling herbal medicines and begging for food. They travelled around with their snakes kept in cane baskets that they slung on their shoulders and, stopping wherever they could gather a curious crowd, they displayed their animals and made them dance to the plaintive wail of the *been*, a flute sculpted from a gourd. That had been their ancestral profession for as long as Kalia Jogi could remember.

It was not that the Jogis had always been like this, Kalia Jogi said, spreading his hands haplessly about him to indicate the desperate poverty in which he and his clan lived. 'We are Naths, followers of Mahadev Shiv-ji, and of Gorakhnath and

Machhinder Nath. They had great magical powers, born from years of asceticism. People, even Brahmins, used to regard them in great esteem.'

Most Jogis in Sindh were Hindus but, following the Partition, several families had converted to Islam, and for a variety of reasons. For some, it was a means of upward social mobility and to escape the inferior status to which caste Hindus had consigned them for centuries. For others, it was a way to gain acceptance among the dominant Muslims, who looked down on the Jogis for being Hindus. But Kalia Jogi claimed to have gone beyond conventional religion. He sat thoughtfully for a while, his head swaying this way and that. Then, clearing his throat, he sang:

> A true Jogi is one
> Who has transcended man-made identities.
> He realizes the light of God
> In every particle of His creation.
> Neither Hindu nor Muslim am I.
> That I know.
> But what I really am
> Is what I still struggle to realize.

This was the *kalam*, Kalia Jogi said, of a Jogi saint, a distant relative of his, who had been a disciple of a Sufi from interior Sindh.

But this was not how most people understood God, Kalia Jogi lamented, although, he said, it was only this way of approaching the Divine that could heal the wounds that the Muslims and the Hindus and the 'high' and 'low' castes had inflicted on each other for centuries. Getting that message across, even to many of his fellow Jogis, was, he admitted, virtually impossible. He pointed to a cluster of hovels behind a line of cacti that marked the end of the Jogi settlement. 'Those huts belong to the Gurgulas. They earn their livelihood by working on the roads or by selling cosmetics and toys. Like us, they are Hindus, and are even poorer than us. But, the Jogis have nothing at all to do with them,' he explained. The Jogis consider the Gurgulas to be their inferiors. Eating with them, or even consuming anything cooked by a Gurgula, was considered a sin, a serious violation of the rules of caste. Not surprisingly, the Gurgulas were debarred by the Jogis from praying at the shrine of Goga Pir and Mahadev in the Jogi colony.

Sahu, from the Meghwal caste, was another of Khurshid's Dalit friends in Tando Allah Yar. In his early thirties, he had studied at the University of Jamshoro and now ran a tailoring shop. He was an ardent Sindhi nationalist, a follower of a powerful Sindhi wadera who was known to be stridently anti-Punjabi and whose politics essentially had to do with resisting what he called 'Punjabi colonialism'.

There appeared to be no other topic that elicited as much passion and excitement among the general Pakistani public than politics, though this might seem strange, given the fact that democracy had never been allowed to flourish in the country, where public culture still remained sternly authoritarian. But, and ironically perhaps for that very reason, 'ordinary' Pakistanis—who strongly resented the military or military-backed regimes that had ruled Pakistan for most of its existence and kept politics a narrow preserve of the feudal, military and bureaucratic élite—were irrepressibly passionate about politics. Still, this passion had consistently failed to make much of a dent in Pakistan's authoritarian political system.

Sahu was a typical Pakistani in this respect. Politics seemed to be the only thing he could think and talk about. Like the

many political activists I had met in Lahore, he was a glib
talker and, at the same time, a poor listener. For more than an
hour I was subjected to a long, uninterrupted harangue about
all that Sahu thought was wrong with Pakistan's politics. It
seemed as if all the woes of Pakistan—and he rattled off a long
list of complaints—were entirely attributable to the alleged evil
machinations of the Punjabis. Even the mounting
unemployment among Meghwal and other manual workers in
Tando Allah Yar, so he claimed, was a 'Punjabi conspiracy'
against the Sindhis. Pakistan's Punjabi rulers, so the Sindhi
nationalist wadera whom Sahu so admired had claimed, were
deliberately flooding Sindh with Pathans from the North-West
Frontier Province and Afghanistan to reduce the Sindhis to an
even smaller minority in their homeland and to rob the Sindhi
poor of their jobs.

Mercifully, at this juncture, Khurshid bluntly cut him short.
The nationalist wadera that Sahu was besotted by, he retorted,
was one of the largest landlords in all of Sindh, the owner of
an estate that extended over several thousand acres. And, just
because the wadera did not hesitate to occasionally share a meal
with his Dalit followers, he was not, as Sahu claimed, 'secular'
or genuinely concerned about the plight of the Dalits. After all,
he employed several hundred Dalit haris on his estate, where
they lived in abject poverty. Khurshid admitted that provincial
autonomy and an end to Punjabi hegemony in Pakistan was a
central democratic demand but, at the same time, he insisted
that Sindhi nationalist leaders, many of whom were powerful
waderas, were hardly less exploitative than the Punjabi military
and feudal lords whom they projected as the enemies of the
Sindhi 'nation'. This sort of nationalism, he argued, was
consistently deployed as a cover-up by the Sindhi waderas to
paper over the serious internal class- and caste-contradictions
within their own society in an effort to bolster their hegemony.

Sahu shook his head in disagreement. Khurshid had no

understanding of politics, he angrily retorted. Sahu's devotion
to his wadera political leader, Khurshid shot back, was as
pathetic as the blind faith of Sindhi haris in the supposedly
miraculous powers of the Pirs, descendants of Sufi saints. Sahu
was about to respond when his father interrupted him. 'That
wadera is a cheat! I'm fed up of hearing you constantly praising
him. Stupid boy, you don't realize but he's simply using you
to get the support of the Meghwals,' he mumbled. Thereupon—
and much to my relief—Sahu kept quiet and silently sulked.

Sahu's father, who appeared to be in his early seventies, was
a soft-spoken man. He took an active interest in Khurshid's
efforts to mobilize the Dalits. 'Upper' caste Hindus, he said,
treated the Dalits as Untouchables, considering them as 'Hindus'
only for purposes of the census so as to inflate Hindu numbers
and, on that basis, garner more power for themselves. They still
forbade the Dalits from entering their temples. Most Dalits
followed their own tribal deities, who, he believed, could be
traced to the pre-Aryan Indus Valley Civilization. In actual
fact, he insisted, the Dalits had never been Hindus, in the real
sense of the term, at all.

The situation for the Dalits had drastically changed after the
Partition, when most of Sindh's 'upper' caste Hindus had
migrated to India, he went on. The vacuum created by their
departure had facilitated the process of Hinduizing the Dalits
who remained behind, as a means of their upward social
mobility within the caste system. This process might have been
forcefully resisted by 'upper' caste Hindus had they remained
in Sindh in substantial numbers. But, the role of immediate
oppressors of the Dalits that 'upper' caste Hindus had earlier
played had now been taken over by Muslim landlords.
Consequently, Sahu's father went on, the Hinduization of the
Dalits had received considerable impetus in the years after the
Partition. They had begun to take on more Sanskritized names
for themselves, and some had even started to claim that at some

distant time in the past they had been 'high' caste Rajputs who, for some minor violation of the iron law of caste, had been pushed down the caste ladder by the Brahmins. This process of Hinduization, so Sahu's father believed, posed insurmountable barriers to the Dalit movement that he, along with Khurshid and other colleagues, were seeking to promote in Pakistan.

Sahu's father's interest in Dalit activism had been sparked off while on a visit some years ago to India, when he had accompanied a group of Pakistani Hindu pilgrims to visit various important *tirath*s or Hindu centres of pilgrimage. 'I had always wanted to go to the Ganga. Bathing in its waters, I had been taught, would wash off all my sins,' he said. On their way back to Pakistan, the party of pilgrims reached a town in Rajasthan, where they entered a temple to pray. When the Brahmin priest learned that they were Pakistani Hindus, he was delighted. 'He garlanded us and offered to do a special puja free of cost,' he continued. But, just as he was about to enter the temple, the priest asked him his caste. He answered him, and that, to the priest, was like a brick being flung into his face. He angrily drove him out, showering him with filthy abuse, threatening to have him beaten up for his alleged insouciance.

That incident, Sahu's father said, had transformed him completely. He had then given up on Hinduism, realizing, as he put it, 'that it spelt perpetual slavery for the Dalits.' On his return from India, he had met with Khurshid, who had introduced him to the thoughts of Babasaheb Bhimrao Ambedkar. He was now a staunch Ambedkarite. 'No longer do I greet my fellow Meghwals with the slogan *Ram-Ram*,' he proudly said. 'I insist they should say *Jai Bhim* instead, for Bhimrao Ambedkar, not Ram, is our true hero.'

The next afternoon, Sahu's father took me to the Rama Pir temple, located in the main market area of Tando Allah Yar. More than a century old, it was one of the largest Hindu shrines in the whole of Sindh. It was set inside a large walled compound, and included a recently built *sarai* or rest house for pilgrims and a domed structure that housed separate shrines for various Hindu deities. A statue of a turbaned warrior astride a blue-hued horse stood just below the central dome. This was the Dalit hero Rama Pir, also known as Ram Devji or Ram Shah Pir.

Rama Pir is the most popular folk deity among the Dalits of Sindh, particularly the Meghwals. The principal shrine of the Rama Pir cult is located at Ramdevra, in western Rajasthan, where he is still widely revered. Little is known about this enigmatic figure. Recent research suggests that he might have been born in a Meghwal family, and was probably a convert to the Nizari Ismaili branch of Shia Islam. The Nizari *dai*s or missionaries, who, from the tenth century onwards, were active in Sindh and western Rajasthan, often used two sets of names— their own Islamic or Arabo-Persian name as well as a Hindu one. This, and their liberal use of Hindu motifs and narratives, was a means to appear more acceptable and intelligible to their Hindu, mainly Dalit, audience, among whom they made numerous converts. This probably explains how Rama Pir got his Hindu-sounding name.

The first Nizari missionary to India, the eleventh-century Nur Satgur, who is buried in Navsari in Gujarat, established the practice of spreading Nizari beliefs by using Hindu idioms, presenting the Nizari faith as a fulfilment of the Hindus' millennial expectations of an avatar who would redeem the world before the end of time. This was in line with the Shia practice of *taqiyya* or concealment of belief in order to stave off persecution. Thus, the Nizari faith was presented as the Sat Panth, the Sat Dharm or the Maha Marg, as well as the Nizar

Panth and the Nij Dharm. The Prophet's cousin and son-in-law Ali, a key figure in Shia theology, was depicted as the Nikalank Avatar, the tenth incarnation of Vishnu. Following established Nizari practice, many Ismaili neophytes kept their faith concealed, being what was termed in Indian Nizari parlance as *gupti momins* or 'secret believers'.

The fact that terms such as Nizar, Nijar, Mecca, Nur Satgur and so on were found in verses attributed to Rama Pir strongly suggests that he was probably a secret Ismaili missionary or at least highly influenced by the Ismailis. So, too, is the fact that in several oral narratives related by the Meghwals, Rama Pir has referred to himself as 'Nijari', a corruption of the Arabo-Persian term 'Nizari'. The sacred mantra recited by Rama Pir's followers also contained the word 'Nizar' (*Om Som Nikalank Dev Nizar*). Rama Pir's grave in Ramdevra is fashioned in traditional Muslim style and has Arabic inscriptions—possibly Quranic verses—embossed on it, and this is further possible evidence of his Muslim, probably Nizari Shia, identity.

As in the case of numerous other Dalit religious traditions centred on powerful heroes who dared to challenge Brahminical tyranny, the Rama Pir cult was gradually Brahminized through the centuries. This occurred through a subtle process of appropriation and accommodation of the cult by 'upper' caste Hindus, the consequence of which was to drain the tradition of its radical anti-caste thrust and appeal. Rama Pir's own Ismaili connections were suppressed and, instead, he came to be projected as a form of Krishna, and as having allegedly been born in a family of 'high' caste Rajput rulers. This rewriting of history facilitated the rapid Hinduization of the cult and its greater acceptability among caste Hindus.

This explains how, Sahu's father said, as he took me around the temple, idols of various Brahminical deities had recently been installed there, although the Rama Pir tradition had, since its very inception, been based on the notion of a formless God, similar to that in Islam. The marble statue purporting to be that of Rama Pir, which occupied the sanctum sanctorum of the shrine, was also relatively new.

Sahu's father did not conceal his distaste for what he regarded as the degeneration of the tradition of his ancestors. The Hinduization of the cult of Rama Pir, he said, was tantamount to inverting its fundamental message of social equality, based on the notion of a God beyond physical form. Rama Pir, he said, never claimed to be God himself, although this was precisely what those who considered him as an avatar of Krishna or a form of Vishnu sought to project him as. And, by seeking to convert him into a miracle-working divine being who was to be worshipped rather than emulated, they had stripped him of his humanity and, more importantly, of the inspiration that Dalits could draw from him in their struggle for social justice. In his time, Rama Pir had been ostracized by the 'high' castes for leading Dalits in religious gatherings or the *jama jagran*s that were held in secret at night, probably to avoid persecution, and for eating with them. He struck at one of the major pillars of caste discrimination—the ban on inter-caste commensality—by speaking of the day when, in his own words, 'Brahmins, Banias, Rajputs and Muslims shall eat from the same plate', and that too in a Dalit home, 'when the gathering shall be held in the house of Meghwal Rishi'. But by 'converting' him into a 'high' caste Rajput, and a form of Krishna at that, the 'high' castes who were manipulating Rama Pir's story wanted his Dalit followers to forget that the struggle against caste oppression had been a central aspect of his mission.

Sahu's father also referred to the sinister caste politics behind the transformation of the Rama Pir tradition. 'Upper' caste Hindus had, for centuries, treated the tradition with scorn, for it was closely related to the Dalits. Even now, Sahu's father said, almost no 'upper' caste Hindus worshipped at Rama Pir's

temple in Tando Allah Yar. In recent years, as the cult of Rama
Pir had begun to grow beyond its narrow, almost entirely
Meghwal, constituency to include most other Dalit castes in
Sindh, the numbers of pilgrims to his temple had rapidly
multiplied. One reason for this, he opined, was the pervasive
sense of insecurity among the Pakistani Dalits, living as a
marginalized minority in a Muslim-dominated society. This
had been further exacerbated by attacks on Hindu and Dalit
shrines across Sindh in the aftermath of the destruction of the
Babri Masjid and the ensuing massacre of Muslims in large
parts of India. The growing fears of threat to their identity, and
their very lives, of Pakistani Dalits was reflected in the swelling
numbers of Dalit pilgrims to Rama Pir's shrine, including non-
Meghwals, who lacked a major folk hero and a temple of their
own. The annual fair at the shrine was now a week-long affair,
attracting tens of thousands of Dalits from all across Pakistan.

As the numbers of pilgrims to the temple began rapidly
mounting, so did the revenues that they brought in. It was this,
Sahu's father explained, that had led to the Meghwal priest of
the temple being replaced, at the behest of some prominent
'upper' caste Sindhi Hindus, by a Brahmin. The new priest did
not last long, however. A staunch Hindu who treated the
Dalits as Untouchables, he is said to have been driven out by
a group of Bhils angered by his refusal to let Bhil pilgrims
touch his feet for fear of being 'polluted' thereby. He was
replaced by a Maheshwari Bania, for whom Sahu's father had
no kind words either. He had been appointed to the post, he
said, simply to garner money from the Dalit pilgrims, but did
nothing for them in return. He was also bent on Hinduizing
the shrine and the cult of Rama Pir even further, for that
helped strengthen 'upper' caste Hindu claims over the shrine
and its substantial income.

The Marwari-speaking 'Hindu' Mehtars or sweepers occupied a separate settlement on the edge of Tando Allah Yar. In the vicinity were distinct enclaves inhabited by Gujarati- and Hindustani-speaking Mehtars. Although all three of these non-Muslim Mehtar groups shared a common occupation and position in the caste system, they remained separate endogamous caste groups. Despised, shunned and considered as being at the bottom of the caste pyramid, they, along with the Muslim sweepers, known as Bala Shahis, played a vital role in the town's life. Were it not for the valuable services that they rendered, Tando Allah Yar, miserably filthy as it already was, would certainly have been completely unlivable.

Ironically, the Marwari Mehtar locality appeared to be an islet of order and cleanliness set amidst the sea of squalor that comprised the rest of the town. The dozen or so houses in the locality were all made of brick and were neatly whitewashed—an oddity in Tando Allah Yar, where almost every house was left unpainted and appeared either incomplete or else in a state of considerable ruin. Ribbons of bright orange bougainvillea ringed the low-level walls that enclosed the houses. At the entrance to the locality was a cement platform, on which were placed cone-shaped stones painted a bright ochre and a vase containing incense sticks—a *thaan* or shrine dedicated to Bala Shah, the patron saint of the sweepers.

Raju Chamaria, another of Khurshid's Dalit friends, was one of the few educated members of the Marwari Mehtar caste in Tando Allah Yar. He insisted I lunch at his home. He lived in a neat two-storey house, on which, he said, his father had spent all the precious savings he had made as a sweeper employed by the local municipal committee. The drawing room where we sat was comfortably done-up. The soft, sweet smell of sandalwood floated about the room. From my comfortable perch on a sofa, I surveyed the house. There was nothing that I could see that was even remotely suggestive of the stereotypical notion of the despised Mehtar that many Hindus and Muslims continue to espouse.

Unlike most of his relatives, Raju did not do sweeping work in the streets of Tando Allah Yar. Instead, he spent most of his time collecting and reading books. Some years ago, he had published a booklet about Rama Pir. He was now collecting material for a book that he planned to write on Hinglaj Mata, a form of the goddess Sati, whose temple was located in Makran, in the Baluchistan desert. She was also revered by some Baluchi Muslims as Nani Ma or 'Grandmother'.

According to Hindu mythology, Sati, the daughter of King Daksha, was the consort of Shiva. Annoyed with her father for not having invited her husband to a sacrifice he had organized, she leapt into the sacrificial fire and burnt herself to death. Shiva's wrath on hearing of his wife's death knew no bounds. He lifted Sati's corpse in his arms and began roaming around the world, threatening to set it ablaze. In an effort to calm him down and to prevent him from dancing the deadly *tandav* that would have reduced the entire earth to ashes, Vishnu intervened by chopping Sati's corpse into fifty-one pieces which, so it is believed, were scattered over various places across India. The most important of them, Sati's head, landed at Hinglaj, and hence the shrine there is considered to be the most revered of the numerous Shakti Peeths. Raju believed that Hinglaj Mata or Sati represented an ancient pre-Aryan Dravidian religious tradition associated with the Indus Valley Civilization.

Raju was deeply pained by the plight of his community. The Mehtars were treated with scorn and disdain, as being 'worse than animals', he said, by Hindus, Muslims and even by the other Dalit castes. 'The Hindus do not consider us to be human beings, leave alone fellow Hindus. The Muslims mistake us for Hindus, and that makes them look down at us even more. Many Muslims follow the Hindu caste system and treat not just us, but also the Muslim Mehtars, as despicable and unclean.'

As one of the few educated members of his community, Raju considered it his duty to work for his own people. Writing about the history of Dalit heroes was his way of doing this. 'We need to create within ourselves a positive identity, a sense of self-worth, a consciousness that we, too, have produced heroes and great people,' he explained. 'Only then can we work towards changing the way other people perceive us.'

Raju asked me if I knew of any book about noted Indian Mehtars. I did not. 'But there are so many Mehtars in India,' he exclaimed in surprise, 'and you Indians are so much more educated than us Pakistanis. Surely you must know of some Indian scholar who has written something on that subject.' I shook my head, embarrassed. Caste discrimination, I answered, continued to thrive in India, even in universities, which remained dominated by 'upper' caste Hindus. This explained why despised castes like the Mehtars continue to be ignored, even by many self-styled progressive Indian writers.

'But I see Indian movies regularly,' Raju countered. 'They never mention caste, so the situation of the Mehtars in India could not be as bad as you seem to make it.'

I could not suppress a cynical snigger, impolite though Raju may have thought me to be. I glanced at the posters of fair-skinned, scantily dressed Bollywood heroines that hung on the wall in front of me. None of them, of course, was a Dalit. Dalits probably had no presence in Bollywood, save, perhaps, in occasional films, where they might be used as dark-skinned accomplices of smugglers and dacoits. In short, Bollywood, like much of the rest of India, had little or no room for the Dalits, and I said as much to him.

'You will be shocked, Raju,' I concluded. 'There is little difference between India and Pakistan as far as the treatment of your people is concerned.'

The late Asad Ali Kaim Khani, Khurshid's father, had bought a couple of acres of sandy land some twenty kilometres from Tando Allah Yar, which he had converted into a flourishing farm. The farm, or *goth* in Sindhi, was Khurshid's regular hideaway from the squalor and deadening boredom of Tando Allah Yar. In the wake of the Partition, many waderas had grabbed land in the area that had been owned by Hindus who had left for India. Most of these Hindus had been city-based traders and moneylenders, who had managed to take control over the land by methods designed to trap landowners in debts that they could never repay. Some of the land that they left behind had also been allotted by the government to Muhajirs, who streamed in from India. The system of granting land to them had been somewhat arbitrary and riddled with corruption. Muhajirs who had left behind a small patch of land in India, and were, technically, entitled to the same amount of land in Pakistan as compensation, often claimed to have been the owners of plots far bigger than they had actually possessed. In this way, the influential among them were able to more than make up for the land that they had lost. Asad Ali Kaim Khani had been a rare, honest exception, however. He had left behind six acres in Sikar, and he applied for and was granted a plot of the same size outside Tando Allah Yar. He later supplemented that with another six acres, bought with money that he had saved in the course of working as an officer in the Pakistani Army.

Khurshid's goth was located five kilometres off a tarred road. From there, we walked down a sandy track that ran parallel to a canal bringing water to ripening sugar cane fields and mango orchards from the Indus beyond. The fields mostly belonged to Kaim Khanis from Tando Allah Yar. They were absentee landlords, living off the labour of their haris, the vast majority of whom were Dalits. The canal was lined with thorny bushes and tall wild grass—ideal terrain, Khurshid said, for the dacoits who infested this part of Sindh.

A goth was an estate belonging to a single landlord, usually named after the person who established it. It was surrounded by high mud walls to keep out dacoits and strangers. Behind the walls was the *baithak* or mansion of the wadera, who often had an even more opulent mansion in the neighbouring town or city. Surrounding the main house were the miserable hovels of the haris. Because these were owned by the wadera, the haris were entirely at his mercy. They could be evicted at will.

Khurshid's goth was tiny by Sindhi standards, where estates could extend to thousands of acres. His farm was a modest twelve acres in size, but it boasted of rich, loamy soil that delivered two crops of rice a year plus an annual harvest of sugar cane and mangoes. Twenty Bhil families, all related to each other, lived on the goth. Some of them worked on Khurshid's farm, but most worked elsewhere, as daily wage earners. They had been brought there by Khurshid's father when Khurshid was himself a child, and Khurshid considered them as part of his own family.

Balu, whom Khurshid described as 'even closer than a real brother', unlocked the heavily barricaded gate that pierced the high wall that ran all round the goth. His father had been employed by Khurshid's father even before Khurshid was born. Balu and Khurshid were roughly of the same age, and they had grown up together.

Balu was a big, burly Bhil. Broad and almost six feet tall, he towered above me like a giant. His coal-black skin, his finely chiselled face, his thick, well-oiled moustache, carefully twirled up at the ends, the glistening gold caps on his front teeth, the rings that dangled from his earlobes, the red and black block-printed ajrak that was carelessly thrown across his shoulders, and the neatly creased *bandhani* turban that he sported, all lent him a distinct grace and an aura of dignity. He welcomed me with a tight, almost-suffocating, embrace.

After we had freshened up, Balu's children brought in our dinner—thick *bajra roti*s cooked in a clay oven with a tangy chutney made of crushed garlic, onion and chillies lightly fried in home-made ghee. We ate together, Khurshid, Balu and I, from the same large steel thali, sitting on a cot in the courtyard, fed by the warmth of a smoky fire. Leathery bats flitted between the trees. From the canal beyond the walls of the goth, a family of frogs croaked together in concert. The clear night sky spread out into a vast star-sequinned sheet. Balu's nieces and nephews, huddled under patchwork razais on their cots, giggled and guffawed as they kept watch over us.

A chill wind blowing in from the direction of the canal soon drove us inside the farmhouse—a simple yet elegant three-roomed structure. Balu's children brought in bundles of razais, and Balu and his two brothers carried in their musical instruments—a dholak, a harmonium, a *chimta* and a *khartal*. 'When two or more good people gather together, it is time to invoke God and have a *satsang*,' Balu joked.

'I know you are good. I can't say that about myself, though,' Khurshid cackled. 'You are a good, valiant Chauhan Rajput, while I am not.'

Balu let out a full-throated laugh, and Khurshid explained the joke. The Bhils, who claimed Chauhan Rajput descent, as did the Kaim Khanis, had retained their ancestral religion, while the Kaim Khanis had abandoned it. Hence, unlike Balu, Khurshid was no longer a 'good' Chauhan.

We shuffled off our shoes and curled up under the razais spread out on the floor. The satsang began. Balu shut his eyes and drew in a deep breath, retaining it for as long as he could. Then, he recited, in a low, measured tone, an incantation to God and his Guru. *Om Shri Parameshwar, Om Shri Sat Guru, Om Shri Jagat Guru*. He repeated this three times, and we solemnly intoned after him.

The clay lamp was snuffed out and the room was enveloped in a blanket of darkness. A smudge of moonlight struggled to filter in through the closed window. Of Balu only the outlines of his body and the whites of his eyes were visible. As his brothers began tuning their instruments Balu explained the significance of the satsang—'the congregation of the truthful'. It was a means of expressing devotion to God, he said. But, it was also a way for the faithful to bond together, the seed, as it were, of a virtuous community, for a satsang could be done only in a group. It was different from individual worship and devotion. The sadhus and the Sufis of Sindh had used satsang, called *mehfil-e sama* in Urdu and Sindhi, to bring together people of different castes and creeds in common worship of the one formless God.

The satsang went on till well past midnight. Balu and his brothers sang in Urdu, Baluchi, Hindi, Marwari and Sindhi, shifting between the languages with perfect ease. They sang bhajans of the Rajput princess Mira Bai, *doha*s of the weaver-poet Kabir, *shabad*s from the Granth Sahib of the Sikhs, and the *kalam* of the patron Sufi saints of Sindh, Shah Abdul Latif and Shah Inayat of Jhok. They sang of devotion and utter surrender to God, of love for all His creatures, of the fleetingness of this world, of the eternal life after death, of the plight of the poor and the torments that awaited the godless rich in the court of God. They sang about the emptiness of ritualism and of the greed of mullahs and *pujari*s alike. They sang in praise of the soul that had transcended man-made boundaries of caste and community and had finally realized God. They sang with a haunting passion, born of indescribable pain—the pain of being impoverished and Dalit, of belonging to a people crushed by the cruel burdens of history for as long as they could remember. But behind their plaintive appeals to God was also a hint of an irrepressible hope and a fervent refusal to haplessly accept the tragic fate that had been thrust on them and their ancestors. No powerful wadera, no wily politician, no ranting mullah or bigotted Brahmin could suppress that overpowering yearning for freedom.

twelve

the mound of the dead

I woke up the next morning to the frantic squawking of a pair of red-beaked parrots that had made their nest in the mango tree outside the window of my room and the puffing of a pump hauling water from the canal just beyond the walls of the goth. The fog was lifting gradually, and from the window I could see Balu's wife vigorously milking her buffalo. A group of Bhil women made their way out of the goth, carrying spades and pickaxes on their shoulders and balancing their babies on their hips. They worked in the fields of neighbouring waderas but lived on Khurshid's goth, where they felt safe.

Hemu, Balu's eldest son, knocked on my door, bearing a mug of tea and a basket of hot rotis. We ate together, and then we walked across to the Bhils' houses. There were some fifteen of them, neatly laid out in a row. They were made of mud and reinforced with stones and shafts of bamboo. Their carefully trimmed thatched roofs sported white flags painted with the sacred symbols of the Rama Pir cult—the sun, a crescent moon and a pair of footprints. Framed pictures of Hindu deities and Bollywood film stars nudged against each other on some of the walls.

At the far end of the settlement, near where the animals were

235

tied, was a stone platform plastered with a fresh coat of cow-dung. A red rag was tied across it, in which was placed a crudely carved piece of wood half a foot long and painted bright crimson. Only its eyes and breasts could be distinguished, and these were exaggeratedly large and were made of bits of silver paper. This, Hemu explained, was Jog Maya, the patron goddess of the Bhils. Adjacent to her shrine was another squat platform, on which was placed a bundle of green cloth, tied up like a little pillow. It represented, Hemu said, the *nishan* or symbol of 'Sufi Sahib'—a Muslim saint whose shrine he had once visited but whose name he could not remember.

I had expected that we would spend the day lazing about on the goth, but just then Khurshid hollered out for me. 'We are leaving in exactly half an hour for Moenjo Daro. Hurry up and get ready! We can't wait endlessly for you, you oaf!'

That was Khurshid being true to form. At more than seventy, he was still a prank-playing child at heart.

In less than ten minutes, I stuffed my belongings into my bag, washed my face and changed into the loose shalwar-kameez and Sindhi-style mirror-work cap that Khurshid had gifted me. I threw an ajrak across my shoulders, which trailed down to my knees. 'You look like a bumbling wadera!' Khurshid chuckled as he watched me dress.

Unbeknown to me, Khurshid had made elaborate arrangements for us to travel all the way to Moenjo Daro— almost 600 kilometres to the north, a journey of some ten hours—and, on the way back, to take a detour to visit some of the most venerated Sufi shrines in Sindh. It would be a hurried, two-day trip, he said, because Hemu, whose recently acquired second-hand pick-up truck we would be using, had to return soon to deliver a consignment of mangoes to Karachi.

Balu joined us reluctantly. 'Why go all the way to an abandoned town where people lived six thousand years ago?

Why spend all that time, money and energy just to see a couple of derelict buildings?' he asked.

Khurshid insisted that we could not do without Balu. What if we were accosted by dacoits on the way? Only Balu the brave Bhil could fight them off, he joked. It was he, Khurshid reminded him, who had single-handedly chased away a band of dacoits who had attacked the goth some years ago. They had been a menace to the waderas and haris of the area, but after Balu had valiantly repulsed them they had dared not show their faces again, and for that the landlords had garlanded him in gratitude at a public function.

And then, Khurshid continued, Moenjo Daro was no simple town. It was built by the Dravidians, the forefathers of the Bhils, Balu's own ancestors. It was the world's largest and most glorious city, he said to him, till the marauding Aryans had invaded it and put to the sword all its inhabitants or else had forced them into servitude as 'low' castes. Did Balu really want to miss out on the opportunity of visiting his 'ancestral home'?

Khurshid's pep talk worked wonders. All at once, Balu relented and changed his mind. 'Yes, of course I have to come with you. I can't let you go alone,' he insisted. 'And, how can I refuse to see the city of my ancestors?'

Khurshid and Balu joined Hemu in the front of the truck. I swung up the steps at the rear and was about to lunge in when an angry black face narrowly missed hitting me. It snorted out curls of hot air from its gaping nostrils. It was Dheema, one of Balu's buffaloes, who was suffering from a bad stomach and was being taken to the veterinary doctor in Hyderabad. She was evidently not in good health at all. A large, and continuously expanding, pool of watery dung spread across the floor of the truck. A noisy jet of pungent sulfurous farts spluttered out from her ample backside as she fixed her angry eyes on me, oblivious of the inconvenience she was causing to the rest of the passengers. Besides the ailing Dheema, at the back of the truck with me, were three Bhil women from the goth who were travelling to the weekly market in Hyderabad along with their children. There was no room to squat, and so I stood at the edge, as far from Dheema as possible, clinging on to the railing.

Boats on River Indus

We drove past Tando Allah Yar and then into Hyderabad, where, much to my relief, Dheema left us and the Bhil women and children piled out. Beyond Hyderabad, the suburbs appeared even more squalid than the city. Mountains of rubbish lined the road, as did mile after mile of depressing, ramshackle houses. We then swerved on to the main Larkana highway, crossing the Indus via the Kotri Barrage. The river appeared stagnant, but country boats gently moved down with their sails billowing in the breeze, as they had for thousands of years.

Shortly after, we passed into the Jamshoro district. The countryside here was flat and bare, save for a few thorny trees. Isolated patches of green stood out against the relentless

monotony of the stony desert. Low-lying hills of slate folded
upon each other in bizarre patterns. Dalit women—
distinguishable by their distinct, brightly coloured dresses—
walked along the road in groups, bearing pots on their heads,
heading for the nearest source of water, which might be miles
away from their miserable hovels. Barefoot children dressed in
rags stood outside the one-roomed stone structures that were
their homes, waving as we passed by. Skinny, dark-skinned
peasant men drove donkey-carts laden with piles of wood,
straw and vegetables to the nearest market.

The road skirted the banks of the Indus, although the river
remained invisible. As we drove farther north, passing into the
Dadu district, the desert receded into the distance behind a
string of hills. Fertile farmland spilled out on either side,
stretching far into the hazy distance. For miles, though, no
house was to be seen. Almost all that land, Khurshid pointed
out, was owned by less than a dozen waderas, who lived in
Karachi and only occasionally visited their estates. This was
Sindh's notorious feudal heartland.

Soon, however, farmland gave way to the encroaching salt-
crusted desert. All this had once been fertile land, but, massive
water-logging, caused by the construction of numerous dams
on the Indus upstream and the indiscriminate use of water
from canals for irrigation, had now rendered it totally unusable.
If the Government of Pakistan went ahead with its plans for
building the mammoth Kalabagh Dam on the Indus in Punjab,
much of the rest of Sindh would turn into desert in the same
way. Not surprising, then, that the Sindhis were up in arms
against the dam, which they regarded as the latest manifestation
of Punjabi colonialism.

We drove past the occasional village and a few small towns.
All of these were uniformly characterized by stark deprivation
and neglect. From my perch at the back of the truck, I did not
notice a single school building, agricultural cooperative or

bank. Probably, I thought, they simply did not exist. I had heard that up to half the government schools in large parts of rural Sindh did not function at all, owing to opposition from the waderas, who did not want their haris to be educated and start demanding their rights. The only sign of the presence of the state, it seemed, were ugly electricity poles coiled with serpentine wires that straddled the road, and cylindrical towers, shaped like minarets, that served as police outposts. These had diminutive entrance doors that were kept tightly shut. Narrow slits halfway up their flanks provided just about enough space for the men holed up inside to survey the countryside and fire their weapons. Their major targets were dreaded dacoits who were said to infest this part of Sindh. Most of the towers were named after various *shaheed*s or martyrs—policemen who had lost their lives fighting off marauding bandits.

The sun was rapidly slipping behind the hills in the far distance by the time we reached the town of Larkana. 'Indian Oppressors Quit Kashmir!' announced a massive poster slung across the road at the entrance to the town. 'Kashmir is the Jugular Vein of Pakistan!'

We turned up the main road, lined with large shops flashing colourful neon signboards and a couple of schools set in neatly trimmed lawns. Larkana seemed an island of prosperity in an ocean of desperate deprivation. It was, after all, the home-town of the Bhutto clan that had produced two Pakistani prime ministers. It was also where many rich waderas from the surrounding countryside had their palatial mansions.

There was little to see in Larkana, though. The town's main Hindu temple was located opposite the restaurant where we had dinner that night, and Balu and I sauntered across while

Hemu and Khurshid went to the market to make some purchases. It was a sprawling structure, with separate chambers for different gods. Verses from the Gita and the Ramayana, crafted in the Arabo-Sindhi script, were etched into slabs of marble fitted into the walls. The evening puja was on, and a crowd of well-dressed men and women stood before the pujari while he intoned Sanskrit verses and swung a pot of incense before them. Balu did not join the congregation. Instead, he stood outside the pillared hall, his eyes transfixed on the idol half-hidden behind a diaphanous curtain at the far end of the corridor. He was afraid that the 'high' caste Hindu worshippers might drive him out if they found out that he was a 'low' caste Bhil.

We rejoined Khurshid and Khemu and strolled down the main street. A posse of Pajeros zipped past us and screeched to a sudden halt outside a mini supermarket. A corpulent middle-aged man hauled himself, with some difficulty, out of the first of these ponderous vehicles. His face was almost completely hidden behind a pair of thick-framed dark glasses. The doors of the other Pajeros in the convoy snapped opened and out poured an entire retinue of turbaned guards brandishing rifles, who rushed to surround the man. Onlookers bent low before him, folding their hands in abject servility.

'He's one of the most notorious waderas in the area,' Khurshid whispered. 'His word is law in these parts.'

We trudged on ahead till we came to the family home of the Bhuttos, reputed to be the largest mansion in Larkana. A whitewashed wall, twenty feet high or more, ran along till the far end of the street, enclosing the mansion within it. The *kothi* was carefully hidden from the prying eye of the public and could not be seen from the outside. The heavily guarded complex occupied an entire block. In the same area were numerous other palatial estates belonging to other waderas, although none of these even closely rivalled the opulence of the Bhuttos. And that, Khurshid caustically remarked, spoke eloquently of their much-vaunted commitment to democracy and socialism about which the Bhuttos had never tired of trumpeting.

We spent that night—31 December—in a grubby lodge. It was too late to scout around for a more comfortable place. The room was bare, save for five steel cots and a naked bulb that dangled precariously from the ceiling. The blankets stank of urine and sweat, but we were too exhausted to make a fuss about it. We slipped into the new year without any fanfare. No crackers went off at midnight. There were no revelries. It was just another day for the denizens of Larkana.

The call to the *fajr* or early morning prayer pierced through the cardboard-thin walls of our room. We washed up, hurriedly packed and piled into the truck. A few stray slivers of pale sunlight lay scattered about, like untidy strands of gossamer, at the foot of the eastern sky. The road was empty, and we drove uninterrupted towards Moenjo Daro, thirty kilometres to the south-west, through lush green fields bursting with ripening wheat and sugar cane. We passed rows of ramshackle mud-and-wattle huts of haris, a couple of modest-sized mosques with short, stump-like minarets, and a dargah of compelling beauty, its façade flecked with intricate blue, green and yellow tiles in geometric patterns. A caravan of camels plodded along a sandy track that wound its way over a stretch of dunes in the far distance. The soil, fed for millennia from the nearby Indus, was rich and loamy, but the people whose houses we drove past all seemed desperately poor. Ironically, they were probably the progeny of the founders of the Indus Valley Civilization, which is said to have been among the most developed and prosperous civilizations of its times.

The towering citadel that presides over the extensive ruins of Moenjo Daro ('Mound of the Dead' in Sindhi) was visible from the road much before we arrived. The excavated ruins of the town cover an area of some 100,000 square metres, but this is estimated as being only under a tenth of the total area that had been occupied by Moenjo Daro at the pinnacle of its glory some six thousand years ago, when it served as the nerve centre of the Indus Valley Civilization. The ruins of the town that still remain unexcavated stretch as far as the banks of the Indus, three kilometres to the north, making Moenjo Daro the largest known Bronze Age town in the ancient world, covering a vast expanse of more than 3 million square metres. Excavations at the site had, however, not gone much beyond the ruins uncovered in 1922 by Sir John Marshall, the then director-general of the Archaeological Survey of India. This was probably because the Archaeological Survey of Pakistan has been strapped for funds, but Khurshid suspected that it might also be due to a distinct reluctance of Pakistan's rulers to highlight and promote the country's pre-Islamic past, fearing that this might undermine its official 'two-nation' theory. It might also have to do with distaste for anything that might further embolden Sindhi nationalists, whose ideology rest on the claim of being a distinct nationality that preceded the arrival of Islam and that traced its roots to the Indus Valley Civilization.

The town was built around the citadel, and comprised separate residential, ritual and commercial quarters. A series of drains covered with baked covers and perforated with soak pits for the disposal of waste stretched along a line of brickwork structures that had once been houses and shops. This indicated a remarkable drainage system that, I could not help thinking, seemed quite unknown in much of contemporary Pakistan. The houses were of varying sizes, possibly indicating a rudimentary sort of class system. At the same time, the bigger and the smaller houses were clustered together; this probably suggests that class distinctions were not extreme and that people of different classes lived in the same localities. Beyond the houses lay the massive granary and the giant bath. Brick-paved roads, some as broad as thirty feet, criss-crossed the town, dividing it into blocks of roughly even size. A series of brick stairs wound around the citadel, which had been converted into a Buddhist stupa in around 1500 BCE, and had remained in use for that purpose until the town was finally abandoned, for reasons that archaeologists and historians continue to heatedly dispute. The citadel commands a panoramic view of the ruins below and the countryside beyond, and of the numerous unexcavated mounds that lie buried under a jungle of tall grasses and thorny bushes that stretch to the banks of the Indus.

I scrambled down from the citadel and pushed into the surrounding bushes, ignoring Khurshid's warnings of hidden dacoits. On each mound that I ascended I found hundreds of shards of brick and baked pottery stuck in the mud. I scratched the ground with a stick and uncovered a piece of what appeared to be the side of a bowl, decorated with a faintly visible streak of black paint. What valuable ancient treasures, I wondered, might lie hidden below the dozens of mounds around that had been left to sink into the encroaching forest? The well-kept museum nearby had salvaged some of them—massive stone vats, clay figurines, metal and stone weights and measures, gold and silver jewellery, pendants made of semi-precious beads, stone implements, metal weapons, copper mirrors, toy carts and miniature animals, seals bearing images of animals and letters in an as-yet undeciphered pictographic script, the bust of a dancing nude woman and a bearded priest wrapped in an embroidered shawl. Also on display were human skeletons dating back 6000 years ago. But below the mounds that spread before me there must, I thought, certainly lie an even richer wealth of ancient artefacts, that, had the Government of Pakistan so willed, could easily have been excavated, thereby adding immeasurably to our limited knowledge of the Indus Valley Civilization and the history of the whole of South Asia.

But perhaps it is just as well that the Pakistani authorities seemed to exhibit no interest in expanding the excavated area around Moenjo Daro. In that way, the precious artefacts that the unexplored mounds contain would remain protected from the very real threat of theft, ironically at the hands of officials of the museum and of the Archaeological Department themselves. These officials had been implicated in a number of alarming scandals over the years. Numerous complaints had appeared in the local press alleging that the authorities had turned a blind eye to the theft of artefacts from the ruins. Some years ago, more than 170 rare objects were robbed from the museum only to be spotted later at auction houses in Europe, where they fetched astronomical sums. In 2002, a gang of robbers broke into the museum and carted off over forty invaluable seals. Inquiries conducted by the local police revealed the involvement in the daring heist of some senior officials of the Archaeological Department as well as a Britain-based archaeologist. The police claimed to have unearthed solid evidence that the three main accused in the theft had met with some archaeologists a fortnight before the robbery who might have assisted them in their plans. Ironically, they had met at a seminar, organized by the UNESCO, to discuss measures for preserving the ruins of the Indus Valley Civilization. One of the robbers, who was later apprehended, confessed that he had sold the priceless seals to a businessman from the United Arab Emirates after failing to get the price he had hoped for in the black market for antiquities in Britain. The police also discovered that more than a hundred seals from the museum had been replaced with replicas, obviously with the connivance of senior museum officials. This raised, the police said, serious doubts about the authenticity of the remaining artefacts in the museum.

There had also been reports of massive financial irregularities and rampant corruption involving money generously granted by the UNESCO to the Government of Pakistan for the preservation of Moenjo Daro. According to newspaper reports, the local councillor of the Larkana district had shot off several letters to the Pakistani government, asking it to hand over the responsibility for the upkeep of the ruins to the district

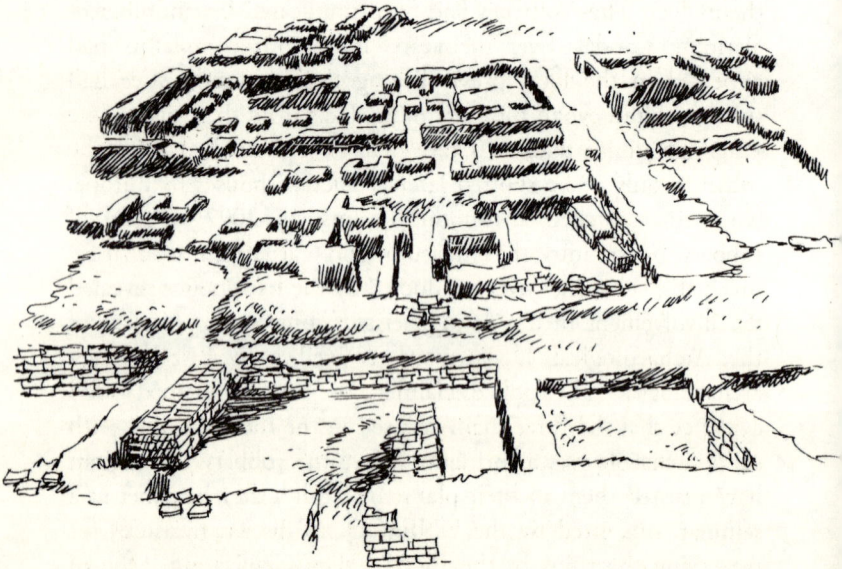

Moenjo Daro

government or else to send experts and funds to preserve the
site from further decay. To his horror, he discovered that a
letterhead 'Committee for the Preservation of Moenjo Daro'
already existed and that its members were drawing fat salaries
from funds allocated by the UNESCO. All the members of the
committee were based in Islamabad, more than a thousand
miles away from Moenjo Daro, and, it was alleged that they
had taken not the slightest interest in the work that they were
paid for. Local journalists demanded to know why the committee
was based in Islamabad, Punjab, if its work was in Moenjo
Daro, Sindh, but the government, naturally, could not come
forth with a convincing reply. It was also reported that several
millions of dollars granted by the UNESCO for the upkeep of
Moenjo Daro had not actually been used for that purpose.
Some of the money had remained unspent, but much of it had
gone into the pockets of officials and other influential people
in Islamabad. Fed up with reports of corruption, the UNESCO
had even threatened to stop funding Moenjo Daro and to
remove it from its list of World Heritage Sites.

Meanwhile, Sindhi newspapers had published alarming reports
of how Moenjo Daro was being threatened with virtual
extinction. Half of the almost 370 walls of structures in the
town were on the verge of collapse, owing to heavy rains and
periodic flooding. The rapid rise in the water table in the
surrounding areas, caused mainly by the cultivation of paddy,
had caused tons of salt to come to the surface, which was badly
corroding the foundations of many buildings. It was also
claimed that people from neighbouring villages were pillaging
the ruins, stealing bricks to build their own houses.

Yes, I told myself again, it was all to the good that those
mounds had remained ignored. They were, I knew, better
protected by the encroaching jungle.

thirteen

in the courts of the sufis

By noon we were back in the truck, heading southwards to the town of Sehwan, taking a slight detour on our way back to Khurshid's goth. The road ambled through endless acres of wheat and mustard ready to be harvested. Schools of swallows dived and darted about in the empty sky. We whizzed past peasant men astride skeletal donkeys, and buffalo-carts laden with bales of straw and bundles of firewood. Standing at the back of the open truck, the wind howled about me. Sharp bullets of sand whirled up from below and bombarded my face. But, dressed in my Sindhi attire, and perched like a potentate above all I could survey, I felt good.

Balu slipped a tape into a recorder. *Sindhari, Sindhari, Medi Pyaria Sindhari* 'Sindh, Sindh, My Beloved Sindh!' sang a woman with irrepressible gusto, set to a throbbing beat. I begged Balu to play that song over and over again till he could take it no more. The woman exulted in the beauties of her Sindh, its rich, alluvial soil, its lush, green fields, its haunting mountains, its world-renouncing Jogis and Sufis, and what she called its noble people. Admittedly, there was more than a small element of exaggeration in her fulsome adoration of her homeland. But, yes, she was right. It did feel good to be in Sindh.

248

The road twisted and turned as we lunged ahead through a low-lying range of stony hills. We crossed into the Dadu district near the township of Radhan, where we stopped for lunch. The only eatery of which Radhan boasted was a little tin shed that was set on the banks of a vast lake of garbage. A giant cauldron hissed on a diminutive kerosene stove. We lunched on the only dish that was available—a watery curry made of daal mixed with bits of buffalo meat, and swimming in fulsome oil. 'Hygiene is half of the faith,' the Prophet Muhammad is said to have announced, and by this eminently sensible criterion the denizens of Radhan, like much of the rest of Pakistan, the self-styled 'Land of the Pure', had ample reason to hang their heads in shame.

The entry to the town of Sehwan was through a pass over a string of knobbly hills—the Lakhi range—bare, stony knolls, bereft of all greenery. The hills trapped the wind flowing in from the surrounding desert, making Sehwan one of the most inhospitable places in Sindh. Sehwan is said to have once been a flourishing city, among the oldest known settlements in the region. According to some historians, the town's name was a corruption of the original 'Shiva Sthan', after a massive temple dedicated to Shiva which had once stood there and which had been a major Hindu centre of pilgrimage. It had been the capital of a Shaivite Hindu king, said to have been defeated by Alexander of Macedon, who captured the city and built a fort nearby, the crumbling ruins of which are still visible. In the early eighth century, the Arab commander Muhammad bin Qasim conquered Sehwan. Two centuries later, it came under the sway of the Ismaili Shia rulers of Multan. Their rule did not last long, for the Ismailis, who were regarded as heretics by other Muslims, were soon vanquished by invading Sunni Turks from Central Asia.

Sehwan's contemporary fame is owed essentially to the mausoleum of a saintly figure that stands atop a high hillock, at the base of which the town has grown and spread out. Centuries after his death, the saint still commands an immense following. Little of confirmed historical evidence is available about the man, the enigmatic thirteenth-century Lal Shahbaz Qalandar. Confusion abounds as to the very identity of Lal Shahbaz. Many Sindhi Hindus consider him an incarnation of Raja Bhartihari, brother of the Hindu king Vikramaditya. It is possible that he might have been an Ismaili Shia missionary, but his shrine is now controlled by a rival branch of the Shias, the Ithna Asharis. On their part, many Pakistani Sunnis claim that he was actually one of them, and that he was named Syed Usman at birth, in memory of the third Sunni Caliph, whom the Shias abhor. On the other hand, the Shias contend that his real name was Syed Husain, and that he was named after the martyred grandson of the Prophet Muhammad, whom the Shias deeply revere.

Most accounts maintain that Lal Shahbaz was born sometime in the latter half of the twelfth century in the town of Marwand, near the city of Tabriz, in present-day Iran. An Urdu booklet that I picked up at his shrine claimed that he was a direct descendant of the Prophet Muhammad, and that his father, Syed Ibrahim Mujab, was the caretaker of the shrine of Imam Husain in Karbala, now in Iraq. Syed Ibrahim, it was said, was a deeply pious man. Indeed, so the booklet claimed, so great a devotee of Imam Husain, 'the King of the Martyrs', was he that the Imam used to speak to him from 'the hidden worlds' and answer his queries, whence his title of *Mujab* or 'he whose prayers are answered'.

One night, so the booklet related, Imam Husain appeared to Syed Ibrahim in a dream, telling him to marry and promising him that he would be blessed with a pious son. Syed Ibrahim is said to have been a venerable seventy-five-year-old at that time. Shortly after, his wife gave birth to a son, who was named Syed Husain. Apparently, from his infancy itself, Syed Husain exhibited signs of being a man of God. At the young age of seven, it is said, he memorized the entire Quran, and some years later, he was initiated into the Qalandar mystical order. The word Qalandar, explained the booklet, meant 'one who is free of boundaries'. Lal Shahbaz Qalandar could free himself from the power of gravity and was able to fly in the air, and that was why he was also called 'Shahbaz' or 'king of falcons'. His soul, the booklet went on, 'soared like a falcon, high up into the boundless heavens'.

The shrine's recently renovated gilded dome, visible from afar as we swerved down the Lakhi Hills and entered a narrow valley, quivered in waves of heat that radiated around it like a protective halo. The road was clogged with crowds—literally thousands of people—weaving their way to the dargah. They came in trucks, buses and jeeps, the richer ones in fancy Pajeros. They came on the bare backs of donkeys, in litters balancing gingerly on the backs of camels, and in bullock- and buffalo-carts. Many of them simply walked—and several of these were without any footwear. It seemed to be some sort of a holy day. They shouted and jostled against each other. They laughed, sang and celebrated. *Jhooley Lal! Karo Beda Par!* 'Jhooley Lal! Help Us Cross the Ocean!' they boisterously beseeched the saint. From a tape recorder slung on the frame of a tractor trailed a female voice singing a hugely popular *qawwali* to the haunting thump of a dholak, and the excited crowds heading to the shrine joyfully repeated after her:

O Lal Muhinji Pat
Rakhiyan Bhala Jhooley Lalan.
Sindhiri Da, Sehwan Da
Sakhi Shahbaz Qalandar
Dama Dam Mast Qalandar

O Lal! Keep us safe
Jhooley Lal of Sindh

The generous one of Sehwan
The Qalandar, King of the Falcons.
Hail to the intoxicated Qalandar!

Dozens of brightly coloured canvas shamianas had been put up in the open square outside the sprawling dargah complex. A loudspeaker strung on a pole relayed the haunting rhythm of a party of Shia men beating and flailing their chests to mourn the murder of Imam Husain. Green- and saffron-frocked *faqirs* squatted under gnarled trees, sucking away at clay pipes. Some of them did brisk business, selling coloured stones, silver rings, votive flags, brass *panja*s in the shape of an outstretched hand (representing the *panjatan pak* or five 'holy ones'—the Prophet, his daughter Fatima, her husband Imam Ali, and their two sons Hasan and Husain) and tawiz—bits of cloth stuffed into carved metal boxes embossed with Quranic verses—which, so they promised, could stave off the evil eye or bring good luck. Some faqirs seemed to be high on hash, which was apparently easily available in the area. They sprawled out on the bare earth in a stupor, their glassy eyes unmoving.

The massive walls that enclosed the tomb of Lal Shahbaz were fit for the mausoleum of a king. From top to bottom, every inch was covered with blue, white, yellow and green glazed tiles. Bits of polished black stone that interrupted the tiles were delicately crafted to form complex geometrical patterns, blooming buds, looping tendrils and verses from the Quran. Dozens of copper bells were strung along the doorway that led into the dark inner hall that contained the grave of the saint. Soft Persian-style carpets stretched from one end to the other, the patterns that once adorned them now only faintly discernible. Clouds of smoke curled out of enormous incense-holders. Through narrow slits that pierced the stone screens built into the inner walls, faint shafts of light slithered through, scattering across the carved wooden canopy built over the grave of the saint which, buried under silken sheets and layers of fresh rose petals and marigolds, was invisible, except for a stone turban on its head.

A party of Iranian pilgrims, all dressed in black in the Shia fashion, sat at the foot of the tomb, swaying to and fro while intoning the names of Allah and invoking the blessings of the saint. A family of Dalits, identifiable by the dress of their women, circumambulated the grave, their hands folded before their faces. An old man with a turnip-shaped turban was bent in prayer on a rug in a corner. Behind him sat an enormous woman, only her eyes and nose visible under the black *naqab* that was wound around her face. 'Ya Husain! Ya Husain! Ya Husain!' she implored and sobbed, shaking her head uncontrollably.

Shrine of Shahbaz Qalandar

Khurshid had befriended a group of wandering Jindawaras in my absence, and he introduced me to them when I returned. They were dressed in rags and held begging bowls in their hands. Their faces were stained with dirt. Bholu was the head of the family, and with him were his wife, Sita, and their twin daughters, Champa and Radha. The girls giggled and gnawed at their fists when I greeted them, and hid behind their mother, clutching at the pleats of her heavily patched ghagra.

There were some twenty Jindawara families in Sehwan, and they lived together in a slum behind the shrine. Making and selling grinding-stones had been their caste occupation for as long as they could remember, but, Bholu said, they had recently abandoned this profession as people now preferred to buy ready-made flour and spices from shops instead. As a result, the Jindawaras were rendered unemployed, and now managed to survive simply by begging. Although they were Hindus, the Muslim shopkeepers of Sehwan and the pilgrims who thronged the shrine gave them food to eat, and that was enough to just about survive. 'The Pir there,' said Sita, pointing in the direction of the dargah, 'loves and helps everyone, Hindus and Muslims, alike.'

We left Sehwan in the late afternoon. I had proposed that we spend the night in the sarai adjacent to the dargah, but Khurshid would have none of it. 'You must be out of your mind,' he scolded me. 'Some fake faqir might poke you with an opium-laced needle, and bedbugs might suck you dry.' He insisted that we leave at once, for darkness was falling fast and the road was not safe. There was every chance of being waylaid by dacoits, he warned, and so we climbed into the truck and wound our way back towards Hyderabad. Sadly, I laughed to myself, we encountered no dacoits. That would have added some excitement to the book I planned to write.

We spent that night in Khurshid's goth, but left early the next morning for the town of Bhit Shah. The shutters of the shops that lined the dusty road leading to the centre of the town were all firmly shut against the early morning cold. A dozen or so families huddled closely together on the bare earth under thick shawls. An elderly man, with a henna-stained beard that trailed down his chin, sat by the road, picking at the glowing embers in the clay cup of his hukkah with a pair of tongs. Another man was busy arranging booklets—in Urdu and Sindhi—on a wheeled cart. A framed picture, hanging from a nail driven into the wooden frame of the canopy that covered the cart, displayed a frail, bearded man dressed in a saffron robe. His head was crouched over his knees and his eyes were shut to the world. A faint trace of a beatific smile quivered on his lips. That, Khurshid indicated, was a portrait of Shah Abdul Latif, the patron poet-saint of Sindh, whose magnificent tomb at Bhit Shah had made the town one of Pakistan's major Sufi centres. No visit to Sindh could be considered complete without paying homage at his magnificent 'court' or *darbar*.

Of the dozens of renowned Sufis of Sindh, venerated by Sindhi Muslims and Hindus alike, Shah Abdul Latif was undoubtedly the most popular. Born in the late seventeenth century in a family of Sindhi Syeds, he had received an elementary education at a village mosque-school, but it was through his intimate interactions with numerous Sufis and Jogis in Sindh and beyond in the course of his numerous travels, that he is said to have traversed the various stations of the mystical path.

Shah Abdul Latif's magnum opus, the *Shah Jo Risalo*, was considered to represent the pinnacle of Sindhi literature. It contained several hundred verses, composed over a period of several years, and were set to various classical ragas and *ragini*s. They were thus meant to be sung, rather than simply read or recited. The contents of the *Shah Jo Risalo* were centred on an ethical monotheism that transcended narrow, man-made divisions of caste and community.

Shah Abdul Latif's understanding of Islam appeared to have been expansive and universalist, and he did not hesitate to celebrate virtues in other faiths and their followers. One of the principal reasons for his immense popularity was that he was a people's poet par excellence. In contrast to many ulema or Muslim clerics, who wrote mainly in Persian and Arabic, he made Sindhi, the language of the 'common' folk, the vehicle to express his views. His verses were laced with idioms and images that 'common' people, grounded in poverty and misery, could readily identify with. His was no world-renouncing mysticism. Rather, it was a thoroughly socially engaged spirituality that, while calling people to devotion to the one God and to consciousness of the life to come after death, it powerfully critiqued and challenged class- and caste-oppression and communal bigotry.

After spending years wandering through various lands, Shah Abdul Latif had decided to settle down at Bhit, now known after him as Bhit Shah, on the banks of a lake not far from the town of Hala. It was a desolate spot—a *bhit* or 'sand hill' made of sandstone—the ideal place for him to spend the remaining years of his life in meditation and silent contemplation.

Barely a month before his death, Shah Abdul Latif retired to an underground room, where he devoted himself to prayer and fasting. Then, some days later, he emerged from the chamber and asked his disciples to sing the praises of God. The music went on for three days without stop till his followers, concerned about their motionless master, discovered that he had already departed from the world and had returned to his Lord.

As befits his status as the unparalleled people's poet of Sindh, Shah Abdul Latif's darbar is vast and breathtakingly magnificent. It was built some years after his death by the Baluch ruler of Sindh, Ghulam Shah Kalhoro. Intricately crafted blue-and-white glazed tile-work adorn its walls, in which are placed lattice screens and sculpted verandas. Crowds streamed into the dark recesses of the tomb-chamber, massaging the marble fence that encircles his grave and bringing their hands to their lips and foreheads in a sign of devotional surrender. A Jogi, identifiable from the wooden rings that hung from his ears, the unstitched saffron-hued cloth that wrapped his body and the enormous mound of matted hair wound round his head, sat in silent meditation at the foot of the grave. A gang of children tapped on a pair of giant kettle drums, a gift to the shrine from the Hindu raja of Jaisalmer. In a quiet corner of the chamber, a cluster of peasant-women fiddled with their prayer beads, their lips quivering as they counted their tasbihs. In the porch outside, an elderly man reclined against a wall, singing verses from *Shah Jo Risalo* in a cracked voice to the accompaniment of a harmonium. Ever since Shah Abdul Latif had shuffled off the mortal coil, his *Risalo* had been publicly recited in this fashion in the porch of his shrine, every day, twenty-four hours a day.

Korren kani salamu achio a'atanda unna jay

Countless pay homage and sing of peace at his abode.

Located an hour's drive to the south of Bhit Shah is the most venerated Hindu shrine in all Sindh—the tomb of Jhooley Lal,

also known as Uderolal. The township of Uderolal, where the
saint was buried and which is named after him, holds a special
significance for many Sindhi Hindus, for Jhooley Lal had, in
the post-Partition period, come to be regarded as their principal
deity.

A fortress-like wall encompasses the vast complex of the
shrine, which is located on the outskirts of the nondescript
town. At the far end, scattered over a hillock, are blocks of
newly constructed houses, financed by rich Sindhi Hindu seths
from India, that serve as sarais for visiting Hindu pilgrims. A
flight of stairs trail up into a pillared hall, which leads to an
enormous domed structure that houses three separate chambers.
One of these serves as a Hindu temple. Conches, brass bells,
necklaces made of *rudraksh* beads, and framed pictures of
Hindu deities line shelves built into the walls. Placed on a
raised marble plinth in the centre of the room is an enormous
framed portrait of an old man bearing a ponderous crown
on his head. A flaming red tilak is smeared his forehead,
and a bushy white beard frames his face. He is comfortably
perched on a large, smiling *palla* fish in the middle of a river
in spate.

'This is the samadhi of Sain Jhooley Lal, the saint of the
Indus,' explained a young man in a hushed voice. 'He appeared
at a time when the Hindus of Sindh were being forced to
become Muslims. The son of Ratanchand and Mata Devaki, a
Lohana couple, he was an avatar of the god Varun. He saved
us from forced conversion to Islam by showing Mirak Shah,
the tyrannical Muslim ruler of Sindh, many miracles, thereby
suitably humbling him.'

'Don't let the Muslims who hang around here mislead you,'
the man cautioned me after I had introduced myself as a visitor
from India. 'They will tell you that Uderolal was a Muslim, but
that is not true. They've concocted this story just to grab the
enormous amounts of money that Sindhi Hindu devotees,

including many rich seths from all over the world, send to this shrine.'

In a room on the extreme right of the complex, I heard a different story. The Muslim-style grave housed in the chamber, the Muslim custodian told me, is the *qabr* of Jhooley Lal. 'He was a pious Muslim faqir,' he explained. He had been born, so the man said, in a Hindu family but had later converted to Islam and taken on the Muslim name of Shaikh Tahir. 'Because he was such a devoted man of God, the Hindus too venerate him.'

Uderolal

I did not know which story to believe. Obviously, one was true and the other false. Or perhaps, could it be that both were fabrications? But there was yet another possibility. Was it possible that there was an element of truth in both versions of the legend about the enigmatic saint?

I turned to Khurshid for an answer. He was not very helpful.

'Why fret about the dead? Think of the living instead,' he chuckled. 'If you ask me, both stories are probably fictional. But, in any case, if both Hindus and Muslims worship here together in peace, that's enough, and who needs to know anything more?'

fourteen

heading back home

I had spent more than a fortnight in Sindh, and there was less than a week for my Pakistani visa to expire. There was still much that I wanted to do, though, and scores of places that I had dreamt of visiting. Zulfiqar, a friendly college student I met when we returned to Tando Allah Yar, offered to take me to Jhok, to the hallowed dargah of Sain Inayat Shah, to the Hindu shrine on the island of Sadhu Bela in the middle of the Indus, to the sprawling necropolis at Makli, probably the largest in Asia, and to the desert in Thar Parkar. He was the nephew of a big landlord, a powerful Pir who had disciples in all those places with whom we could stay, he suggested. The offer was enticing, almost too irresistible to let go. But good sense prevailed over temptation. I had no desire to spend the rest of my life languishing in a Pakistani prison for overstaying my visa or for visiting places that my visa did not permit me to.

But, on the other hand—and this I had to admit reluctantly to myself—I was now tired. The constant travel was beginning to take its toll on my nerves. The chaos of Pakistan was now beginning to feel intolerably overwhelming. Suddenly, I wanted urgently to go back home. To India. To my mother and to my dogs in Bangalore.

To get back to India, I needed to travel all the way to Lahore and then cross the border at Attari, taking the same route that I had taken on my way from India to Pakistan. It would, of course, have taken much less time and effort to return via Karachi, from where I could fly to Bombay, but the inflexible visa rules between India and Pakistan did not permit of that easier option.

The trains heading north from Hyderabad to Lahore were all full for the next fortnight. I breathed a sigh of relief. I had spent an entire night crouched on a stiff, narrow seat on the Karakoram Express on my way from Lahore to Hyderabad, and the prospect of enduring the ordeal again was simply too forbidding to consider. I decided to take the overnight train to Multan, and then travel to Lahore by coach.

'Don't think that will be any less traumatic,' Khurshid winced as he helped me drag my luggage into the train. 'You are in for a taste of hell.'

The driver of the train sounded the first of three whistles announcing our imminent departure. Khurshid slapped me on the back and pulled me into a tight embrace. His cheeks were wet. So, I found, were mine. We knew it might be the last time we would ever meet. He was too old, he said, to consider travelling to India again, and he might, he added, never see his 'motherland' again before he died.

Khurshid leapt off the train just as its wheels began to creek. I scrambled to the door of the carriage, waving out to him till he finally disappeared out of sight as the train entered the enveloping darkness.

I settled in my seat and looked about. My travelling companions were a pair of corpulent women and three noisy children. The women, dressed in black enveloping burqas, had drawn their face-coverings tightly above their mouths, only letting enough space for their eyes to peep out. The children were glued to the windows, sucking lollipops.

The women's eyes were fixed on me, I noticed. They seemed distinctly hostile.

'How did you get in here?' one of the women, the fatter of the two, finally asked. She spoke in Urdu, and from her accent she appeared to be a Muhajir. 'We are women here. Can't you see?' chimed in the other woman. 'Leave, and go elsewhere.'

I was aghast, stunned beyond belief. Leave? And go where?

'Yes, you must leave. You are a man, and you cannot sit with us women. Go and find another seat somewhere else,' cried the first woman angrily.

I cringed at this raw display of what I considered self-righteous religiosity that these women appeared to wear, quite literally, on the sleeves of their burqas. They obviously believed that I had transgressed Islamic norms and invaded the space of the *zenana*, women's hallowed territory where no 'strange' men may ever enter. They seemed to consider all males as sexually charged beings, against whom women must constantly be carefully protected. They had probably been taught to believe that that was what their religion mandated.

'Why don't you get up?' whined the second woman, seeing that I was in no mood to listen. 'If you don't, we will have to call the ticket collector.'

I steadied my nerves. The insult they had inflicted was simply too brazen to brush aside. I would not budge from my seat; I decided I would fight back.

I whipped out my ticket from my pocket and flashed it about. 'Here,' I said firmly, bringing it close to their faces and deliberately shifting nearer to them, 'it says that this is my seat. I refuse to go anywhere else.'

As if by chance, just then, the ticket collector stopped at the entrance to our compartment. I spotted him before the women did, and pre-empted them by lodging an angry complaint. 'I'm from India, brother,' I said to him, conscious of a sudden burst of patriotism that I did not till then know I harboured, 'and in our country such awful behaviour would never be tolerated.

We have no such bizarre rules.' 'In any case,' I added, 'I see no reason why these women should object to my presence. Why should they see all men as threatening?'

My protest worked a sudden transformation in the women. 'Oh, brother, are you really from India?' the first woman gently cooed. 'My father was born there, in Agra, the city of the Taj Mahal. My mother was from Benaras. I'd love to go to India.' The second woman joined her, letting her hijab fall from her face. 'I, too, am originally from India. My parents came to Pakistan from Delhi. I hear it's so much better there.'

Witnessing the sudden burst of bonhomie between us, the ticket collector smiled, handed back our tickets and left us to gossip among ourselves late into the night.

By midnight, when the train had passed out of upper Sindh and into southern Punjab, the women and the children were fast asleep. I tossed about on the hard, narrow berth. The compartment was like a tin box. Its walls were rusted, cracked and badly stained. It was suffocating inside—the windows were shut tight and the fans did not work. The floor of the compartment and the aisle outside were littered with islets of garbage rotting in pools of foul-smelling water.

Sleep eluded me completely that night. Distracted, I heaved myself out of the berth and headed towards the toilet. A middle-aged man squatted on his haunches near the door, urinating into a cranny on the floor. I asked him why he did not use the toilet instead.

'Look inside the toilet for yourself,' he replied brusquely.

I pushed open the door of the lavatory. Heaps of human excreta in various hues decorated the floor. I slammed the door shut and turned back. The man gave me a knowing smile through his broken teeth. Khurshid was right about the train, I thought. A veritable piece of hell.

The train chugged into Multan railway station at nine in the morning, four hours behind schedule. My visa did not permit me to visit Multan, and this posed a major logistical problem that, after much fretting, I decided it was best to leave unsolved. I had permits to visit both Hyderabad and Lahore, but my visa did not mention the mode of transportation that I would have to take to travel between the two cities. Since I was travelling by land, and not by air, did that mean that I could stop for a while at any place en route from Hyderabad to Lahore? And, if obviously, so I wanted to believe, the rules were flexible enough to allow me to break journey at a convenient place for a meal or to change a bus or a train, did they also permit me to do a little more—perhaps a wee bit of sightseeing as well? Or, was that interpreting the rules a bit too liberally for my convenience?

Well before the train got to Multan I had decided to shunt the matter of the rules aside. There was no way, I told myself, that I would deny myself the opportunity of doing a hurried tour of the town, about which I had heard and read so much.

I hired an autorickshaw and instructed the driver to take me on a quick round of Multan. We crawled through the chaotic traffic that stretched like an impenetrable wall from the railway station to the far end of the town. Multan did not appear any different from the other Pakistani towns that I had visited. Barring a stretch along a wide avenue, lined with sprawling bungalows that belonged to the local élite and the impressive new campus of the Bahauddin Zakariya University, Multan was a run-down, cheerless and rapidly decaying city. Many of the ancient Sufi tomb complexes that inhabited it were in a state of advanced disintegration, a pale reminder of a distant past when Multan had been a major centre of Sufism. The breathtaking dargahs of the twelfth-century Suhrawardi saint, Bahauddin Zakariya, and the thirteenth-century Ismaili missionary, Pir Shams, and that of another popular saint,

Shah Rukn-e Alam's dargah

Shah Rukn-e Alam, hidden behind towering walls richly decorated with beautiful tile-work, stood as mute testimonies of a heritage that had been brutally destroyed. The crumbling remains of the Mul Sthan or 'Main Temple', a Hindu shrine dedicated to Surya, the sun-god, built long before the arrival of Islam in the region, and from which Multan derived its name, lay scattered about in a heap along a busy highway. Considered as having been among the most sacred Hindu temples of ancient India, it had withstood the arrival and spread of Islam, comfortably coexisting for centuries with the dargah of Bahauddin Zakariya that stood adjacent to it. Mobs had torn it down in 1992, however, in the wake of the destruction of the Babri mosque in Ayodhya in India by Hindu vandals.

There was, of course, much more to see in Multan, but darkness was rapidly falling and I decided to return to Lahore. A friendly shopkeeper advised me to take the Daewoo bus. 'It's a Korean company, so the buses are smooth. Make sure you take it, and not any Pakistani bus, because those are simply awful. There's no other word for them,' he said. 'And what is more,' he added with a naughty wink, 'Daewoo has women conductors! The only such company in Pakistan.'

I bought my ticket and walked towards the waiting bus—a sleek, brand new van. A pale-faced woman dressed in a tiger-striped shalwar-kameez stood outside the door. A diaphanous chiffon dupatta dangled provocatively from her head. She wore heavy make-up, though her lipstick was smudged and streaks of it smeared her chin. *'Slamalikoom,'* she cooed, twisting her lips into a pout and a forced smile as she checked my ticket.

From my comfortable seat, I watched middle-aged men file into the bus after me, appearing shifty and excited while handing the woman their tickets. As soon as the bus filled up, Daewoo's star attraction who, I suspected, many of the male passengers had hoped would escort us all the way to Lahore, suddenly disappeared.

It was dark outside, and through the dense fog I could only make out the occasional pale light of fires outside peasants' homes as we trundled through the Punjabi countryside. Six hours later, I was back in the snug comfort of Sheila's home in Lahore.

I had just three days left to leave for India, but there were still things I needed to do in Lahore. One of these was a visit to the University of Punjab which, I had been told, was ranked among the top universities of Pakistan.

Sheila's friend Salim took me on a whirlwind tour of the campus. It was, or so he said, one of the largest university campuses in Asia. Building blocks were scattered about all over, and some of them seemed impressive from the architectural point of view. We met up with some of Salim's friends for coffee at the men's-only cafeteria. There was a separate cafeteria for women students, Salim explained. Succumbing to the threats of the Jamiat ul-Tulaba-e Islam, the students' wing of the Jamaat-e Islami—Pakistan's foremost Islamist outfit—the vice chancellor of the university had decreed that members of opposite genders could not interact on campus, even over a cup of tea.

Jamiat vigilantes—Salim contemptuously termed them as 'fascist foot soldiers'—carefully patrolled the campus, not hesitating to use intimidation and even violence to curb any sign of what they regarded as 'un-Islamic' behaviour. Salim spoke of Jamiat activists and their rivals engaging in running gun-battles that, in some campuses across the country, had resulted in numerous kidnappings and even murders. Student groups other than the Jamiat, Salim complained, were effectively banned from the Punjab University, probably on the vice chancellor's orders. Like the heads of most other Pakistani universities, he was a retired Army general and, like most generals, he wanted to clamp down on even the feeblest voices of dissent on campus. Indeed, Salim surmised, that was possibly why the Pakistani government had awarded him that plush assignment in the first place.

We took a hurried round of the university's library. Vast and well-stocked, it could compare favourably with the best of Indian libraries. Yet, Salim complained of rapidly falling standards in the university. It boasted of almost no internationally recognized scholars. Even PhD students could hardly speak decent English, he said, and the level of their scholarship was pathetic. Few university professors—who were all paid a fat salary that came along with attractive frills—had published anything substantial at all.

On my last day in Pakistan I decided to spend my remaining Pakistani rupees. The entire trip had not cost me even half of what I had expected—friends I had stayed with and even stray acquaintances I had met had refused to let me pay for almost anything. I thought I might want to spend the money that I had left doing some shopping but there was little that I could find in Lahore that I could not get in India. The price of almost everything—cigarettes and mobile phone cards were notable exceptions—was significantly higher in Pakistan than in India, though Pakistani goods, other than fabrics and dry fruit, were generally of a much lower quality. I decided to splurge on books instead, and headed for the busy Mall Road, the only place in Lahore for English books.

It did not take me much time to scout around all the bookshops on Mall Road. They were less than half a dozen in number, most of them modestly sized. I failed to find anything worth picking up. The vast majority of the English titles on sale was published in the West, and to my surprise, in India as well. Ironically, most of the books about Islam in English were imported from India, from Delhi-based Muslim publishers. Even more strikingly, almost all the English books dealing with the vexed issue of Kashmir, the major bone of contention between India and Pakistan, were works by Indian authors published in India, and almost certainly representing the official Indian position on the disputed territory. Such, I discovered to my horror, was the pathetic state of scholarly discourse in Pakistan.

I thought I might strike better luck at the Urdu shops

because, while the standard of English remained low in Pakistan, Urdu thrived, being the country's national language. I wound my way to the legendary Urdu Bazaar in Lahore's Old City. I had heard much about the bazaar that dated to pre-Partition times. It was said to be the major centre for Urdu books in Lahore and, indeed, the largest in the entire country.

Narrow unpaved lanes, scarred with crater-sized potholes and lined with clogged sewers, connected the vast expanse of Urdu Bazaar. Several hundred Urdu bookshops and publishers had their premises in the area. Most were gloomy, single-roomed structures. Only a few were large, brightly lit, clean and airy.

I spotted some interesting titles on display, including translations of the Ramayana, the Gita, the Dhammapada, the Guru Granth Sahib and works by Osho Rajneesh, which, I learnt to my pleasant surprise, sold exceptionally well. Several shops specialized in classical Urdu literature, but these I avoided. I was keen to pick up books on contemporary Pakistani politics and society, but, after spending almost the entire day scouting around the market, I could locate hardly half a dozen decent titles. This suggested—and Sheila confirmed my suspicion when I raised the issue later that evening—that the state of critical social science research was abysmal in Pakistan. 'Our professors don't do any empirical research, original work or any thinking at all. The few good ones we had have all fled the country—out of fear of the mullahs, the Islamists and the dictatorial state, or in search of greener pastures,' she bemoaned. 'The Islamists want us to think like them, and our rulers don't want us to think at all. Both want us to be illiterate morons, whom they can manipulate at will.' That, in short, she pronounced, was why well-researched social science books about the country were almost impossible to come by.

Admittedly, many bookshops in the market did sell books about Pakistani history and culture. There were books about

Islamic rituals, including such matters as the prescribed rules for bathing, combing one's beard and having sex, polemical tracts inveighing against rival sects and religions, booklets about the Sufi saints and leading maulvis of Pakistan, and thick leather-bound multivolume commentaries on the Quran. There were scores of hagiographical accounts of Muhammad Ali Jinnah and Muhammad Iqbal that repeated the same pious clichés about their alleged passionate devotion to Islam and to the cause of a separate state for the Muslims of India. And then there were shoddy tomes that lionized Pakistan's leading Islamist ideologue, Sayyid Abul Ala Maududi, and the American-sponsored military dictator, General Zia, or lavished fulsome praise on Zulfiqar Bhutto and his daughter Benazir. I spotted almost nothing, however, about 'ordinary' Pakistanis, in whose lives I was interested. I made a few purchases: some books on Sindhi saints, a critique of the Pakistan demand penned by the noted Indian Muslim scholar, the late Husain Ahmad Madani, an account of the revolt of the Muslims of Poonch against the oppressive Dogra regime in Kashmir, and a volume in praise of Guru Nanak, written by a Pakistani Sufi scholar.

On my way out of the labyrinth of the market, I chanced upon a bookshop, above the entrance of which was slung a cloth banner that hailed what it called 'The Brave Jihad of Our Brethren in Kashmir'. Curious to know more, I stepped inside. Men, sporting shaggy beards that clung like mangled wasp-hives to their cheeks and trailed down their chins, shuffled about, plucking books from display shelves and loading them into boxes. The labels pasted on the boxes indicated that they were being dispatched to various places across Pakistan and to the Gulf.

The stern appearance of the men, and their hideous beards in particular, at once suggested to me that they were associated with the Ahl-e Hadith, a brand of self-styled Islamic purists akin to the Wahhabis of Saudi Arabia. I glanced about the

room. Pasted on the walls were posters hailing the dreaded
terrorist outfit Lashkar-e-Tayyaba and its parent organization,
the Markaz Dawat ul-Irshad, self-proclaimed heroes of Islam
who believed that the time had come for Muslims to launch a
global jihad to establish what they called 'Islamic rule' all over
the world.

For a moment, I stood transfixed, scared out of my wits and
not knowing what to do. The Lashkar had called for, and was
deeply implicated in, what it styled as a jihad against the
'infidels' of India. It was responsible for scores of terrorist
attacks across India that had taken a heavy toll on human lives.
Lashkar activists had slain scores of perfectly innocent Hindus,
as well as Muslims who opposed them or did not agree with
their version of Islam, without any compunction or the least
provocation. The men who milled about the shop, and who, I
presumed, were key Lashkar activists, could easily have thought
me an 'Indian' or 'Hindu' agent and slit my throat at that very
instant.

I gathered myself together. I tried to appear as normal as I
could in the circumstances. I studied the books on display.
Some of them were violent diatribes against the Shias and the
Barelvis, upholders of popular Sufism, both of whom the
Lashkar, in line with the general Ahl-e Hadith and Wahhabi
position, considered to be dangerous heretics and outside the
pale of normative Islam. Others were stories about the Prophet
and his companions, focusing particularly on their military
conquests. But the bulk of the books on sale was devoted to the
Lashkar's self-styled jihad in Kashmir. There were entire volumes,
containing testimonies—real or fabricated, I cannot say—of
the parents of Lashkar 'martyrs', hailing the deaths of their sons
who had crossed into Kashmir to fight the Indian forces. They
were all sure to find a place for themselves in heaven, they
fervently insisted, where they would live in massive mansions
and be waited upon by doe-eyed houris. There were pamphlets

proclaiming that the Prophet Muhammad had allegedly prophesied a grand battle that would be waged by a team of Muslims against India—the *ghazwat ul-hind*. Those who participated in this war, so they claimed the Prophet had announced more than fourteen hundred years ago, would be saved from the fires of hell. It was precisely this war, they asserted, that the Lashkar was waging against India. There were also scores of tracts that spewed venom against the Hindus, branding all of them as inveterate foes of Islam.

Lashkar-e-Tayyaba militants

I purchased a booklet. Its contents appalled me, of course, but, I felt, it was necessary to study it in order to critique and expose the Lashkar's patent falsehoods. The Lashkar was playing havoc with innocent lives, in Pakistan, in Kashmir and in India. With its venomous rhetoric against the Hindus, it was further fuelling the flames of Hindutva fascism in India, and this had alarmingly ominous consequences for most Indians, particularly the Muslims of the country, Hindutva's principal victims. The Lashkar, like the Hindutva chauvinists it claimed to so vociferously oppose, spoke a language of hate, violence and bloodshed. It saw the world in the same frighteningly Manichaean terms. Posturing as inveterate enemies, they actually fed on each other. Indeed, they desperately needed each other to survive.

Standing there in that bookshop before its ugly, gnome-like owner, who made a living out of selling and spewing undistilled venom, I wanted to take my revenge. The only way I could do that was to expose the lies of the Lashkar. And that, I decided, I simply had to do when I got back home.

I paid the man, picked up the booklet that I had selected, walked out into the street and lunged into a waiting autorickshaw. It chugged out of the bazaar and I let out a heavy sigh of relief.

Finally, the day to return to India arrived. I hardly slept the previous night. I lay in my bed, tracing in my mind the one-month journey that I had undertaken: the bus trip from Delhi across the border to Lahore; the walks around Lahore's Old City; the hurried visit to Kasur; the three days I had spent with Ammar and his family in Gujranwala; the train ride to

Hyderabad, and from there to Himmatabad; the week with Khurshid in Tando Allah Yar, in Goth Asad Ali Khan, and then in Moenjo Daro, Sehwan, Bhit Shah and Uderolal; the short break in Multan; and then the bus ride back to Lahore. I had travelled across Pakistan, to sprawling cities, small towns and isolated hamlets deep in the interior of the countryside. I had met Dalit bonded labourers and Leftist human rights activists, maulvis and madrasa teachers, journalists and peasants, Punjabi university students, Baluchi landlords, Sindhi nationalists, Bania shopkeepers, Mehtar sweepers, Jogi mendicants, and men and women of Muslim background who defined themselves as liberals, humanists, communists and even atheists. It had been a truly momentous journey, like none other that I had previously undertaken.

I thought of the many people I had met, the concern and affection that I had received from scores of them, although—or perhaps even because—I was from India. Several had become close friends. They had changed my life in a major way and my perception of their country. They had helped disabuse me of some of the worst prejudices about Pakistan and its people that, like most other Indians, I had been reared on since infancy. They had been helpful and hospitable hosts, great companions, truly wonderful human beings. Once back in India, behind that impenetrable border, I would probably gradually lose touch with, or perhaps only vaguely recall, many, indeed most, of them. That would be tragic, I knew, but it was true.

I thought of Nani and Nana's ancestors, whose ashes lay inseparably mixed with the soil of Pakistan, in remote villages I had not had the opportunity to visit—and probably never would. Leaving Pakistan was like tearing away from a part of my own self. I shuddered as I thought of the blind, raw hatred, packaged as patriotism and piety, which most Indians felt for Pakistan and its people, and vice versa. I wondered how many hundreds of thousands of innocent lives, of Indians and Pakistanis, who shared more in common than most of them would admit, had been sacrificed at the bloody altar of national chauvinism and fake religiosity. How many more would be, in the future?

Admittedly, however, in a way I was glad to be going back. Pakistan had not been easy to negotiate. Travelling in the country had been thrilling, but tiring, too, and, at times, unnerving, even exasperating. There were occasions when I had simply given up and wanted to flee back to India. There was much about the country that appalled, even frightened, me. My visit had reinforced some of the worst stereotypes about the country. The filth and squalor, the weak and thoroughly inefficient system of governance, the untrammelled power of the feudal lords, the stark inequalities, the pathetic plight of the country's religious minorities, the growing influence of hate-spewing Islamist outfits and the dismal state of scholarly discourse, all this and more I had found deeply distressing. A month in the country had been just about as much as I could have possibly handled.

Sheila was up and about at that early hour. The bus was to depart at 5 a.m., but she had woken up three hours before and was rustling up breakfast for me when I climbed down the stairs from my room. 'Eat, puttar,' she said, placing a plate of steaming parathas before me. 'You have a long journey ahead of you.' She went back to the kitchen and came out with a cloth bundle. It contained a box full of parathas, a tin of daal and a bottle of orange juice. 'You'll need this on the bus,' she said.

That was how Sheila was. Bossy and caring. She had been something of a mother to me.

We drove to the office of the Pakistan Tourist Development Authority through still, deserted streets. We exchanged barely a word. I let the tears stream out till I had none left.

The bus, owned by the Pakistan government, was distinctly smaller than the Indian vehicle I had taken to Lahore from Delhi. The seats were narrow, stiff and uncomfortable. It was suffocating inside—the air conditioning did not work and the windows were tightly sealed. The conductor, an unwashed burly lout, flung my bags inside the underbelly of the bus and demanded *baksheesh*.

The bus let out a shrill honk, and I tore myself from Sheila's embrace. I scrambled aboard and took my seat. The bus trailed out of the terminal and swerved on to the road leading to the border, barely twenty miles away.

It took us an hour to reach Wagah. We were ordered out of our bus and herded to a booth, where our passports were stamped by Pakistani immigration officials. The officials at the Customs counter, huddled closely together on a wooden platform under a razai and sipping tea, shooed us away irritatedly.

We piled back into the bus. The conductor slammed the door and the vehicle chugged ahead, towards the massive granite gateway that stood at the border like a stern sentinel. I twisted in my seat and looked through the window. To my utter amazement, I saw Sheila there, a hundred metres or so behind the bus, squatting on the bonnet of her car. She had travelled all the way from Lahore to the border just to make sure that I passed through smoothly. I could not call out to her, for the window was firmly sealed. I waved, trying to catch her attention, but she could not see me through the dark glass of the window.

The passengers, who had all along been excitedly chattering away, suddenly fell silent. The bus crawled through the gateway. Tears welled up in my eyes, and a stormy sea of tangled

Pakistani side of the border

emotions rushed through my body. I heard an army official bark, and the gates swung open.

The bus passed through the gates. It stopped, for just a brief moment, on the white line painted on the tarmac that marked the final limit of Pakistani territory. And then it silently slipped across the line and into India.

We got off the bus at the Attari checkpoint, barely fifty metres from the border, and filed into a large, swanky hall. Compared to the grubby box-like cement structure at Wagah on the Pakistani side, the Indian checkpoint seemed positively luxurious. The suave officials at Attari were definitely a contrast to their bumpkin counterparts at Wagah. Yes, it felt good to be back home in India.

When I got to the hostel where I then lived in Delhi later that evening, I bumped into a friend from Ahmedabad—Naseem, a Muslim Gujarati woman, who had seen over a dozen members of her family, including her husband and children, speared to death before her very eyes by Hindu hoodlums during the infamous Gujarat genocide in 2002. Hers is a tragic tale that the world has conveniently forgotten. Justice still evaded Naseem and thousands of people like her throughout India. Meeting Naseem that evening moderated somewhat the joy of being back home. Perhaps India and Pakistan were not so different, after all.

Indian side of the border

One afternoon, a month after my return from Pakistan, I received a call from the officer in the Pakistan High Commission who had arranged the visa for me.

'I read your article in the *Indian Express* about Pakistan yesterday,' he said curtly. 'Can we meet for tea? I want to discuss the article with you.' He sounded distinctly unpleasant.

I knew why the officer was cross with me. The article in question dealt with the dismal economic and political conditions that I had observed in Sindh. Obviously, he had not taken lightly to that.

I was not at all keen on meeting the man. But, I knew I could not refuse or else it would be virtually impossible to get a visa to visit Pakistan again. I agreed to catch up with him the following afternoon at the India International Centre, a favourite watering hole for Delhi's chattering classes.

Half an hour past the appointed time, the officer strode into the restaurant of the India International Centre, followed by two officious-looking colleagues. He spotted me seated in a corner and nodded lightly. Wagging his index finger in my direction, he indicated I should join him at the table he was settling at. I obliged.

The man did not care to reply to my greeting. He busied himself scanning the menu, while a handsome white-uniformed waiter hovered behind him.

'You have chicken *tikka*?' the officer asked.

The waiter nodded.

'Is the chicken *halal* or *jhatka*?'

'Sir, I don't know what that means,' spluttered the waiter.

'You don't know what that means?' barked the officer. 'Arey yaar, fierce communal riots have broken out over halal and jhatka and you say don't know what that means!' He let out a loud huff, and settled for tomato sandwiches instead.

'Yes, Mr Sikand,' he now turned to me, looking at me straight in the eye, and said, 'that article of yours. What you have written is absolutely wrong.'

Unable to control my rage, I shot back. 'I stand by everything I've written. I've seen things for myself in Sindh. The poverty, the stranglehold of the waderas, the pathetic plight of the haris, the filth and the squalor.'

He cut me short, now visibly irate. 'Poverty is much worse in India,' he burst out. 'There are no cycle-rickshaws in Pakistan, but in India, millions of poor people have no other source of livelihood. Did I not suggest that you should note that in your writings when you came to me for the visa?'

I admitted he had mentioned to me the absence of cycle-rickshaws in his country when I had first met him and that he had specifically advised me to write about that phenomenon. But my article, I protested, was not a comparative study of economic conditions in India and Pakistan, let alone of rickshaw-pullers in the two countries.

'No, no, Mr Sikand,' he shook his head violently as he gobbled his sandwich. 'You are a very biased person. I never expected this when I gave you the visa.'

I knew, then, that as long as this man remained at the Pakistan High Commission in Delhi I would never be able to return to Pakistan.

postscript

In the year that passed after my return from Pakistan, I received several invitations to visit the country. The first was from a Sufi centre in Lahore, which was organizing a conference devoted to Sufism and inter-faith dialogue; the second from the organizers of the World Social Forum in Karachi. But, as I had expected, on both these occasions my application for a visa was scuttled by the officer in the Pakistan High Commission in New Delhi who had taken a strong dislike for me. I received a third invitation, from the South Asian Free Media Association, to participate in a conference in Islamabad. The conference aimed at promoting free media exchange between the various South Asian countries, particularly between India and Pakistan, and was to be inaugurated by the Pakistani minister for information and broadcasting. But, the officer at the Pakistan High Commission, whose ire I had kindled by my frank portrayals of his country in the media, obviously did not believe in that concept. He sabotaged my visa application but granted visas to the rest of the Indian invitees. So much for the commitment of the Pakistani government to a free South Asian media, I wrote to the organizers of the conference, who were courteous enough, so I heard, to make a note of my protest and lament the shameful behaviour of the officer in the inaugural session of their meeting.

My angry retort, I was convinced, would snuff out all hopes

that remained of my ever visiting Pakistan again. And so, when, a little less than two years later, in May 2008, I received an invitation from a Pakistani NGO to participate in a conference in Islamabad, I wrote back to the organizers expressing my inability to attend because I felt that my application for a visa would inevitably be turned down.

The redoubtable Farrah Parvaiz Saleh, head of the Lahore-based Citizens' Commission for Human Development and organizer of the conference, was not the sort to take 'no' for an answer. A fiery social activist, mother of a member of Pakistan's National Assembly, wife of a senior Pakistani bureaucrat and part of the inner circle of the ruling Pakistan People's Party, she had all the right connections in the right places, she assured me, and so there was no way that I would be refused a visa to attend *her* conference. I took her assurance good-humouredly, and although I did not expect anything to come of it, I sent her the documents she required for processing my visa application.

Several days passed, and I got no news about the visa. Then, just a day before the conference was to begin, Farrah called up. 'I've spoken to the relevant people in the relevant ministries, and your visa application is now cleared,' she gushed excitedly. 'Rush to Delhi at once, pick up your visa and hop on to the next flight to Islamabad.'

I hesitated for a bit. I was sure, I told her, that, despite what she had said, the Pakistan High Commission in Delhi would refuse to grant me a visa. It was pointless my flying down all the way from Bangalore, where I then was, to Delhi, only to be turned back, I said.

'Don't be silly,' Farrah scolded me. 'When I say something I mean it. Go to Delhi at once. And that's an order!'

I caught the early morning flight the next day to Delhi and rushed straight from the airport to the Pakistan High Commission. I handed my papers to a foul-faced man at the visa counter. He glanced through them and rummaged through an enormous file placed on the desk before him. My application had not been approved as yet, he said as he flung my papers back at me. 'Wait for a few more days,' he growled.

'But I've been told by the organizers of the conference that the Prime Minister's Office in Islamabad has informed the High Commission to issue the visa immediately. I have to catch a flight to Pakistan this afternoon,' I protested, struggling to conceal my irritation and trying to sound important.

'Ha! Prime Minister's Office indeed! Whom do you think you are fooling?' the man mocked. 'If his office had sent such an instruction, do you think I would be sitting on my chair like this? There'd be fire here, fire!'

I called up Farrah and explained the matter to her.

'Arey yaar, Yogi, don't get worried. Relax. I'll do the needful,' she answered coolly. 'Take it easy. I'll fix it up in five minutes.'

True to her word, five minutes later, Farrah called back to announce that my visa was ready and that I should collect it from the main gate of the High Commission.

I rushed to the gate, where I was handed back my passport. It had a week-long visa stamped in it, which allowed me to visit Islamabad and to transit through Karachi on the way in and through Lahore on the way back.

I rang up Farrah to inform her. I asked her how she had managed it. 'Yaar, Yogi, don't ask silly questions! I assured you, na, that I would do the needful? And I generally keep my word, you see.'

We burst out laughing.

It seemed too good to be true. Finally, it appeared, I was going back to Pakistan. My fears of never being able to return to the country had proven wrong, and I was truly elated.

It took a little more than two hours for the Pakistan International Airlines flight from Delhi to get to Karachi, where I boarded another flight to Islamabad later that evening.

Islamabad was definitely among the most well-organized cities that I had seen. 'Islamabad is not Pakistan. It is not even in Pakistan,' joked a Lahori friend of mine when I informed him of my arrival in the city. 'It's a piece of Switzerland transplanted into the massive bog that is Pakistan, with which it has nothing at all in common. It's for those Pakistanis who have nothing to do with the rest of the country,' he fumed.

He was right, in a way. Pakistan's capital city, designed by a Greek architect in the 1960s, was decidedly élitist. It was strictly reserved for those with power and pelf. It was a city that clearly, and in no ambiguous terms, announced that it was meant solely for the rich and the famous. Settled at the foot of the Margalla Hills that led on to Kashmir and beyond, it was divided into a number of sectors, each of which had its own shopping complexes, hospitals and schools. Enormous bungalows were hidden behind high walls, and wide grassy banks lined the broad boulevards that criss-crossed the city. Carefully manicured gardens and thickly wooded parks stretched on for miles. Hardly any pedestrians were to be seen, for almost every family in the city owned at least one car. The poor who toiled in the houses of the rich did not live in the city. Instead, they commuted daily by mini-van and horse-cart from squalid slums in Rawalpindi, Islamabad's twin city, located only a few miles away.

I have a special dread of academic conferences and an instinctive aversion to armchair academics who presume to be 'experts'. From the dozens of conferences that I have sat through in India and abroad over the years, I must confess I have learnt but little. Farrah's conference turned out to be quite different, however. The first initiative of its kind in Pakistan, the three-day meeting, held at the plush government-run Convention Centre in the heart of Islamabad, a stone's-throw distance from the Pakistani Parliament, brought together dozens of activists and journalists from different parts of South Asia to discuss the problems of, and the prospects for, democracy in the region. It was easily one of the most engaging and lively conferences that I have ever attended.

A number of leading Pakistani political figures made their appearance over the three days of deliberations. Among them were the sophisticated Raza Rabbani, Leader of the Senate of Pakistan and senior member of the ruling Pakistan People's Party, the Baluch politician Faisal Karim Kundi, deputy speaker of the Pakistan National Assembly, an arrestingly attractive man whose presentation made no sense at all, and the cricketer-turned-politician, Imran Khan. Some of the Pakistani speakers were plainly propagandist, uttering the expected pious homilies about democracy and justice, but several others were extremely critical about the way their country was heading.

The trenchant critiques of ruling-class politics and American imperialism, and the fierce condemnation of the misuse of Islam by reactionary forces by leading Pakistani activists who addressed the conference, indicated to me a vibrant civil society in the country of which few foreigners are aware. Voices for democracy and social justice and against terror in the name of Islam, they suggested, were becoming increasingly strident in Pakistan, even as the country was being further hurtled into the throes of probably interminable crises with the rising clout of radical Islamist groups, who were now engaged in deadly duels with the Pakistani Army and in indiscriminate killings of fellow-Muslim Pakistanis. Both the Islamists and the US-led so-called 'war on terror', the Pakistani participants unanimously stressed, now threatened to hurl the country into the throes of a civil war, from which it could never extrictate itself.

Pakistan's Parliament

The conference gave over with a valedictory address by the suave, doe-eyed Syed Yousuf Gilani, Prime Minister of Pakistan. He spoke the expected, about human rights, the struggle for democracy in South Asia and the need for a balanced relationship between the army and civilian authorities in Pakistan. Like his fellow Pakistan People's Party leaders who spoke before him, Gilani also subtly critiqued the then-military-dictator President of Pakistan, General Musharraf, suggesting, although not explicitly, that it was time for him to step down as he had become a liability. Almost all of this was, of course, trite and general, but that, I supposed, is how most politicians talk, anyway. It was thus hardly surprising that the very next day newspapers quoted Gilani as showering fulsome praise on Musharraf and blessing him as a 'democrat'.

After the prime minister's homily concluded, the foreign participants in the conference were taken to meet him. 'Foreign delegates, stand in a queue please,' ordered a matronly Pakistani woman. Delegates? It sounded utterly officious and stupidly pretentious.

An Indian 'delegate' strode up to Gilani, grabbed his hand in his and announced, 'Please make sure you work for good

Indo–Pak relations. You just have to.' A Bangladeshi 'delegate' nudged the Indian aside, and, introducing himself to the prime minister, declared, in a forced American twang, 'Myself is the professor from the Bangladesh. Respectable sir, the Bangladesh is willing to offer you all services.'

The mild-mannered Gilani appeared to be somewhat taken aback by this unsolicited and ungrammatical offer of Bangladeshi assistance, and he smiled condescendingly. I squirmed as I stood in the queue, waiting to shake hands with him, dreading that he must have thought all of us 'delegates' to be a bunch of eccentrics.

My second trip to Pakistan had been very different from the first that I had undertaken two years before. The foreign 'delegates' had all been put up at the mock-colonial Islamabad Club, the favourite haunt of Islamabad's super élite—serving and retired military generals, top-notch bureaucrats and politicians, powerful feudal lords and billionaire industrialists. I permitted myself to indulge in the vulgar luxury of the Club, ever mindful, of course, that this island of comfort bore no relation whatsoever to the rest of the country. The people I met at the conference were an entirely different bunch from those I had met on my previous trip. They included CEOs of international NGOs, English-language journalists, noted social activists, leading university professors as well as a stream of well-known politicians. Most of them spoke English fluently, many with clipped Oxbridge accents. Unlike on my earlier visit, I met a number of well-educated women, decidedly Westernized, most of whom worked with various international development organizations. In all, they represented the fledgling Pakistani liberal upper-middle class that, as was clear from their views, saw itself as increasingly beleaguered by the American-backed Pakistani military, on the one hand, and radical Islamists and conservative mullahs, on the other. They gushed about the desperate need for democracy, social justice and secularism in their country, unanimous that the very real threat of what they called the 'Talibanization' of Pakistan had to be forcefully resisted before it was too late.

Faisal Mosque, Islamabad

The foreigners among us were treated as honoured guests by our hosts. We were driven around town in a fleet of limousines to see the various sights, admittedly few, of which Islamabad boasted: the President's Palace, Parliament House, the Supreme Court, the Pakistan National Monument, an abandoned Hindu temple on the banks of the sprawling Rawal Lake, the ugly, post-modernist Faisal Masjid and the International Islamic University attached to it, a string of fancy restaurants at Pir Sohava, and the Lake View Park, where we were invited to a sumptuous dinner hosted by the suave Kamran Lashari, head of Islamabad's Capital Development Authority.

The plush surroundings in which we stayed, the slick buildings and sprawling monuments that we hurriedly visited and the upmarket eateries where we dined, belonged to a world entirely different from that which the vast majority of Pakistanis inhabited. The newspapers were full of alarming news about the way that the world of 'ordinary' Pakistanis was heading. There had been a fresh round of sectarian killings in southern Punjab; Baluchistan was aflame; there was trouble in Karachi; the Taliban were threatening to capture Islamabad itself; and almost all Pakistanis were now unanimous that Musharraf must quit. It was quite clear that democracy, which was what we had gathered in Islamabad to discuss, was sorely missing in the country and, at the same time, was being loudly demanded by vast numbers of Pakistanis.

We had a three-hour stopover at Lahore airport on our way back to Delhi from Islamabad. I spent my remaining Pakistani money at a government handicrafts emporium, picking up onyx vases and ashtrays and a brightly hued handmade tapestry. 'I wish I could stay on in Pakistan longer!' I said to the friendly manager of the shop as he totted up my bill. He smiled, and, taking my hand firmly in his, said, 'Inshallah, you will be back soon'.

I walked over to the cafeteria. A handsome waiter handed me a cup of tea. I repeated the same phrase—about wishing that I could stay longer in Pakistan—meaning every word of it. He answered in identical fashion. 'Inshallah, you will come back again,' he assured me.

We got chatting. His name was Habib. He had recently taken to working as a waiter at the airport, having previously worked in a local band. He had composed over a dozen lyrics, he said, and on my pleading he sang his latest composition— a Punjabi song about the pangs of separated lovers.

A voice crackled over the loudspeaker, announcing the imminent departure of Pakistan International Airlines' flight to New Delhi. A line formed around a counter, and I joined it at the end. 'I really wish I could stay on longer,' I said to the lady who checked my boarding pass before I headed through the gate that led to the waiting aircraft. 'Inshallah, you will be here soon,' she coyly replied.

Within five minutes of our departure, we flew out of Pakistani territory and into Indian airspace. Less than an hour later, the plane began to descend over Delhi, the sprawling urban jungle of the city visible below a thick blanket of grey clouds. But just then, and all of a sudden, the plane began to heave violently, up and down, this way and that, hurtling into deep air pockets, and going completely out of control. Menacing black clouds swelled outside the window. The darkness was broken by massive bolts of lightning, and rain came crashing down on the plane in violent torrents.

All around me, the passengers began to shriek frantically. I instinctively grabbed the hand of an elderly Pakistani woman seated next to me as she cried out to Allah, exhorting Him for protection. Death had finally arrived, I thought, as the plane tossed about helplessly in the relentless storm. My mind scrambled to focus on God, begging for forgiveness of sins and for His acceptance. If a violent death in an air crash was what He had decreed for me, then so be it, I told myself as I struggled to control myself from collapsing. All this while, frenzied appeals to Allah, Ishwar and God grew louder and more desperate, as all of us, Indians and Pakistanis, Hindus and Muslims, finally united before our common creator in the face of what we feared was imminent death.

The ordeal lasted for almost twenty minutes and, given that I am an exceptionally nervous air traveller, it was nothing short of a miracle that I managed to retain my wits about me for that long. Then, just as the plane appeared to be plunging down through the blinding blanket of clouds, the microphone was switched on. The air hostess coughed and waited for a bit before making an announcement. I feared the worst. Was she going to swing open the door of the plane and order us to jump out? Or, worse still, was she going to tell us that there was no way we could survive and that we should now prepare to meet our end?

'Lady and Gentleman,' announced the air hostess in broken, heavily accented English. 'Because very terrible weather in Delhi we go now back Lahore. Sorry for inconvenience to you caused.'

The plane veered around suddenly. Wisely, the pilot took a slightly different route back, skirting the rain-swollen clouds. But, until we touched down at Lahore an hour later, we were all stunned into an eerie silence in our seats, whispering our prayers to the one God with multiple names.

'See, I told you that, Inshallah, you'd come back to Pakistan soon,' beamed the keeper of the handicrafts emporium at the airport when he caught sight of me. Habib, the young singer-turned-waiter whom I had earlier met at the airport restaurant, welcomed me with a warm hug and an identical reply.

Yes, indeed, it was good to be back, to be back on terra firma, to be back in Lahore, to be back in Pakistan, to be back alive.

The passengers of the aborted flight were directed to a Pakistan International Airlines counter in the departure lounge. There, we were informed that there was no scheduled flight from Lahore to Delhi for the next four days. We could wait till then, we were told. I wished I could have availed of that option, for that would have given me four extra days in Pakistan, but I could not, since my visa was to expire the very next day. We were advised to take an alternate route: to fly to Karachi the next evening and from there to Delhi, a long and tedious journey. I would not have minded that option either, for in that way I could have got to see a bit of Karachi gratis. But the grumbles of protest grew louder and more aggressive, and an Indian Muslim man who had appointed himself spokesman of the stranded passengers, announced that stern action would be taken against any of us who broke rank and accepted the offer. Followed by half a dozen angry Indian and Pakistani women, he surrounded the airline staff, raising shrill slogans, rudely hectoring them and even threatening to go on a hunger strike if immediate arrangements were not made for a special flight to take us to Delhi directly. His brusqueness, I thought, was entirely uncalled for, considering the valour of the intrepid pilot (a woman, it turned out) who had steered us safely through what could have been a deadly killer storm. But, because most of the other passengers had already joined in the noisy chorus demanding a special flight, I kept quiet. Finally, it was decided by our strike leader that we, a bunch of some fifty Pakistanis and Indians, roughly equal in number, should refuse to fly to Karachi and, instead, should press on with the demand for a special flight to Delhi immediately.

Three hours later, the airline officials relented and graciously announced that they had organized a plane to take us to Delhi the next evening. Meanwhile, they said, they had arranged for us to spend that night at an inn not far from the airport.

We filed into vans waiting outside the terminal and were driven to the inn—a grubby lodge in the Defence Housing Society area on the outskirts of Lahore, definitely not the luxurious five-star hotel that some of us were expecting. The lodge was short of space, and so we were to be put two to a room. The allotment was done in an entirely random fashion, which was all to the good, because many Indian and Pakistani passengers found that they were compelled to share rooms with a person of the other nationality.

The near-death experience on the aborted flight seemed to have instinctively bonded together the passengers, Indians and Pakistanis, Hindus and Muslims, who had been herded into the inn. In a short while, I was on first-name terms with at least half of them, and was already privy to some of their most private details. There was Asim from Thatta, in Sindh, whose first wife had eloped with a friend of his, and who was on his way to attend a Sindhi conference in Delhi. There was Nathu, a Sindhi Hindu trader from Sukkur, who was passionate about Sufism and was going to meet with his guru in Agra. There was Najma, a corpulent Shia woman from Lahore, who was visiting long-lost relatives in Lucknow. There was Haji Shams, a soft-spoken maulvi from Sargodha, who had been invited to a conference on ethics and biotechnology in Delhi, and who frankly confessed that he had no idea what he would speak on as he had not the faintest clue of what biotechnology was all about. There was Husaini, a frail, elderly woman from

Hyderabad in Sindh, who was heading for a city with the same name in India for a medical operation. Then there was Rehan, a cheerful businessman from Jhelum, with whom I shared a room, who was travelling to Rohtak to purchase seeds and agricultural implements for his farm. And so on.

The next afternoon, we were informed that the plane that Pakistan International Airlines had arranged for to take us to Delhi would depart later that evening. When we got to the airport and learnt that the plane which had been set apart for us was an old and rarely used forty-seat propeller-driven craft, angry protests broke out again. The plane was simply too frail to weather a storm, the passengers insisted. It was a toy plane, hardly a real one, they pointed out. Given the harrowing experience that we had gone through the day before, they demanded that the least that Pakistan International Airlines could do was to put a decent Boeing or Aerobus at our disposal. And then, they complained, the scheduled time of departure of the flight was the worst that could have possibly been chosen for, in the late evenings at that time of the year, fierce squalls had a nasty habit of breaking out over Delhi.

The passengers' angry outcries had no effect on the adamant staff of the airlines who were, no doubt, in a desperate hurry to get rid of us as soon as possible. There was no other craft available, they firmly told us.

I climbed up the ladder leading to the tiny plane, stricken with a deep sense of fear and foreboding. I wished there were some other way of getting back to Delhi. But there was none, since my visa strictly required me to return to Delhi by air from Lahore, and so, I told myself, it was pointless fretting.

Then, in a short while, we were airborne. The sky was

remarkably clear, a brilliant, cloudless blue. The plane sailed majestically, like a swallow in spring. Barely half an hour later, it began its descent into Delhi. How utterly strange it seemed, I thought—we had been in Pakistan just thirty minutes earlier, and we would be in India in half that time. How near the two countries actually were—and yet how very distant.

Just then, an idea struck me. I grabbed a scrap of paper—actually an airsickness bag kept in the pocket of the seat before me—and scribbled down the following lines:

Dear Friends,

Yesterday's near-brush with death has brought all of us, Pakistanis and Indians, so close together. If, in the face of death, our common and ultimate destiny, we can be so close, then why not in life, too? In order to celebrate our friendship, I propose that the moment the plane lands in Delhi, Allah/ Ishwar willing, we should raise the following slogan:

Pakistani–Hindustani Bhai Bhai!
Hamari Dosti Zindabad!

For the benefit of those of you who might not know Hindi/ Urdu, it means, 'Pakistanis and Indians are brothers! May our friendship last forever!'

Please read this note and pass it around.

I read the note again. It expressed something in which I strongly believed. On the other hand, however, I felt, some passengers might think me naïve, even stupid. But, then, I thought, I really could not care. I was not going to meet them again in any case, so why worry about what they might think? I passed the note to the passengers sitting behind me, and it gradually wove its way round the plane. Just to make sure that everyone had got the message, after a while I stood up and read the note out aloud.

A panic-stricken air hostess, hearing my impassioned speech, rushed to my seat, wondering what had happened.

'I'm doing my politics,' I told her. She broke into a hearty, approving laugh when I explained what my declamation was all about.

Five minutes later, the little plane gracefully touched down at New Delhi airport, and I heard a loud chorus repeat after me:

Pakistani–Hindustani Bhai-Bhai!
Hamari Dosti Zindabad!